Cognitive-Behavioral
Therapy for
Adult ADHD

Practical Clinical Guidebooks Series

Cognitive-Behavioral Therapy for Adult ADHD

An Integrative Psychosocial and Medical Approach

J. Russell Ramsay

Anthony L. Rostain

Routledge
Taylor & Francis Group
New York   London

Routledge
Taylor & Francis Group
270 Madison Avenue
New York, NY 10016

Routledge
Taylor & Francis Group
2 Park Square
Milton Park, Abingdon
Oxon OX14 4RN

© 2008 by Taylor & Francis Group, LLC
Routledge is an imprint of Taylor & Francis Group, an Informa business

Printed in the United States of America on acid-free paper
10 9 8 7 6 5 4 3 2

International Standard Book Number-13: 978-0-415-95501-0 (Softcover) 978-0-415-95500-3 (Hardcover)

Library of Congress Cataloging-in-Publication Data

Ramsay, J. Russell.
   Cognitive behavioral therapy for adult ADHD : an integrative psychosocial and medical approach / J. Russell Ramsay, Anthony L. Rostain.
      p. ; cm. -- (Practical clinical guidebooks series)
   Includes bibliographical references and index.
   ISBN-13: 978-0-415-95500-3 (hb)
   ISBN-10: 0-415-95500-9 (hb)
   ISBN-13: 978-0-415-95501-0 (pb)
   ISBN-10: 0-415-95501-7 (pb)
   1. Attention-deficit disorder in adults--Treatment. 2. Cognitive-behavioral therapy.
I. Rostain, Anthony L. II. Title. III. Series.

[DNLM: 1. Attention Deficit Disorder with Hyperactivity--therapy--Case Reports. 2. Cognitive Therapy--Case Reports. WM 190 R179c 2007]
RC394.A85R36 2007   616.85'89--dc22   2007001557

Visit the Taylor & Francis Web site at
http://www.taylorandfrancis.com

and the Routledge Web site at
http://www.routledge.com

This book is dedicated to the loving memory of my father, J. Roger Ramsay (1939–1998), and to my beloved daughters, Abigail and Brynn Ramsay, who collectively inspire me to strive to do my best in my most valued job: "Dad."

J.R.R.

I dedicate this book to the loving memory of my mother, Gita Alfandary (1926–2004), and my stepfather, Sol Lefkowitz (1927–1991), and to my wonderful kids, Isabelle, Julian, Sam, and Gen, who have taught me what it really means to be a dad.

A.L.R.

Contents

Preface

Mark Twain described a classic book as one that everyone loves but no one has read. This description is apropos for the psychiatric syndrome called attention-deficit/hyperactivity disorder (ADHD): it is a disorder about which everyone has an opinion but one to which very few people, even seasoned mental health professionals, have had much more than superficial exposure. Part of the problem rests with the complexity of the disorder and its variable presentations; another part of it comes from historical controversies surrounding the classification of children who do not follow rules or pay attention in class; and yet another part of the problem stems from the inevitable debates among scientists and clinicians from a multiplicity of disciplines regarding what causes the disorder and how it is best treated.

ADHD is currently understood by those who study and treat it as a highly heritable neurodevelopmental syndrome of impaired functioning in regions of the brain associated with planning, foresight, initiating and sustaining attention, and self-control. The core symptoms of ADHD consist of developmentally inappropriate symptoms of inattention, impulsivity, and hyperactivity. These symptoms, in turn, create significant functional problems in daily life over time and across different situations such that they negatively affect afflicted individuals' reciprocal interactions with the environment throughout the life span. Although some of the symptoms of ADHD are nonspecific (for example, poor concentration can also be seen in depression or anxiety disorders), the ADHD symptom profile is considered to be valid, unique, and not better explained by other existing psychiatric syndromes.

Some of the confusion and misinformation surrounding ADHD is a product of the fact that the types of problems commonly associated with ADHD—impulsivity, inattention, hyperactivity—are, in some form, familiar to all of us. Who has not misplaced car keys, had difficulty paying attention during a lecture, felt exceedingly restless when a situation called for stillness, or acted on a whim only to later regret not having considered the obvious (in retrospect) consequences of doing so? These experiences, so common to everyone, create the sense that, rather than suffering from a significant neurobehavioral disorder requiring treatment, those children and adults diagnosed with ADHD simply have not learned to deal with the requisite difficulties of life and simply need to "toughen up and get over it."

To consider the issue from a different perspective, however, most individuals have experienced a significant fright or period of intense worry, which includes physical feelings of nervousness and other bodily symptoms of anxiety that result from sympathetic nervous system arousal. For most of us, these sensations subside in a reasonable time and with little, if any, residual ill effect and are not indicative of the presence of a psychiatric disorder. We can describe these experiences as normal anxiety, which serves an adaptive function. Individuals with diagnosed anxiety disorders have similar feelings of worry and dread, the difference being that these are more frequent, more intense, more enduring, more pervasive, and, consequently, may interfere with their lives to a degree that necessitates professional intervention. In addition to recognizing that anxiety disorders represent extreme manifestations of normal biological processes, people seem generally willing to accept that many people may vary regarding their genetic predispositions for developing anxiety disorders that interact with mediating environmental factors. Available pharmacological and psychosocial treatments are viewed as reasonable ways to address anxiety problems, and individuals with anxiety disorders must take responsibility for following treatment recommendations—which most often include a certain degree of facing one's fears. Patients with anxiety disorders, though, are not viewed by most people as being "weak-willed" but rather as struggling with a valid clinical condition.

We have a similar dimensional view of ADHD. We all experience varying degrees of difficulties associated with its symptoms, but those diagnosed with ADHD fall at the extreme end of the continuum and face a daily struggle with trying to cope with their symptoms. Current scientific evidence indicates that ADHD has earned its place as a valid psychiatric disorder, similar to the aforementioned anxiety disorders. If anything, ADHD is the most widely researched and validated diagnostic category in child psychiatry. The symptoms of ADHD reflect inefficient functioning in regions of the brain thought to guide and coordinate planning, organization, working memory, self-regulation, and so forth—various components of what we consider to be self-control. These cognitive abilities, known collectively as the *executive functions*, have important downstream consequences for many other mental mechanisms we rely on for daily functioning, such as attention, impulse control, emotional regulation, effort, memory, and motivation.

In the century since childhood ADHD was first described in 1902 by the British pediatrician Sir George Still (see Still, 1902/2006, for excerpts from the original lectures), society has slowly come to recognize that affected children suffer not from poor parenting or poor character but rather from a serious, though treatable neurobehavioral disorder. Until relatively recently, however, ADHD was viewed as a developmental delay that affected children would grow out of by adolescence, maybe young adulthood at the latest. It was thought that it was the rare exception for an individual to display residual symptoms of ADHD in adulthood.

The notion of adult ADHD seemed to spring *de novo* into the public consciousness in the past decade with the publication of several popular self-help books related to the topic (for example, Hallowell & Ratey, 1994; Murphy & LeVert, 1995). In fact, there had been growing recognition among researchers and clinicians over the past 30 years that the symptoms of ADHD did not inexorably remit in the course of adult development. There were even hints of this phenomenon in some studies conducted in the 1960s using samples of young adults who presented with symptoms of hyperactivity and impulsivity and who had also experienced similar problems in childhood. It has since been established that although there is often a decrease in the visible symptoms of hyperactivity (for example, inappropriately leaving one's seat) with increasing age, there continue to be difficulties with inattention, impulsive behavior, and an ongoing sense of internal restlessness for the majority of individuals who were diagnosed with ADHD in childhood.

Many ADHD adults were able to get through childhood and adolescence by relying on their intelligence to overcome difficulties related to inattention or restlessness; or on the support of sympathetic parents, teachers, and friends. However, they may have experienced increasing difficulties as they progressed through high school, only to fall apart upon reaching college or entering the work force. Other adults with unidentified ADHD may have been able to struggle through college and even enter graduate or professional programs, or find an occupational niche in which they were able to function. Most of these adults carry around the notion that they are not fulfilling their true potential and are frustrated by the way in which the seemingly manageable demands of academic, work, or home life pose significant problems for them. Unfortunately, there are countless others whose struggles with undiagnosed or untreated ADHD in childhood and adolescence led to them dropping out of school, being underemployed, developing substance abuse problems, or having arrest records.

As with other psychiatric disorders, those who suffer from ADHD experience a range of symptom severity and impairment, from relatively mild symptoms that require short-term intervention to manage a particular problem area to those with chronic, severe symptoms of ADHD and coexisting mood, anxiety, or substance abuse problems that can prove debilitating in a number of domains of life. Although ADHD is represented by a discrete diagnostic category, its effects for adult patients are wide-ranging and varied.

Our interest in adult ADHD and the original impetus to establish the University of Pennsylvania Adult ADHD Treatment and Research Program in 1999 was twofold. First, from a scientific standpoint, we recognized that, although we considered the popular psychology books on adult ADHD that emerged in the mid-1990s to be clinically useful and written by skilled clinicians, we foresaw a need for research to establish evidence-based treatments for these patients, particularly considering that most cases are made complex by comorbid disorders and many functional problems. Second, from the standpoint of being practicing clinicians, we understood the challenges involved in personalizing treatment to the individual needs and temperament of each patient. Thus, our mission was to strive to develop treatments that were empirically supported and clinically useful.

This book represents a summary of our combined treatment approach for adults with ADHD. In addition to our own research and clinical experience, its contents also reflect an effort to describe the research, clinical interventions, and expertise of our professional colleagues and predecessors who continue to strive to better understand and to treat adult ADHD. We are grateful to our contemporaries in the fields of clinical work and research for their published works, formal presentations, and informal conversations, correspondence, feedback, and support in the development of this book. That said, we assume full responsibility for the content of this volume.

We hope this book will be relevant for many readers. First, we have written it to be a clinician-friendly resource for experienced mental health professionals who seek guidance for structuring treatment with their adult patients with ADHD. Second, we hope that this book will be relevant for clinical training programs for mental health clinicians. We have found that graduate and medical students generally are not exposed to the diagnosis and treatment of adult ADHD in the course of their education. This book could be used as a resource for students, training directors, and clinical supervisors to fill a gap in clinical training. Finally, we hope this book will be useful for professionals involved in clinical research in adult ADHD. Although we have attempted to present an evidence-based treatment approach for adult ADHD, it is clear that more research is needed to improve available treatments, not to mention to further understand the neuropsychological functioning and life experiences of individuals with ADHD. If young researchers find some unanswered empirical questions raised in the pages of this book and embark on research to answer them, we will have viewed our work as being successful and worth the effort.

The first chapter provides a description of ADHD symptoms seen in adult patients, commonly encountered comorbid disorders, daily functioning problems experienced by these patients that are not described in the official diagnostic criteria, information about the prevalence of adult ADHD, and current scientific data and theories regarding its etiology. Such information is important in order to understand the problems experienced by adults with ADHD and to educate these patients. The first chapter culminates with a review of the necessary components of a comprehensive diagnostic evaluation for adult ADHD. For the many individuals whose symptoms of ADHD have gone undiagnosed until adulthood, receiving an accurate diagnosis is often the first therapeutic intervention. That is, when the symptoms of adult ADHD are accurately diagnosed, individuals often describe a cognitive shift from viewing their long-standing problems as resulting from a character flaw or stupidity to recognizing that there is a sound neurobiological explanation for the difficulties they have encountered. The attention then turns to helping individuals to overcome their difficulties.

The second chapter focuses on describing the treatment strategies commonly used for adults with ADHD. In particular, we describe structuring a pharmacotherapy treatment regimen, with particular attention paid to issues of comorbidity and medication compliance. We also provide a summary of our cognitive behavioral therapy (CBT) framework for understanding and treating adult ADHD. Finally, we outline a course of combined treatment using both medications and CBT, including specific cognitive, behavioral, and skill-based interventions within a 20-session model of treatment extending over about 6 months. Although we acknowledge that this time frame may not be applicable for certain patients—some may require fewer sessions, some may require many more sessions—it is a useful heuristic for thinking about setting up therapy.

The third chapter reviews the current research support for the pharmacological and psychosocial treatments discussed in Chapter 2 as well as the limitations of the current empirical literature. In particular, psychosocial treatments for adults with ADHD have not yet been widely studied—as of the publication of this book there have been only nine published outcome studies—and there is a need for further research. Pharmacologic studies of adult ADHD are more numerous and advanced than studies of psychosocial treatments, although these studies face the complexities of the high frequency of comorbid disorders and complicated dosing issues seen in adult patients. Moreover, pharmacologic studies rarely use outcome measures other than the symptom clusters used to define the diagnosis. It is not clear that improved attention span and concentration necessarily lead to improved functional status (for example, decreased procrastination), especially with respect to strategies for coping with the difficult aspects of daily life for people with ADHD.

Chapter 4 focuses on presenting several case examples with which we illustrate commonly encountered presenting problems, assessment procedures, and our combined treatment approach in action. In particular, case examples include snippets of dialogue from CBT sessions to demonstrate for clinicians how to implement the interventions described in previous chapters. Likewise, we describe how to address common medication issues, both in CBT and during medication management sessions.

Chapter 5 reviews complicating factors that may arise in the course of treatment of adult ADHD. Among the issues discussed are how the symptoms of ADHD affect treatment follow-through (for example, forgetting appointments, poor follow-through on therapy homework), patients' misuse of medications (issues of both underutilization and abuse), dealing with comorbid disorders and substance abuse, addressing patients' sensitivity to failure and rejection, unrealistic expectations for what treatment can offer, and managing the therapeutic alliance (including common mistakes made by therapists).

The sixth and final chapter addresses issues related to relapse prevention and helping patients maintain their effective coping after treatment ends. We make clear that the goal of CBT is to make the therapist obsolete by empowering patients to use their coping strategies independently, to make lifestyle changes in order to learn to manage their ADHD symptoms, and, when necessary, to seek help in the form of booster sessions or other assistance. We also discuss how to address various factors related to the long-term use of medications to manage ADHD symptoms.

The appendices provide readers with quick references for additional resources to provide to their patients, such as reputable self-help books and Web sites. Additionally, we have provided tables outlining (1) a typical session of CBT for adult ADHD; (2) a 20-session course of CBT; and (3) commonly prescribed medications, dose range, and side effects.

ADHD can be an exquisitely confounding disorder. For those who suffer from it, ADHD makes the mundane details of life difficult and the anticipated challenges of life seem insurmountable, leading many to feel that they are not fulfilling their potentials or that they have failed in life. For clinicians who want to help these patients, ADHD adds layers of complexity to assessment and treatment, and poses challenges to standard pharmacotherapy and psychotherapy approaches. We hope that this volume will prove useful by helping clinicians to better understand the symptoms of adult ADHD, to formulate more effective treatment plans, and to assist their patients as they attempt to achieve their goals. By doing so, we hope that it will be helpful for students, supervisors, clinicians, and, most importantly, for adults living with ADHD.

Acknowledgments

The authors wish to thank many individuals, without whom the development and completion of this book would not have been possible. First, the University of Pennsylvania Adult ADHD Treatment and Research Program is indebted to Fred Shvetz, David and Shirley Toomim, and Jack Parker, who have all made generous gifts in support of our program's ongoing mission to develop better treatments and to give away our knowledge to other professionals and to the public.

In particular, we want to acknowledge the incredible generosity and encouragement of David and Shirley Toomim, of whom we have grown inordinately fond since first meeting them in 2002. This book represents the culmination of one of the visions of the Toomins, who wished to encourage the development and research of effective treatment approaches that could be disseminated, thereby making a tangible difference in the lives of those affected by attention-deficit/hyperactivity disorder (ADHD). Their unwavering support of our fledgling efforts to design, evaluate, and disseminate our collaborative model of care made it possible for us to gain the expertise and to develop the tools that we have brought together in this volume. Sadly, David Toomin died before he could see the end result of his gift, though, in line with their generosity and modesty, even during her grief, Shirley Toomin encouraged memorial donations for her husband to be used to support the mission of our program. Our hope is that the publication of this book makes manifest the Toomins' original vision and, in some small way, repays a portion of the debt we owe to them for their steadfast support of us and our work.

We thank our colleagues in the Department of Psychiatry at the University of Pennsylvania School of Medicine and its Chairman, Dr. Dwight L. Evans, who create a professional environment that encourages the pursuit of clinically relevant research that makes a difference in the lives of our patients. We also owe a deep debt of gratitude to the many individuals who have been a part of the Adult ADHD Treatment and Research Program over the years, including our research coordinators:

Andrea Fabricatore, Jennifer Elliott, Lisa Mimmo, Stacey Garfield, Sarah Charlesworth, and Marissa Fernandez; research assistants: Lanre Dokun and Caitlin Howarth; clinical associates: Brad Rosenfield, Hollie Levy-Mack, Meghan Leahy, Lofton Harris, and Bruce Berg; professional colleagues with whom we have collaborated: William Culbertson, Paul Moberg, Roberta Waite, Amishi Jha, Edward Moss, and John Listerud; and administrative staff at Penn (who we all know *really* are in charge of getting things done): Michele Cepparulo, Tina Inforzato, Melissa Kahane, and Rosellen Taraborelli.

We thank Routledge/Taylor & Francis Group, namely Dana Bliss, who originally approached us about writing this book and who has been supportive of us throughout the editorial and publication process. We view the *Practical Clinical Guidebooks Series* as very important for mental health professionals devoted to providing evidence-based clinical services, and we were honored to be asked to contribute this volume.

Finally, we wish to acknowledge the patients living with ADHD whom we have been privileged to serve since our program started in 1999. We have been honored to witness their resilience and dignity in managing and ultimately transcending the effects of ADHD.

I (J.R.R.) would also like to thank two of my teachers, Dr. Leonard I. Jacobson, my undergraduate mentor, and Dr. Anita L. Greene, my dissertation chair and graduate advisor, who were wonderful role models for maintaining high standards of professionalism in both research and clinical work. These standards were further reinforced during my predoctoral internship at CPC Behavioral Healthcare in Red Bank, New Jersey. My colleagues at the Center for Cognitive Therapy at the University of Pennsylvania School of Medicine and its Director, Dr. Cory Newman, have provided unwavering support and encouragement of my professional development since I arrived as a postdoctoral fellow and, more recently, in my attempts to find ways to adapt cognitive behavioral therapy (CBT) to meet the needs of adults with ADHD.

I would never have ended up as a specialist in adult ADHD without having been approached by Dr. Tony Rostain in 1999 with the proposition to collaborate on developing a program dedicated to providing high-quality, evidence-based treatments for a group of adults with ADHD who did not seem to be benefiting from the standard treatments offered by our outpatient psychiatry clinic. The project has been the centerpiece of my career, and my relationship with Tony Rostain, who is equal parts mentor, collaborator, and friend, is one that I treasure. In some small way I hope that our working alliance and mutual professional respect serve as an example for other psychologists and psychiatrists to work together in a truly bio-psycho-social model for understanding and treating psychiatric disorders.

I have been able to focus on my career development in no small part because of the support of friends and family I have outside of my professional life. In particular, I wish to thank my teammates over the years on the Jeff's Demos soccer team. The enjoyment of playing in the games each week is matched only by the team's camaraderie afterward. The friendships with my teammates, representing all walks of life, are among the oldest and most valued in my life.

I would not have been able to pursue my educational and professional goals without the loving support through the years of my grandmother, Harvena Felty, my parents, Mary Ann Ramsay and the late J. Roger Ramsay, and my sister, Jennifer Ramsay.

My biggest debt of gratitude goes to my daughters, Abby and Brynn, and to my lovely wife, Amy. I am unable to adequately describe the great affection, pride, and love I have for my daughters and I hope they know how blessed I am to be their father. Finally, Amy has been an unfailing partner throughout every step of my adult life, which has consisted mostly of "ups" but with our fair share of "downs," and I am bewildered that she still puts up with me. I cannot envision my life without her beside me and I remain, as ever, passionately enamored of her.

I (A.L.R.) would also like to thank the mentors who offered me boundless support and encouragement when I first began treating ADHD patients at The Children's Hospital of Philadelphia (CHOP) in the mid-1980s: the late Dr. David Cornfeld, the late Dr. Robert Leopold, Dr. Alberto Serrano, and Dr. A. John Sargent. Their intellectual companionship and professional advice were invaluable in fostering my development into a truly bio-psycho-social, developmentally oriented family systems clinician and researcher. I also want to recognize the close collaborative relationships that grew up around the founding of the CHOP ADHD program by thanking my colleagues Dr. Tom Power, Dr. Susan Levy, Dr. Marianne Glanzmann, and Dr. Larry Brown. I am extremely grateful for the hours we spent together learning to make sense of the world of ADHD children and adolescents, and finding new ways to help them and their families. No small debt of gratitude is also owed to my professional colleagues and friends at the Philadelphia Child Guidance Clinic, who understood the importance of developing new approaches to ADHD within a systems-oriented framework that enabled me to broaden my view of the nature of the disorder and its treatment. And a special note of thanks is due to my teachers and colleagues in the Department of Psychiatry of the University of Pennsylvania, who enabled me to make the transition from pediatrics and child and adolescent psychiatry into the world of adult psychiatry: Dr. Peter Whybrow, Dr. Gary Gottlieb, Dr. James Stinnett, Dr. Trevor Price, Dr. Steve Arnold, Dr. Paul Moberg, Dr. Sydney Pulver, and Dr. George Ruff. With their assistance, the vision of creating a program for treating ADHD adults became a reality.

Of central importance in the evolution of my work with ADHD adults has been my relationship with Dr. J. Russell Ramsay, who has become my closest professional colleague, partner, and coconspirator. It is hard to describe how naturally our teamwork has evolved over the 8 years we have worked together, and how exciting it has been to develop our approach to treating adults with ADHD. Russ Ramsay is an incredibly talented therapist, a diligent and hardworking researcher, a remarkably intelligent thinker, and one of the funniest people I know. His energy, enthusiasm, modesty, good nature, and positive attitude have made it both rewarding and fun to work and to travel to the far reaches of the globe together. This book represents the culmination of the first phase of what I expect will be a long and productive professional relationship and friendship.

Of course, no one can hope to undertake the demanding and time-consuming work of caring for psychiatric patients without a strong social support network. I am extremely fortunate to be blessed with the most wonderful family and friends that anyone could ask for. I am thankful for the love and support of my parents, Jacques and Gita; my stepfather, Sol; and my siblings: Carine, Tanina, and Alain Rostain; Laura Engel and David Blanco. I also want to salute my friends whose comradeship has gotten me through the best and worst of times, especially Matt Alexander, Mike Felsen, Louis Freedberg, Steve Hecker, Rob Hoffnung, Red Schiller, Don Schwarz, and Michael Silver.

I especially want to recognize the incredible love and support of my wife, Michele Goldfarb, who has been my closest friend and my source of inspiration for 10 years. Her generosity of spirit and her loving kindness have been constant and unwavering throughout the roller-coaster ride of this past decade. And finally, I want to give special thanks to my children, Isabelle and Julian, whose love has given my life special meaning and immeasurable joy; and to my stepchildren, Sam and Gen, who have allowed me to become an important part of their lives, for which I am grateful beyond words. Thanks to all of you for putting up with my crazy work schedule and my passion for doing the best I can do to help others. I love you all so much!

CHAPTER 1

Adult ADHD
Diagnosis, Symptoms,
Etiology, and Assessment

Mary was visibly flustered as she entered the doors to the waiting area of the clinic. She was 30 minutes late for her first meeting with a doctor whom she had waited months to see. She had planned to leave in plenty of time to arrive early for her scheduled appointment (for once); however, an hour before she had to leave she decided to take a look at the packet that had been mailed to her by the doctor's office. She had received the packet several weeks ago and remembered the doctor's assistant mentioning something about being sure to bring it along with her to the appointment. Mary only recalled having the envelope the previous day and had spent an hour searching for it in her apartment, growing so frustrated she almost called the doctor's office to ask for another copy to be sent to her by fax. Thinking she would prepare for her appointment by reading through the informational material, she was shocked to discover there were numerous questionnaires for her to complete before her appointment. Mary felt a wave of anxiety beset her as she worried that she might have to reschedule her appointment if she did not have completed paperwork to hand over. She felt simultaneously angry at the doctor for sending her so much paperwork and at herself for having waited so long to open the manilla-colored envelope that so obviously, in retrospect, held important contents. She scribbled as fast as she could but then remembered that she had not showered and dressed for her appointment. She rushed around her apartment trying to "tie up loose ends" before departing. Mary was disturbed as she drove to the appointment, even unwittingly running a stop sign in her neighborhood and driving well above posted speed limits as she tried to think of the best route to the office. She felt increasing tension as she encountered unexpected heavy traffic and difficulties finding a parking space near the doctor's office. Now, after eventually finding her way to the office and having given her name to the receptionist, she felt scattered and on edge. Her feelings only worsened when the receptionist said that there was no record of the appointment. Mary had the fleeting thought that "I screwed up and showed up on the wrong day." She felt her eyes fill with tears as the receptionist called the doctor on the intercom. Mary looked down at her paperwork, trying to find the appointment information to see if she had arrived on the wrong day and only then realized that the questionnaires were double-sided and that she had only completed the front of the pages. Mary silently cursed at having put herself in yet another embarrassing position. The receptionist got off the intercom and confirmed that the doctor was expecting her and that he had simply forgotten to inform the front desk of Mary's appointment. The receptionist asked for the nature of the appointment and Mary said with a trembling voice choking back tears, "I'm here for an evaluation to see if I have ADHD."

Attention-deficit/hyperactivity disorder (ADHD) is an exquisitely puzzling condition. For those affected by it, many aspects of daily life that most people take for granted are rendered more difficult by the symptoms of ADHD. Although these symptoms may appear innocent and merely annoying nuisances to observers, if left untreated, the persistent and pervasive effects of ADHD symptoms can insidiously and severely interfere with one's ability to get the most out of education, fulfill one's potential in the workplace, establish and maintain interpersonal relationships, and maintain a generally positive sense of self.

ADHD is equally confounding for mental health professionals. Most clinicians have not received formal training in the assessment and treatment of ADHD, particularly in adult patients. Its symptoms can be difficult to differentiate from other, more familiar psychiatric disorders, increasing the likelihood that the diagnosis of ADHD will be missed. On the other hand, it is equally possible to overdiagnose ADHD based on a limited snapshot of a patient's life and a handful of reported symptoms without adequately reviewing the relevant history of functioning and considering alternative causes of problems that may be unrelated to ADHD. The very name *attention deficit* can be misleading because individuals with ADHD report the ability to pay attention to tasks that are interesting, rewarding, or otherwise compelling in some way. These various difficulties have led to the perception of ADHD as a controversial psychiatric diagnosis.

A good deal of the controversy and confusion surrounding ADHD, particularly adult ADHD, stems from a misunderstanding of the diagnostic criteria and how they are utilized by clinicians. It is common to hear people proclaim that "everyone has ADHD," "ADHD is not really a disorder," or "doctors are trying to make normal behavior a diagnosis." We recognize that there are limitations inherent in any attempt to categorize human behavior, particularly when attempting to identify problematic behaviors to the extent that they are deemed "disorders" requiring clinical attention. The symptoms of ADHD are especially difficult to define because it is hard to draw the line at where normal levels of impulsivity and distractibility end and clinically significant levels requiring intervention begin. Although more work needs to be done, particularly in defining developmentally relevant symptoms of adult ADHD, the current diagnostic criteria (when used as designed) and research of the unique manifestations of ADHD symptoms represent substantial progress in this area.

The overarching goal of this chapter is to provide a description of the phenomenology of ADHD; in particular, how its symptoms are manifested in adult patients. Knowing how the symptoms of ADHD impinge on the lives of affected adults is an important precursor, first, to performing accurate diagnostic assessments for adult ADHD and, second, to formulating and implementing effective treatment plans. We will start our discussion with a review of the current official diagnostic criteria of ADHD. However, these symptom criteria were developed specifically for children and do not accurately reflect the experiences of most adults with ADHD (McGough & Barkley, 2004; Ramsay & Rostain, 2006a). In lieu of official diagnostic criteria for adults (see Barkley & Murphy, 2006b, for a list of research-based adult ADHD criteria), we will augment our discussion of diagnostic criteria with a review of the distinct symptoms of adult ADHD. This discussion also will include the commonly encountered coexisting or comorbid disorders that complicate assessment and treatment. We will summarize research exploring the epidemiology, prevalence, and different possible etiologies of ADHD. The chapter concludes with a review of the standard features of a competent and comprehensive diagnostic assessment for ADHD in adult patients.

DIAGNOSTIC CRITERIA AND SYMPTOMS ACROSS THE LIFE SPAN

According to the current diagnostic nomenclature as set out in the most recent edition of the *Diagnostic and Statistical Manual of Mental*

Disorders (4th ed., text revision [*DSM-IV-TR*], American Psychiatric Association [APA], 2000), ADHD is listed in the section on "Disorders Usually First Diagnosed in Infancy, Childhood or Adolescence." It is further classified under the subheading of "Attention Deficit and Disruptive Behavior Disorders."

There are nine symptoms for each of two subtypes of ADHD, with a minimum of six symptoms of at least one subtype required to be present to warrant a formal diagnosis. To fulfill diagnostic criteria, an individual must exhibit persistent (that is, for at least 6 months), maladaptive, and developmentally inappropriate symptoms of "Inattention," "Hyperactivity–Impulsivity," or both. According to *DSM-IV-TR* guidelines, some symptoms causing impairment should have been evident before the age of 7 and should have been present in at least two settings (for example, school, home, peer settings).

These symptom categories yield three potential classifications of ADHD: predominantly inattentive type, predominantly hyperactive–impulsive type, or combined type (if criteria for both subtypes are fulfilled). There is an additional diagnostic category called ADHD, not otherwise specified (NOS), which reflects the presence of prominent symptoms requiring clinical attention that do not fulfill full criteria for an existing subtype (that is, subthreshold symptoms). The *DSM* also notes that adolescents and adults who currently have symptoms that no longer fulfill full diagnostic criteria (presumably having previously met full criteria) should be specified as "in partial remission."

It is important to acknowledge that the specific symptom criteria were developed to identify observable behaviors commonly displayed by children with ADHD. Although it is acknowledged that ADHD persists into adulthood for up to 70% of children diagnosed with ADHD (Klein & Mannuzza, 1991; Mannuzza & Klein, 1999; Mannuzza et al., 1993, 1998; Rasmussen & Gillberg, 2000; Weiss & Hechtman, 1993; Wilens, Biederman, & Spencer, 2002), developmentally appropriate diagnostic criteria for ADHD designed to identify difficulties commonly encountered by adult patients have not yet been integrated into the *DSM*, though DSM-V committees will begin deliberations in 2007, with a tentative publication date of 2011 for the revised manual. Thus, we will discuss the developmental course of the symptoms in our review of subtypes below.

Before doing so, we want to address the commonly heard comment that "everyone has ADHD sometimes." It is true that we all experience variations in our ability to focus our attention, feelings of restlessness, and impulse control. However, research has indicated that when using strict diagnostic guidelines to assess symptoms—including the requirements for chronicity, severity of symptoms, and impairment—non-ADHD individuals rarely report problems, whereas individuals diagnosed with ADHD report significant numbers of problems (Barkley, 2002; Barkley et al., 2002). Thus, everyone does *not* have ADHD, just as everyone does not have mood disorders simply because they experience variations in their moods.

ADHD, Predominantly Hyperactive–Impulsive Type

It is hyperactivity, or excessive and developmentally inappropriate levels of motor (or vocal) activity, that comes to mind for most people when they think of ADHD. Impulsivity is closely related to hyperactivity and is generally defined as difficulty delaying gratification and regulating one's behavior, or "acting without thinking." Despite being the quintessential type of ADHD, it is the least common subtype, affecting less than 15% of all individuals with ADHD (Millstein et al., 1997; Wilens et al., 2002). Hyperactive children are described as "being on the go or driven by a motor," "unable to sit still," "always in motion and getting into things," and "always talking or making noises," among other signs. Impulsivity in children often is captured by descriptions such as "doesn't think before acting," "doesn't learn from mistakes," "doesn't think about risks or effects of actions," and "says things without thinking." These behaviors cause problems both in structured settings with clear rules (for example, getting out of his seat without permission in school) and in unstructured settings (for example, cannot wait her turn during play with peers).

The hyperactive–impulsive type, particularly when combined with conduct disorder, is associated with high risk for additional psychiatric, substance use, and behavioral problems. Individuals with the hyperactive–impulsive and combined types often experience greater emotional and behavioral impairments in all stages of life than the primarily inattentive subtype (Fischer et al., 2002; Satterfield & Schell, 1997; Wilens et al., 2002).

The observation that older adolescents and adults with ADHD only rarely manifest such extreme levels of hyperactivity–impulsivity lent credence to the now antiquated and inaccurate bromide that children with ADHD would eventually and inexorably "grow out of it." While there is a reduction in symptoms of hyperactivity and impulsivity with age (Barkley, 2006a; Hart et al., 1995; Weiss, Murray, & Weiss, 2002; Wender, 1995, 2000; Wilens et al., 2002), ADHD adults often report a subjective sense of restlessness, fidgetiness, or subtler signs of physical restlessness, such as bouncing their legs, playing with things with their hands, or excessive talking.

Many adults with ADHD report what they describe as "mental hyperactivity," such as having their train of thought easily disrupted by new thoughts or ideas. These various internal distractions continue to create functional difficulties for affected individuals, interfering with their motivation for and follow-through on tasks and negatively influencing academic functioning, occupational performance, interpersonal relationships, and even recreational pursuits. Furthermore, individuals with the hyperactive–impulsive subtype have an elevated risk for substance abuse (Wilens et al., 1997), cigarette smoking (Pomerleau et al., 1995), driving problems (for example, accidents, citations; Barkley, 2006b; Barkley, Murphy, & Kwasnik, 1996a), and oppositional or antisocial behaviors (Barkley, 2006a; Fischer et al., 2002) that could result in later health, interpersonal, and legal problems (Wilens et al., 2002).

ADHD, Predominantly Inattentive Type

About 20 to 30% of all individuals with ADHD exhibit the inattentive type (Wilens et al., 2002). The label of attention deficit is a bit misleading since individuals with ADHD exhibit seemingly intact attention in certain situations and most people without ADHD report having periodic difficulties concentrating and being easily distracted on certain tasks. What is particularly problematic in ADHD is the inability to willfully focus and allocate attention and concentration efficiently, particularly when tasks are not inherently enjoyable, such as studying, paying bills, or planning projects. Attention is not a one-dimensional construct, and emerging scientific findings suggest that there are several attention networks in the brain that subserve a variety of interrelated functions that pertain to attention, such as arousal, alerting, orienting, focusing, sustaining, and so forth. For any individual reporting inattentive symptoms, one or more of these functions may be impaired. From the clinical perspective, when difficulties related to inattention arise across many situations (including recreational environments) and remain chronic over time such that they lead to pervasive functional difficulties that interfere with quality of life, then the ADHD diagnosis applies.

Adults with ADHD have difficulty resisting the lure of distracters when they offer immediate positive reinforcement (for example, something enjoyable) or negative reinforcement (for example, an opportunity to stop and leave a less compelling or distasteful task before them). In such cases, an individual with ADHD is more likely to seek activities that are more immediately reinforcing and more pleasurable than to be vigilant about less exciting, though ultimately more important, tasks. Further, once interrupted, individuals with ADHD have greater difficulty than non-ADHD individuals reengaging in an activity. Thus, they have greater difficulty initiating, persisting with, and working to completion on tasks that are not intrinsically appealing to them.

Unlike symptoms of hyperactivity and impulsivity, which wane with age, symptoms of inattention and subsequent information processing problems remain relatively constant across the life span (Biederman, Mick, & Faraone, 2000; Hart et al., 1995; Wilens et al., 2002). Further, demands for the ability to concentrate, to be organized, and to manage one's time and effort increase in adulthood, and the negative consequences associated with inattentiveness and disorganization become more severe. Self-reports of adults and corroboration from others who know them (for example, spouses, roommates) confirm that ADHD patients are likely to report greater numbers of symptoms of inattention than controls (Barkley et al., 2002; Murphy & Barkley, 1996b). In addition to the *DSM* symptoms, adults with ADHD describe problems such as "losing things," "appearing spacey or in a daydream," "having difficulty getting started on and finishing tasks," and "being easily distracted by interruptions and things that have nothing to do with the task at hand," among many other complaints (Weiss & Murray, 2003). There is growing interest in difficulties associated with sluggish cognitive tempo (SCT), a subset of individuals diagnosed with the primarily inattentive type who are characterized as anxious, "daydreamy," lethargic, and sluggish. Individuals with SCT tend to have difficulties related to social dysfunction and withdrawal and fewer externalizing behaviors, and these symptoms, which create equal levels of impairment as traditional ADHD symptoms, do not seem to respond to ADHD medications (Barkley, 2006a, Carlson & Mann, 2002; Hartman et al., 2004).

Unlike hyperactive–impulsive or combined type ADHD patients, adults who are primarily inattentive often do not report as many behavioral problems at home or at school when they were younger (Wilens et al., 2002). Rather, inattentive adults were likely to have experienced academic problems and received feedback from teachers noting their need for more supervision in completing work, to pay better attention in class, and to develop better study skills. Their grades were likely to suffer from turning in assignments late, incomplete, or forgetting to turn them in altogether. Because their difficulties generally were internalized and did not lead to disruptive behaviors that would capture the attention of teachers, these patients' difficulties often were not identified until college or later in adulthood. Not surprisingly, predominantly inattentive symptoms are often associated with comorbid internalizing disorders, such as anxiety or depression (Nigg, 2006; Tannock, 2000).

ADHD, Combined Type

The combined type is the most frequently encountered subtype of ADHD in clinical settings, affecting about 50 to 75% of all individuals with ADHD (Millstein et al., 1997; Nigg, 2006; Wilens et al., 2002). These individuals experience the combination of inattentive and hyperactive–impulsive symptoms, creating a "double whammy" of cognitive and behavioral difficulties. Considering the distinct risk factors associated with externalizing behaviors, individuals in this category are often lumped together with those fulfilling diagnostic criteria for the hyperactive–impulsive subtype.

In fact, there is debate in the ADHD literature regarding whether or not the hyperactive–impulsive and combined types of ADHD represent distinct disorders from the inattentive type (Hinshaw, 2001; Lahey, 2001; Milich, Balentine, & Lynam, 2001; Nigg, 2006). Further, hyperactive–impulsive type behaviors in childhood appear to be a precursor for later development of combined type features (Barkley, 2006a). Regardless, individuals with the combined type tend to be the most impaired of the three ADHD subtypes owing to the combination of prominent symptoms of inattention that may contribute to academic impairment and high incidence of behavioral and emotional comorbidity (Wilens et al., 2002).

ADHD, Not Otherwise Specified (NOS)

This final category reflects individuals who, although their symptom profiles do not fulfill diagnostic criteria, may seek help for significant functional difficulties related to limited, subthreshold symptoms of ADHD, such as disorganization, procrastination, or poor time management. According to the *DSM-IV-TR*, this category is also used for individuals fulfilling full criteria but whose onset of symptoms occurred after the age of 7. It should be noted that experts in adult ADHD acknowledge that this is an arbitrary age of onset and that evidence of symptoms appearing prior to age 12 and persisting into adulthood is sufficient to warrant a diagnosis of adulthood ADHD (McGough & Barkley, 2004), with recent evidence suggesting 16 years old as a sufficient age of onset (Barkley & Murphy, 2006b). In fact, Faraone (2006) presented evidence that there is no difference in symptoms and impairment between adults who had been diagnosed with ADHD prior to age 7 and those with a later onset of symptoms. There are differences, however, for individuals with subthreshold symptoms, indicating that the diagnosis must be used carefully.

The NOS diagnosis is appropriate for individuals who have been accurately diagnosed with ADHD earlier in life and who are seeking maintenance treatment of their symptoms, often described as "residual" ADHD. In such cases, the individual is often already on a therapeutic dose of medications and has developed good coping skills, which means that the review of current symptoms and testing results will likely fall within normal limits. However, ADHD is a chronic disorder requiring ongoing management. For other individuals for whom this diagnostic category applies, there are attention problems, albeit subthreshold, that create difficulties in functioning for which some manner of clinical intervention is appropriate, unless, of course, it is clear that these symptoms can be explained better by another disorder or by some sort of secondary gain.

Although it is increasingly recognized that symptoms of ADHD persist into adulthood for more than 50% of affected individuals (and upwards of 80%), until recently the prevalence of adult ADHD was not well known because many individuals who experienced symptoms as children were not identified and assessed until adulthood. The notion of age-dependent decline of symptoms (for example, Hill & Schoener, 1996)—that children eventually grow out of ADHD—is now understood as an artifact of how symptom profiles of ADHD change with age and how (and by whom) symptoms are assessed (Barkley et al., 2002; Mick, Faraone, & Biederman, 2004). Relying solely on patient responses on self-report questionnaires to establish the diagnosis is insufficient. Barkley, Fischer, et al. (2002) found very low persistence rates when using *DSM* diagnostic thresholds for the reassessment of young adults who had been diagnosed with ADHD in childhood. However, when defining persistence as self-report of symptoms that fell two standard deviations above the mean (for example, top 7%) of a normative sample, then the same responses by the same individuals resulted in increased persistence. Parents' reports of symptoms for this same sample of young adults revealed 66% persistence. Similarly, Biederman et al. (2000) reported about 40% syndromatic persistence (that is, meeting full diagnostic criteria) among a sample of young adults (18 to 20 years) who were reassessed after having been diagnosed with ADHD in childhood. However, when defining persistence in functional terms (that is, at least five *DSM* symptoms and a Global Assessment of Functioning scale score of 60 or lower), there was 90% symptomatic persistence among this same sample of young adults that might require clinical attention.

The next section will review the emerging prevalence data for adult ADHD and the life outcomes of adults living with ADHD.

PERSISTENCE AND PREVALENCE OF ADULT ADHD

Many of the difficulties involved in establishing diagnostic criteria for ADHD also hinder efforts to accurately gauge the prevalence of ADHD. The prevalence range most often cited is 3 to 7% of the childhood population in the United States, a number derived from expert consensus (APA, 2000), though published studies estimate upwards of 10% of boys and 5% of girls of elementary school age fulfill criteria (American Academy of Child and Adolescent Psychiatry [AACAP], 1997; Faraone, 2005). Some studies report even higher prevalence figures; however, when relying solely on symptom checklists to establish the diagnosis instead of a full clinical evaluation, these statistics reflect "screening" prevalences of ADHD (Nigg, 2006). There is corroborative empirical support for the more conservative prevalence figures, and similar results are obtained in international samples, indicating that ADHD is not simply an American phenomenon that results from a fast-paced, media- and technology-saturated culture (Biederman & Faraone, 2004; Faraone, 2005; Faraone et al., 2003). However, there is variability in international prevalence rates depending upon how ADHD is operationally defined and on how symptoms are measured (for example, more focus on observable signs of hyperactivity than on symptoms of inattention) and cultural differences in disclosing symptoms (Gingerich et al., 1998).

Barkley (2006a) has noted that some critics of the ADHD diagnosis point to data that show that large numbers of non-ADHD children have been found to have some of the symptoms of ADHD. Scrutiny of these studies, however, reveals that they often cite findings based on individual symptoms rather than the minimal symptom requirement (that is, at least six symptoms) and the severity of symptom requirement of the *DSM* (that is, symptom must occur "often," thus reflecting developmental inappropriateness).

Barkley (2006a) summarized prevalence studies of ADHD that employed established diagnostic criteria (*DSM* or *International Classification of Diseases, ICD,* World Health Organization, 1993) and diagnostic interviews of children and adolescents. The prevalence rates ranged from 2 to 9.5% of children and adolescents when using *DSM-III* (APA, 1980) criteria (average 4.9%); 1.4 to 13.3% when using adult ratings of *DSM-III-R* (APA, 1987) criteria (average 5.9%), and 1.4 to 8.9% when using *DSM-III-R* (APA, 1987) criteria. Nigg (2006) reported a 6.8% median estimate of prevalence from his review of five studies utilizing structure behavior ratings and assessment of impairment using *DSM-IV* criteria (APA, 1994), almost equally divided between the combined and primarily inattentive subtypes.

Attempts to establish prevalence rates of ADHD in adulthood suffer from the fact that its study remains in its infancy. Researchers and clinicians continue to search for a consistent set of diagnostic criteria that adequately describe the developmental deficits of adult ADHD relative to normative adult development and functioning. Furthermore, longitudinal studies tracking children diagnosed with ADHD into adulthood vary regarding the use of *DSM* criteria, other measures of ADHD symptoms, and whether the presence of the diagnosis in adulthood is defined as meeting full diagnostic criteria, partial criteria, or the presence of symptoms that require treatment but that may not meet full diagnostic criteria (Biederman et al., 2000). In many studies, the official diagnostic criteria changed by the time children with ADHD reached adulthood. However, a recently completed national comorbidity survey revealed that 36.3% of respondents who had met *DSM-IV* (APA, 1994) criteria for ADHD in childhood continued to meet full diagnostic criteria in adulthood, as assessed by self-report symptoms questionnaires (Kessler et al., 2005). The authors noted that this may be a conservative percentage because *DSM* symptoms were designed for children ages 4 to 17 and many symptoms may not apply to many adults continuing to struggle with ADHD, resulting in an underestimation of adult ADHD.

Another limitation of previous research on the persistence and prevalence of ADHD is that it has generally focused on children; moreover, clinic-referred boys with the hyperactive–impulsive subtype. Such observable behaviors are more easily defined and identified by raters than are the symptoms of the inattentive subtype; thus, individuals in this latter category have been underrepresented in research and are probably less likely to seek treatment until encountering difficulties in adulthood. However, recent research involving community samples of children has revealed that the prevalence and severity of ADHD in both boys and girls is more similar than was previously thought (Biederman et al., 1999; Biederman et al., 2002, 2005). Finally, many studies of adult patients do not include an adequate enough assessment of the history of childhood symptoms of ADHD to confirm a valid diagnosis.

Despite these limitations in defining and studying ADHD, the prevalence rate of adult ADHD has been estimated from 2% of the population (Spencer et al., 1996) to upwards of 5% of the population (Barkley, 2006a; Biederman, 2005; DuPaul et al., 2001; Heiligenstein et al., 1998; Murphy & Barkley, 1996b). A recently completed study of adult ADHD, the National Comorbidity Survey Replication, established a prevalence rate of 4.4% prevalence among U.S. adults (Kessler et al., 2006), with a 4.2% prevalence rate among a subsample of adults in the work force (Kessler, Adler, Ames, et al., 2005). The very fact that ADHD was included in such an important and large study of the occurrence of psychiatric problems in the United States is notable in that it shows that adult ADHD is viewed as a disorder worthy of attention and study. Taken together, the prevalence rates translate to about 8 to 10 million adults affected by ADHD in the United States.

A complicating factor in recognizing and getting treatment for adult ADHD is the fact that it very often coexists with other problems that may mask the symptoms of ADHD. The next section discusses some common comorbid problems observed in adults with ADHD and the many negative life outcomes they experience that make clear that ADHD is a potentially disabling syndrome for which many will require treatment.

COMORBIDITY AND LIFE OUTCOMES
OF ADULTS WITH ADHD

By the time children with undiagnosed or untreated ADHD reach adulthood and seek treatment, it is unusual for ADHD to be cited as their sole or even their primary reason for seeking help. It is estimated that 70 to 75% of adults with ADHD who enter treatment carry at least one additional psychiatric diagnosis (Angold, Costello, & Erkanli, 1999; Biederman, 2004; Shekim et al., 1990; Wilens et al., 2002). The prevalence rates for anxiety disorders (24 to 43%) and depression (major depression: 16 to 31%; dysthymia: 19 to 37%) among clinic-referred adults with ADHD are comparable to those seen in children with ADHD and occur more frequently than would be predicted by chance (Barkley, 2006a; Biederman et al., 1993; Fischer et al., 2002; McGough et al., 2005; Safren et al., 2001; Tzelepis, Schubiner, & Warbasse, 1995; Wilens et al., 2002). The prevalence of substance use disorders among patients with ADHD is twice that found in the general population, with 32 to 53% reporting alcohol use problems and 8 to 32% reporting other substance use problems (Barkley, 2006a; Biederman et al., 1998; Biederman et al., 1999; McGough et al., 2005; Shekim et al., 1990; Tzelepis et al., 1995).

These statistics suggest that comorbidity in the assessment and treatment of ADHD is the rule rather than the exception. This fact makes assessing ADHD symptoms difficult, as it is often tricky to discern whether complaints of inattention or disorganization reflect the chronic and pervasive symptoms of ADHD, result from another disorder, or are some combination of the two.

In addition to psychiatric comorbidity, adults with ADHD are at higher risk for a number of serious life problems that affect their ability to function. When compared with adults without ADHD, adults with ADHD consistently complete fewer years of school, have lower levels of employment, earn lower salaries, change jobs more frequently, receive more negative ratings of work performance, have higher divorce rates, have lower relationship satisfaction, are at higher risk for psychiatric and substance abuse problems, have higher rates of pessimism and lower life satisfaction, and are more likely to report impairment that interferes with keeping up with the demands of daily life (Barkley, 2002; Barkley, Murphy, & Kwasnik, 1996b; Biederman & Faraone, 2005; Biederman et al., 2006; Faraone & Biederman, 2005; Fischer et al., 2002; Murphy & Barkley, 1996a; Rasmussen & Gillberg, 2000; Weiss & Hechtman, 1993).

Recently completed surveys of the life outcome of adults with ADHD compared with non-ADHD controls reveal a number of functional problems associated with a diagnosis of ADHD that have a negative impact on identity, satisfaction, and life options. When compared with non-ADHD controls, adults with ADHD who were asked to recall their experiences in childhood and adolescence rated themselves as less likely than peers to participate in extracurricular activities (including organized sports) and educational/cultural activities outside of school, to go on dates, and to spend free time with family or friends (Biederman et al., 2006; Faraone & Biederman, 2005). Adults with ADHD were less likely than non-ADHD peers to recall being liked by teachers, parents, and peers and were more likely to describe themselves as having negative attitudes and social experiences. Adults with ADHD were significantly more likely than non-ADHD adults to have not finished high school and reported lower grades despite being more likely to have received special academic help. Of adults with ADHD, 72% said their symptoms have had a lifelong impact and they were significantly more likely than controls to report workplace and relationship impairment. Not surprisingly, adults with ADHD were significantly more negative in their outlooks on life and had lower ratings of self-acceptance.

Adults with ADHD were less likely to be employed regardless of academic attainment and had lower household incomes than matched controls (Biederman & Faraone, 2005). In fact, assuming that the reported differences in educational attainment and achievement are fully attributable to ADHD symptoms, the estimated annual individual income loss associated with a diagnosis of ADHD was estimated at upwards of $10,300 to $15,400 per person, which reflects a total annual income loss of $77.5 to $115.9 billion associated with a diagnosis of ADHD.

In addition to lost income due to lower education attainment, ADHD is associated with lower levels of workplace performance (Kessler et al., 2005). In a survey of U.S. workers, ADHD emerged as a significant predictor of overall lost work performance. More specifically, ADHD was associated with 13.6 days of absenteeism (missed days of work) and 21.6 days of presenteeism (underperformance on the job), which adds up to 7 workweeks of lost productivity at an annual salary-equivalent loss of $5661 per worker with ADHD. The projected impact on the U.S. labor force was estimated to be 120.8 million lost workdays per year at a salary-equivalent cost of $19.6 billion.

It was previously thought that if an individual was able to complete college, then she or he could not possibly have ADHD. Research has revealed that symptoms of ADHD can coexist with high intelligence to create a uniquely frustrating combination of strong abilities and executive dysfunction (Brown, Patterson, & Quinlan, 2003). Forty-two percent of a sample of ADHD adults with IQs of 120 or higher reported stopping their postsecondary education at least once (Brown, 2005). Many individuals with ADHD are able to compensate for their symptoms through high school and even college but find themselves facing increasing amounts and complexity of work in graduate school or at work that are difficult to manage and create severe stress and frustration.

Other longitudinal and cross-sectional studies have revealed similar patterns of lower academic and vocational achievement, more frequent job changes, poorer driving records, higher rates of divorce, higher health care costs (even when controlling for psychiatric care), and greater risk for developing substance abuse and psychiatric disorders among adults with ADHD when compared with non-ADHD controls (Barkley, 2002, 2006a, 2006b; Weiss & Hechtman, 1993; Weiss, Hechtman, & Weiss, 1999; Wilens et al., 2002).

Furthermore, a case could be made that ADHD is a highly relevant public health issue. A longitudinal study of children with ADHD followed into young adulthood revealed that adolescents with ADHD began having sex at an earlier age, were less likely to use contraception, and, not surprisingly, had four times the rate of sexually transmitted disease and almost 10 times the pregnancy rate by age 20 when compared with their non-ADHD peers (Barkley, 2002; Barkley et al., 2006). Similarly, individuals with ADHD were more likely than peers to incur major injuries requiring medical attention and to have higher rates of driving violations and automobile accidents (including higher numbers of accidents with injuries and higher rates of monetary damage as measured by driving records and performance on driving simulators).

To this point, we have discussed the diagnostic criteria for, developmental course of, and prevalence of ADHD in addition to the common comorbidities and life outcomes experiences by adults with ADHD. The negative life outcomes associated with ADHD raise the question of what causes its symptoms. The next section will provide a brief overview of research on the etiology of ADHD.

ETIOLOGY

ADHD has strong genetic and neurobiological underpinnings. Research into the heritability of ADHD symptoms has focused on its prevalence in biological relatives, in identical and fraternal twins, and in adoptive families (with no genetic similarities). The findings consistently point to ADHD as being a highly heritable condition, with close to 80% of the variance of the traits associated with ADHD resulting from genetic factors.

Similarly, various neuropsychological and neuroimaging studies of brain structure and function have revealed differences between the brains of individuals with ADHD and those without ADHD. Although more work needs to be done to replicate these findings in larger samples, there is convincing evidence that ADHD is not the result of poor parenting or poor diet or is limited to a hectic American culture, but rather is the result of atypical neurodevelopmental processes. As Martha Denckla has noted (1991), "ADHD is a label for a heterogeneous group of dysfunctions related to each of several nodes along the attentional/intentional network...from cerebellum up to and including prefrontal cortex...[that] includes neural substrates of activation, orientation, motivation and vigilance as these connect with and influence executive function..." (p. x).

NEUROBIOLOGY

Neuroimaging technology has allowed researchers to study the structure and functioning of the brain with increasing specificity. The results of these studies must be approached with caution due to the small numbers of subjects from which the findings are drawn, the inconsistency of findings across studies, and the fact that researchers are still trying to sort out the significance of the activity versus inactivity of certain brain regions in response to different tasks. Despite these limitations, neuroimaging research has started to uncover the neurobiological underpinnings of ADHD (see Pliszka, 2002, 2003, 2005; Spencer, Biederman, Wilens, & Faraone, 2002, for reviews).

Structural Neuroimaging

In the typical human brain, the right hemisphere is usually larger than the left. Studies using magnetic resonance imaging (MRI) to examine the brain's morphology indicate that individuals with ADHD have right hemispheres that are on average 5.2% smaller than in individuals who are not diagnosed with ADHD (Castellanos et al., 1994; Filipek et al., 1997; Hynd et al., 1990; Pliszka, 2003). Thus, the ADHD brain tends to appear more symmetrical than is typically seen in the non-ADHD brain.

There are functional implications of having a smaller right frontal lobe. This region is involved in withdrawal behavior when a person perceives aversive stimuli. In effect, it serves to raise a neurological "red flag" when facing a situation with potentially negative consequences. It is also involved in weighing the consequences of actions and in assessing the risks versus rewards of various choices. A common observation about individuals with ADHD is that they enter situations or take chances with an apparent disregard for or lack of consideration of potential negative consequences and that they tend to persist in unrewarding behaviors for longer periods of time than age-matched controls. While there can be many contributing factors to impulsive or risky behaviors, a deficient warning system would certainly seem to play a role.

Three other specific structures that are found to be smaller in the right side of the brain for ADHD individuals include the cerebellum, the caudate nucleus, and the globus pallidus (Pliszka, 2003). The cerebellum, which lies atop the brain stem, controls the coordinated expression of movement, particularly overlearned, seemingly automatic actions. For example, learning to tie one's shoelaces requires a significant allocation of attention, concentration, and motor coordination. The individual must execute a number of complex, goal-oriented steps to create an intricate shape from two ends of a string that must also adequately secure the shoe. With regular practice, however, tying one's shoe becomes automatic and could be done without looking, without concentrating on the task, and while simultaneously carrying on a conversation. Such skills represent the transfer of control from predominantly prefrontal and parietal regions to the cerebellar region.

Overall cerebellar volume tends to be smaller in children with ADHD and, in particular, the vermis (a midline structure) (Castellanos et al., 1994, 2001; Mostofsky et al., 1998). The vermis is the only part of the cerebellum that receives dopamine. The whole cerebellum receives norepinephrine. The vermis plays a role in the output of both of these neurochemical input systems. It is now believed that some of the neuropsychological deficits that accompany ADHD, such as impaired motor control, inefficient procedural learning, and difficulty with multitasking, stem from cerebellar underdevelopment.

The caudate nucleus and globus pallidus are located near the middle of the brain and serve to translate neurochemical commands into the initiation of action (Pliszka, 2003). Together, they are referred to as the striatum, key components of what is known as the basal ganglia.

Degeneration of structures of the basal ganglia is associated with many movement disorders such as Parkinson's disease and Huntington's chorea. There have been mixed results in different studies of the comparative sizes of caudate nuclei in the brains of children with ADHD (Castellanos et al., 1996; Filipek et al., 1997; Semrud-Clikeman et al., 2000). Some studies found that children with ADHD had smaller right caudates than non-ADHD children, though their right caudates were larger than their left. Other studies found non-ADHD children to have larger left caudates than right, and ADHD children had smaller left caudates than these controls (though their left caudates were larger than their right). Semrud-Clikeman et al. (2000) found that children whose larger left caudates performed better on measures of inhibitory control (that is, Stroop task).

Taken together, findings from structural neuroimaging studies suggest that there are some subtle structural differences in some brain regions for individuals with ADHD when compared with the same brain regions of individuals without ADHD. Further, the brain regions in question play a role in regulating the types of behaviors frequently disordered in individuals with ADHD. Caution is recommended in reviewing such studies, however, in that they are often based on small samples, mostly of children and adolescents, and the aforementioned structural differences may only apply for a relatively small percentage of individuals with the clinical symptoms of ADHD.

Functional Neuroimaging

In addition to structural variations, there have been differences found in the activity of diverse brain regions in individuals with ADHD. In particular, the frontal lobes are implicated in higher order cognitive processing, such as planning, organization, and prioritizing—many aspects of what would be referred to as self-control, which is impaired in many individuals with ADHD (Barkley, 1997a, 1997b; Brown, 2005, 2006).

In a landmark study, Zametkin et al. (1990) used positron emission tomography (PET) to compare rates of glucose metabolism between adults with and without ADHD. Zametkin and colleagues' results showed that adults with ADHD metabolized glucose more slowly in the frontal lobes (about 8% less activity than controls), indicating that this region of the brain was operating less efficiently in adults with ADHD than in adults without ADHD. Ernst et al. (1998, 1999) later reported results from a different PET scan study that revealed that girls with ADHD exhibited global decreases in glucose metabolism when compared with non-ADHD girls, whereas no such difference emerged for boys with and without ADHD (as cited in Pliszka, 2003). Although Zametkin and colleagues have been unable to replicate their initial finding, the frontal lobes and, more specifically, the region of the prefrontal cerebral cortex (located just behind the forehead) have become primary areas of interest for investigators. These regions are thought of as the "command centers" of the brain, the seat of what are known as the *executive functions*.

Dozens of functional neuroimaging studies have been carried out in the ensuing decade to pursue this line of research using various imaging methods (see Bush, Valera, & Seidman, 2005, for an excellent review of this topic). By asking subjects to perform various neuropsychological tests inside the imagers, researchers have identified key differences in the way patients with ADHD process information and solve cognitive problems. For instance, the dorsal area of the anterior cingulate gyrus, which normally assists in the detection of error and is involved in regulating attention, motivation, response selection, and decision-making, is inactive in ADHD adults given a counting version of the Stroop test (Bush et al., 1999). Instead, peripheral areas are activated in the ADHD brain, which are less efficient in completing the same task. Adolescents with ADHD activate more regions of the brain than non-ADHD subjects when asked to suppress a response on a go–no go task, suggesting that this inhibiting behavior is harder and requires more work for them than it is for individuals without ADHD (Schulz et al., 2004).

The emerging data suggest that executive dysfunction is indeed a hallmark of ADHD, and that the interconnected areas of the brain that regulate these processes do not work as efficiently as they do in control subjects. It is also becoming increasingly clear that there is a fair degree of individual variation among individuals with ADHD with respect to the severity and extent of executive dysfunction, as well as the specific brain regions that are most highly affected. The variability among patients with the disorder makes it so difficult to specify the precise pathophysiology of ADHD, and makes the diagnostic use of current neuroimaging techniques unhelpful and impractical.

EXECUTIVE FUNCTIONS

Executive functions are higher order cognitive processes that serve to integrate and coordinate other cognitive functions of the brain that are associated with many of the brain regions mentioned above. The brain has been conceptualized as akin to a Swiss army knife, having many discrete and important skills and functions crucial for solving problems in the environment. These specific functions or modules are thought to be evolutionarily advantageous in that they have conferred on those individuals with them a differential advantage for survival or reproduction (Barkley, 2001; Pinker, 1997). The executive functions, however, do not provide a specific, discrete mental skill, such as language or "theory of mind." Instead, the executive functions seem to operate as a module of metaorganization that oversees most of these higher order cognitive functions that are central to our abilities for self-control, vigilance, learning, and forethought, which are impaired in ADHD (Barkley, 1997a, 1997b; Brown, 2005, 2006). Despite the appeal of this emerging paradigm, not all cases of ADHD can be explained by prefrontal lobe executive dysfunction (Willcutt et al., 2005).

The executive functions may be the organizational processes that most people think of as the brain's flexibility in navigating through different challenges of life. Dr. Thomas Brown of Yale University has focused on deficits in the executive functions as central to the downstream symptoms seen in individuals with ADHD (Brown, 1996, 2005, 2006). Brown posits that the structures and functions that undergird the executive functions are not fully developed at birth but continue to develop and mature into early adulthood. They are dependent upon the processes of myelination, synaptic pruning, and elaboration of the dopamine and norepinephrine systems, all of which result from the interaction of biology and developmental experience. Difficulties in the executive functions can develop from developmental deficits, traumatic injury, disease, and decline in the course of aging. Brown considers ADHD to be a developmental disorder of impaired executive functions and views the hyperactive–impulsive and inattentive types of ADHD as different manifestations of this core impairment. Development of the executive functions in the ADHD brain is delayed when compared with the non-ADHD brain and, in many cases, may not catch up. However, many individuals may have particularly forgiving environments or "scaffolding" that compensates for the effects of executive dysfunction (Brown, 2005). With increased demands for intact executive functioning in adolescence and in adulthood, problems related to ADHD may emerge at any point at which the demands of life exceed one's executive functioning abilities.

In contrast, Dr. Russell Barkley (1997a, 1997b, 2006a) views ADHD as a disorder of behavioral disinhibition: the inability to inhibit a prepotent response to compelling stimuli (that is, a response for which there is immediate and/or previously associated reinforcement). He has put forth an elegant and testable theory of the manner in which behavioral disinhibition interferes with the performance of the executive functions, resulting in the downstream symptoms observed in ADHD. His theory is particularly pertinent for the difficulties encountered by individuals with hyperactivity–impulsivity. Barkley views the inattentive type of ADHD as a qualitatively distinct disorder from the hyperactive–impulsive type, or at least as not falling within his behavioral disinhibition framework.

Despite ongoing debates about the source and precise impact of executive dysfunction, there is agreement about its role in the symptoms and associated difficulties experienced by individuals with ADHD, such as academic impairment in childhood ADHD (Biederman et al., 2004). In fact, research to establish new symptoms for diagnosing ADHD in adulthood revealed that six of the seven best symptoms for identifying ADHD were derived from examples of executive dysfunction (Barkley & Murphy, 2006b). Moreover, executive dysfunction is increasingly associated with differences in the structure and function of the ADHD brain. These differences in neurobiological structure and functioning in the ADHD brain, in turn, seem to be the result of genetic predispositions.

GENETICS

The findings from genetics research consistently suggest that shared environmental factors (that is, social class, home environment) account for 0–6% of individual differences in ADHD symptoms; nonshared environmental factors (that is, nongenetic factors such as neurologic injury or exposure to toxins) account for 9 to 20% of individual differences in ADHD symptoms; finally, genetic factors, on average, account for close to 80% of individual differences in ADHD symptoms, making ADHD one of the most heritable psychiatric disorders (Barkley, 2006a; Coolidge, Thede, & Young, 2000; Faraone et al., 2000; Faraone, Tsuang, & Tsuang, 1999; Gilger, Pennington, & DeFries, 1992; Levy et al., 1997; McGuffin, Riley, & Plomin, 2001; Nigg, 2006; Pliszka, 2003; Rhee et al., 1999; Thapar, Hervas, & McGuffin, 1995; Thapar et al., 1999).

The gold standard of genetics research is the study of identical twins. The goal of such research is to, as much as possible, tease apart genetic and environmental contributions to the occurrence of various disorders. Identical, or monozygotic twins (MZ), develop from the same fertilized egg and, thus, share identical sets of genes. It is nature's version of cloning. Fraternal, or dizygotic twins (DZ), develop from two separate fertilized eggs. These twins share half their genes, just as any other two children of the same biological parents do. When twins are raised together, it is presumed that each has had essentially similar environmental experiences. Thus, it is predicted that MZ twins would appear to be more similar than DZ twins for genetically influenced traits or conditions. In fact, twin studies of hyperactivity and inattention have consistently shown that genetic factors account for a substantial amount of variance for ADHD symptoms (heritability estimates 0.39 to 0.81; Thapar et al., 1999). Studies of adoptive families with ADHD children, in which there is no genetic relation between adoptive parent and adopted child, have been used to compare the influence of environmental factors on children with ADHD. Again, the results from adoption studies indicate that adopted children with ADHD are significantly more similar to their biological parents than they are to their adopted parents, as measured by ratings of behaviors (Sprich, Biederman, Crawford, Mundy, & Faraone, 2000).

Some of the primary candidate genes implicated in ADHD are related to dopamine transmission. For example, the 7-repeat allele of the D4 dopamine receptor, with a worldwide prevalence of about 21%, causes the D4 receptor to be subsensitive to dopamine. It has been found to be a moderate risk factor for ADHD. The dopamine transporter gene (DAT) on chromosome 5 has also been a focus of ADHD research and shows similar promise as a candidate gene for the disorder. The DAT governs the reuptake of dopamine from the synaptic cleft into the neuron, and alterations in its normal functioning have been observed in recent neuroimaging studies of patients with ADHD (Krause et al., 2003; Krause et al., 2006). Since reuptake into the presynaptic terminal is the prime method by which the effect of dopamine is halted (Pliszka, 2003; Swanson et al., 2000), increased activity of the DAT leads to more rapid clearance of the neurotransmitter from the synapse and, hence, to functional dopamine depletion—a highly plausible explanation for the pathophysiology of ADHD. Not surprisingly, there are several other dopaminergic genes that are the subject of intense study (for excellent reviews, see Faraone et al., 2005; Faraone & Khan, 2006).

Despite the important progress of molecular genetics studies, Nigg (2006) provides a clearheaded reminder that the genetics of ADHD are "probabilistic" and not "deterministic." It seems most likely that there are multiple potential pathways to the development of ADHD, making it a complex disorder to study (Acosta, Arcos-Burgos, & Muenke, 2004). Likewise, it is a clinical challenge to assess ADHD in adult patients and to differentiate its symptoms from those of other psychiatric disorders. Careful assessment for adult ADHD is vital in order to avoid misdiagnosis. Though various symptom checklists and brief questionnaires can be useful as screening tools, there are no shortcuts when evaluating for adult ADHD: it requires a full diagnostic assessment by a qualified mental health professional. In the next section, we will discuss the core components of a competent assessment for adult ADHD.

ASSESSMENT OF ADULT ADHD

> I am a little apprehensive about our encounter. I have lost a lot
> of time, and I'm scared of slipping through the cracks again. For
> you, Monday afternoon will be another day at work. For me,
> Monday is another opportunity to pass unnoticed underneath
> the radar screen, or for the hoof beats of a zebra to be mistaken
> for those of a horse. (Female college student before her ADHD
> evaluation)

The previously mentioned difficulties involved in accurately identifying
ADHD symptoms and differentiating them from other disorders reinforce the importance of using a comprehensive diagnostic assessment
battery for adult ADHD. In this section, we will discuss the different
components of a comprehensive evaluation for adult ADHD, which
include review and history of presenting problems, review of developmental history, assessment of past and current ADHD symptoms, and
neuropsychological screening.

Review and History of Presenting Problems

As with any clinical assessment, it is useful to find out how patients
have come to the decision to seek help. It is important to find out what
patients view as problems in their lives and how their difficulties reflect
a change in previous functioning. Inquiring about how various circum-
stantial factors contribute to their difficulties, how their problems are
affecting their daily life, and what they have done to attempt to manage
these problems provides important clinical information about patients'
current situations.

In the case of an assessment for adult ADHD, it is also useful to ask
how the patient became aware of the diagnosis of ADHD, her opinion
of it, and its possible relevance to her current circumstances. In many
cases, individuals have "self-diagnosed" based on reading a popular
book on adult ADHD or from friends commenting that the person
"seems ADD." On the other hand, some individuals may be very skeptical about the diagnosis and are pursuing the evaluation solely at the
urging of a loved one. Such information is useful for the clinician in
case it seems that a particular patient is either over- or underreporting
symptoms based on their opinion of ADHD. When discussing possible
explanations for their presenting difficulties, it is reasonable to ask
patients both "How do you think ADHD might be affecting you and
be contributing to your problems?" and "If it turns out that there is not

evidence of ADHD, how do you think you would explain the problems you are experiencing?"

It is all too easy for patients and clinicians to become overly focused on the ADHD aspect of an evaluation and to forget to adopt a wider range view of the individual's well-being. A simple question along the lines of "Is there anything else going on in your life other than the possible role of ADHD that you think is significant or that you view as a problem to be addressed?" Finally, as always, it is important to assess patients' strengths and their available positive support systems and resources.

Developmental History

Next, it is important to review the patient's developmental history, including any reported problems during pregnancy, delivery, and early development. This review includes actively assessing for the attainment of developmental milestones and ruling out exposure to toxins in the womb (for example, maternal cigarette smoking) or infant and childhood diseases or injuries that could contribute to ADHD symptoms. In such situations, it can be invaluable to get the input of patients' parents or other individuals who knew them in childhood, in person or by questionnaire/letter, whenever possible.

Family History

It is useful to gain an understanding of the patient's family history and current family situation. In addition to eliciting any evidence or history of family conflicts that could affect patients, it is important to review family medical and psychiatric history as a means for uncovering possible genetic predispositions for emotional or medical problems. A comprehensive genogram should be constructed in order to discern the patterns of inheritance that are present in the family. This includes asking explicit questions about siblings, parents, or extended family members who are diagnosed with or appear to have ADHD, learning disabilities, or other problems related to self-control and information processing. Because awareness of ADHD has only relatively recently gained greater attention, it is not surprising to learn that few individuals born before the mid-1960s were identified with ADHD despite the presence of what can be seen in retrospect as clear symptoms of ADHD. However, asking questions about members of the family who seemed impulsive, had problems in school, were disorganized, or seemed to have problems similar to those for which the patient is seeking help may help uncover some clues about family history of ADHD.

Academic History

In most clinical evaluations, ascertaining the number of years of education completed by patients and their terminal degrees constitutes an adequate review of academic history. In the case of an adult ADHD evaluation, however, even if someone has earned an advanced degree, there may be important details about how the patient performed in school that are not reflected in his or her educational attainment. Reviewing academic and behavioral performance at each level of education, including asking about classes failed or left incomplete, grades repeated, summer school, the need for special academic support, and classes dropped in college may provide telling information. Likewise, asking questions about patients' abilities to listen and pay attention in lectures, complete reading assignments, organize and complete written assignments, manage time and maintain organization in their studies, take timed exams, and complete assignments on time provides vital information. We have heard many stories of patients who got by in school without doing any assigned reading or by relying on extra credit assignments and were able to move on to the next level of education without necessarily being prepared for it. In one case, a college student admitted that he was only able to focus on reading the first 10 pages of assigned reading. He compensated by dominating the discussion in the next class based on the few pages he had read and understood. While he earned high marks for class participation, he was unprepared for exams with questions drawn from the material he had not read.

Vocational History

For adults in the work force, a similarly detailed review of work history is indicated. Even when an individual has a seemingly stable employment history, it is useful to ask about the presence of any work-related difficulties, such as getting projects done on time, getting to work on time, disorganization, time management problems, or interpersonal conflicts with coworkers or superiors. It is useful to review reasons for changing jobs in the past and specific job duties or environments that have proven to be consistently challenging for the individual. Self-employed individuals should be queried regarding handling the unique work demands faced by them (for example, customer relations, scheduling work, financial accounting) and whether or not their self-employed status was by choice or by default (for example, "I couldn't hold a job anywhere else."). Finally, stay-at-home parents may face many difficulties keeping up with the demands of parenting and managing a household that are worth investigating.

Medical and Psychiatric History

A standard review of medical and psychiatric treatment history is useful to rule out the presence of medical disorders or brain injuries that could contribute to the complaints of inattention or impulsivity for which the individual is seeking an assessment. If there have been treatments for medical or psychiatric conditions, including ADHD, it is useful to ask about past diagnoses and assessments and response to previous medications and other interventions. In some cases, the clinical interview may unearth symptoms that may reflect a psychiatric or medical condition that could mimic the symptoms of ADHD. A medical consultation may be indicated to rule out suspicions of possible organic causes of symptoms, as in the case of a sleep study to rule out a sleep disorder or for blood work to rule out thyroid problems. A thorough diagnostic interview is crucial to assess for psychiatric disorders that may mask, coexist with, or mimic ADHD symptoms.

Diagnostic Interview

As was mentioned earlier, adults with ADHD are very likely to present with at least one additional psychiatric diagnosis. Furthermore, evaluations for adult ADHD may not necessarily reveal sufficient evidence to support a diagnosis of ADHD, instead indicating that other factors, such as mood, anxiety, substance use, or personality characteristics, are the source of patients' problems. Thus, a structured diagnostic interview is a vital facet of an adult ADHD evaluation.

At the University of Pennsylvania Adult ADHD Treatment and Research Program, we administer the Structured Clinical Interview for *DSM-IV* (SCID) (First et al., 1997) to each patient. The SCID assesses for the presence of substance abuse/dependence, mood disorders (including bipolar disorder), anxiety disorders, psychotic disorders, and eating disorders. As we tell patients, our goal is to obtain a comprehensive view of various factors that might be relevant to the problems they are experiencing.

There is no module for ADHD in the SCID; therefore, we use a combination of clinical interviews, symptoms checklists, objective questionnaires, and eliciting of corroborative information to assess ADHD symptoms. Finally, we administer various mood and personality questionnaires to gather a wide array of objective data about patients' symptoms and functioning that are diagnostically helpful, clinically relevant, and informative for patients.

ASSESSING SYMPTOMS OF ADHD

Of course, the main reason for conducting our comprehensive evaluation is to assess for symptoms of ADHD. Throughout the aforementioned components of our assessment, we are listening for and asking about symptoms of ADHD in patients' lives. A good clinical interview is invaluable in assessing the presence of ADHD symptoms. It is necessary, however, to bolster the clinical data collected in the interview by administering specific objective checklists and measures of ADHD symptoms, both in childhood and adulthood.

Inquiring about ADHD Behaviors

It is useful to inquire directly about patients' functioning in a number of life domains often affected by ADHD. Questions focused on how individuals handle work and/or school, including managing time, organizing paperwork and other materials, working independently, and meeting deadlines (including if individuals find themselves rushing at the last minute) can be informative. Similar questions about how individuals manage their personal affairs, including paying bills (and incurring late fees), keeping up with household chores, keeping appointments, adhering to a financial budget (including questions about impulsive spending), and maintaining organization (including questions about losing things) shed light on how they handle the business of adult life. General questions about patients' assessment of their own abilities to meet day-to-day responsibilities, fulfill personal obligations, learn from mistakes and change behaviors, and, finally, fulfill their own sense of potential can be telling. The answers and stories told by adults with ADHD can be heart wrenching. Most individuals without ADHD may recount isolated incidents in which they encountered limited difficulties. Individuals with ADHD, on the other hand, often report numerous and recurring examples of functional problems that cause them great distress almost every day.

ADHD Symptom Checklists

We use symptom checklists to help assess the presence of both childhood and current adulthood symptoms of ADHD. The combination of checklists and interview allows clinicians to ask follow-up questions about specific symptoms patients may or may not endorse (particularly when there seems to be discordance between interview and checklist responses).

We have found Barkley's symptom checklists and the associated psychometric data he has gathered on them extremely helpful to this end (Barkley & Murphy, 2006a). We ask patients to complete the self-report forms for both childhood and adulthood symptoms in addition to assessing for the same symptoms during the clinical interview. Parallel forms of both adult and childhood checklists are available for observers to rate their perceptions of patients' behaviors. Whenever possible, we ask patients to obtain these scores from their significant others, such as parents, siblings, spouses, and roommates. We expect that the current symptom questionnaires will be modified in the near future to reflect new research identifying symptoms of ADHD specific to adult patients (for example, Barkley & Murphy, 2006b).

As they currently exist, the symptom checklist items are consistent with *DSM-IV* diagnostic criteria and alternate between symptoms of inattention and hyperactivity–impulsivity. The symptoms are rated by the respondent on a 4-point scale of severity of symptoms from those that are/were *never or rarely* a problem ("0" or minimal) to those that are/were *very often* a problem ("3" or severe). According to the scoring instructions, symptoms endorsed as occurring at least *often* ("2" or moderately) are considered diagnostic and are counted for each of the subtypes. If at least six of nine items are endorsed as moderate severity in either category of subtype, the symptoms fulfill criteria for that subtype (and fulfill "combined" if criteria for both subtypes are met). In our clinical practice, however, if individuals report numerous symptoms rated as being "mild" in childhood, describe a history characteristic of an ADHD profile, and are facing problems in adulthood related to executive dysfunction, we would consider these patients as fulfilling criteria for ADHD.

Although we do not use it in our clinic, the Wender Utah Rating Scale (WURS) (Ward, Wender, & Reimherr, 1993) is frequently used in research, and readers should be familiar with it. The WURS is a 61-item self-report rating scale that assesses symptoms of adult ADHD, such as activity level, inattention, impulsivity, mood lability, irritability/hot temper, disorganization, and impaired stress tolerance. These seven symptom clusters reflect Wender's model of adult ADHD and have come to be known as the Utah criteria (Wender, 1995). The WURS has 25 items that are highly correlated with parental report of childhood ADHD behavior and has been used in some studies of adults as a retrospective assessment of childhood onset of ADHD symptoms. Two criticisms of the WURS are that it has not been revised to keep with changes made to *DSM* criteria and its symptoms may not be applicable for individuals with inattentive type ADHD (McGough & Barkley, 2004).

Standardized Adult ADHD Symptom Rating Scales

Although the classic ADHD symptoms can be assessed in adult patients through a careful clinical interview, they often look different in adults than in children. Relying solely on the presence of *DSM* symptom criteria is a necessary but insufficient facet of a diagnostic assessment for adult ADHD, particularly considering that the existing criteria were developed primarily for children (McGough & Barkley, 2004) and may not be developmentally appropriate for the assessment of adults (Barkley & Murphy, 2006b).

Standardized objective symptom rating scales such as the Conners' Adult ADHD Rating Scales (CAARS) (Conners, Erhart, & Sparrow, 1999) and the Brown Attention Deficit Disorder Scale for Adults (BADDS) (Brown, 1996) help clinicians assess a wide range of symptoms of ADHD in adult patients. We have found using both of these scales in our clinic to be beneficial because each provides useful and somewhat nonoverlapping clinical information.

The CAARS: Long Version is a 66-item self-report instrument that measures a wide variety of symptoms of ADHD in adult patients. Similar to the Barkley symptom scales, patients rate each item on a 4-point scale of the occurrence of symptoms ranging from *not at all, never* to *very much, very frequently*. The CAARS yields a total score and subscale scores (that is, Inattention/Memory Problems, Hyperactivity/Restlessness, Impulsivity/Emotional Lability, Problems with Self-Concept) measuring a variety of deficits commonly associated with ADHD. Among the subscale scores are three devoted to *DSM* criteria (*DSM-IV* Inattentive Symptoms, *DSM-IV* Hyperactive–Impulsive Symptoms, and *DSM-IV* ADHD Symptoms Total) and an additional ADHD Index score that are helpful in corroborating clinical data gathered during interviews. Each respondent's responses are tabulated and transformed as *t* scores (mean = 50; standard deviation = 10) on a profile form that is based on norms compiled specific to both gender and age of the respondent. There also are both brief and screening versions of the CAARS as well as an observer form.

The BADDS-Adult Version is a 40-item examiner-administered instrument that measures a wide variety of symptoms of ADHD in adult patients. The BADDS not only examines the ability to sustain attention but also the ability to get started on work tasks, initiate and sustain attention, maintain effort necessary to complete tasks, regulate moods, and recall information encountered in daily life. It yields a total score and five subscale scores corresponding to the previously mentioned components of the executive functions (that is, Activation, Attention, Effort, Affect, and Memory). Each item is rated on a 4-point scale of the occurrence of symptoms ranging from *never* to *almost daily*. Similar to the CAARS, respondents' responses are tabulated and presented as *t* scores on a profile form that is based on adult norms.

Despite the usefulness and quality of such objective measures of ADHD symptoms, there is no single test upon which clinicians can rely to accurately diagnose ADHD. Of course, this statement is true for most psychiatric disorders, as diagnoses are arrived at only after review of history, clinical interview, and, whenever possible, at least one objective measure. However, we would not recommend making a diagnosis of ADHD based on a single score on a single questionnaire. The other aspects of the evaluation are important because some individuals with ADHD may tend to underreport symptoms on various checklists and objective measures (Barkley, et al., 2002). Thus, it is very useful to augment the interviews and symptom assessments with measures of neuropsychological functioning.

Neurocognitive Screening

The conceptualization of ADHD as stemming from executive dysfunction has led to a surge in neuropsychological research geared to study and identify specific deficits in neuropsychological functioning that might help to make the diagnosis. However, the research has not yet provided tests that either reliably predict an ADHD diagnosis or differentiate individuals with ADHD from those without ADHD (McGough & Barkley, 2004). Despite these current limitations, neuroconitive screening can be helpful in combination with assessment of clinical symptoms to identify areas of executive dysfunction and to illustrate for patients their cognitive profiles.

Before discussing some neuropsychological tests we have found useful in an adult ADHD evaluation, we should offer a similar caution made by others who discuss the use of neuropsychological testing for adult ADHD (for example, Murphy & Gordon, 2006). None of these tests has been shown to reliably predict a diagnosis of ADHD and, thus, should not be interpreted in this manner. On the other hand, testing allows clinicians to observe how patients handle various tasks that require sustained attention, impulse control, and working memory and to evaluate their performance. Such clinical data may be helpful by illustrating in finer detail the relative strengths and weaknesses exhibited by patients, at least as measured by these tasks. We inform patients that they will complete a brief cognitive decathlon in which they will be asked to complete a variety of tests to allow us to get a sense of how their brains respond to them.

We have found one test of auditory working memory surprisingly helpful: the Selective Reminding Test (SRT) (Buschke, 1973; Spreen & Strauss, 1991). The SRT is a list of 12 words that is aurally presented to a patient across multiple learning trials. The respondent is instructed that he or she, after hearing the entire list, is to repeat back all the words in any order. After the respondent recalls as many words as possible, the examiner identifies the omitted words and the respondent is instructed to recite the entire list of 12 words again. The test goes on for 12 trials or until the respondent accurately recites the word list three consecutive times, whichever occurs first. The SRT provides a measure of memory encoding, retrieval, and consolidation. The measure is standardized by age and by gender and includes alternate forms for retesting. In order to test delayed recall, the patient could be asked to repeat the list again after 5 minutes of other activities or at greater time increments.

We commonly administer specific subscales of the *Wechsler Adult Intelligence Scale—Third Edition (WAIS-III)* (Wechsler, 1997) to provide a brief summary of intellectual functioning and performance on specific cognitive skills, and as a brief screen for the presence of a learning disorder. We administer the Vocabulary, Block Design, Digit Span, and Digit Symbol Coding subscales to assess verbal skills, nonverbal problem-solving, auditory working memory for numbers, and cognitive processing speed, respectively. Although specific patterns of subtest scores and splits between verbal and performance measures have not been proven to be reliably associated with a diagnosis of ADHD (Murphy & Gordon, 2006), these subscales seem to provide an overview of strengths and weaknesses that patients find helpful.

More frequently used in the assessment of adult ADHD are measures of continuous performance, such as the Conners' Continuous Performance Test-II (CPT-II) (Conners, 2004). The CPT-II is a computerized measure of sustained attention and vigilance that requires the participant to visually monitor letters presented at varying speeds. The participant is asked to respond to targets by pressing the spacebar and to inhibit responses to nontargets as they appear on the screen. Some of the scores derived from the CPT-II are the number of correct responses, number of targets missed (omission errors), number of responses to non-targets (commission errors), and response variability. The measure takes approximately 14 minutes to administer and is supported by normative data for adolescents and adults.

The Penn Abstraction, Inhibition, and Working Memory Test (AIM) (Glahn et al., 2000; Gur et al., 2001) is a computerized test of abstraction, inhibition, and working memory developed by researchers at the University of Pennsylvania to assess some aspects of the executive functions that has been validated on populations of normal and schizophrenic patients. Considering that executive dysfunction is a shared aspect of schizophrenia and ADHD, we have used the test as part of our assessment protocol. The AIM consists of the Abstraction and the Abstraction plus Memory subtests. The Abstraction subtest presents five computer-generated shapes (two shapes in the upper right corner, two shapes in the upper left corner, and one in the center of the computer screen). The goal is to match the center target shape to one of the two sets of shapes, located in the right or left corner. Principles for matching the target shape vary across trials. That is, the rules for what constitutes an accurate match change and the respondent must discern the rules based on feedback (that is, right or wrong choice) during the test and apply them (that is, learn). The Abstraction plus Memory subtest is identical to the Abstraction subtest except that the target stimuli are presented for 500 ms and then disappear. There is a 2.5-second delay before the two sets of shapes appear in their respective corners of the screen. The AIM provides a measure of abstract thinking and cognitive flexibility. The AIM yields z scores of the respondent's accuracy for both the memory and non-memory trials and z scores of the respondent's reaction times for the correct responses for both the memory and nonmemory trials (in addition to calculating total scores for accuracy and reaction time). Normative data are available for healthy adolescents and adults. We have found the review of accuracy scores and reaction time scores for both non-memory and memory subscales to provide useful information about relative strengths and weaknesses for individuals in terms of the relative trade-offs of accuracy and speed of responding, though more research is needed regarding its usefulness for adults with ADHD.

The results for adults with ADHD on these and other neuropsychological tests are mixed (Gallagher & Blader, 2001; Hervey, Epstein, & Curry, 2004; Riccio et al., 2005; Solanto, Etefia, & Marks, 2004), which is the case for neuropsychological tests for ADHD in general (Murphy & Gordon, 2006). That is, by adulthood it seems that individuals have developed adequate compensatory strategies and/or cognitive skills (not to mention improved attention on novel computerized tests) that they seem able to adequately hold it together during a relatively brief test. Thus, adults with clear clinical symptoms of ADHD may score within the normal range on many tests of the executive functions. There is a need for ongoing research of the neuropsychological functioning of adults with ADHD to determine tests that help clinicians to more accurately make the diagnosis.

ADULT ADHD AND COMORBIDITY

Earlier in this chapter we referred to the need for a comprehensive diagnostic assessment to determine the presence of comorbid psychiatric symptoms. On the one hand, this procedure is important to differentiate the effects of other sorts of problems for which people seek treatment from the core symptoms of ADHD. An accurate differential diagnosis and understanding of presenting symptoms is an important first step in crafting a treatment plan that will prove helpful for the individual (Ramsay, 2005c).

On the other hand, as we have attempted to make clear the clinical picture is often not so cut-and-dried with adult ADHD. In most cases, long-standing difficulties experienced by individuals become intertwined with various other developmental frustrations, emotional symptoms, and life problems. In some cases, individuals recognize that they are struggling through life and encountering more than their fair share of disappointments but may not have been able to secure adequate assessment and treatment. Some other individuals may have appeared to outside observers as doing rather well in life, getting through high school, entering college, getting a job, and/or starting a family, with little sign of trouble. However, such individuals, when asked specifically, admit to recurring inefficient behavioral patterns and other difficulties encountered throughout their lives. While not an impairment when they were younger, symptoms required increasing efforts to manage as these individuals faced the progressively more difficult demands of adult life. These individuals go through life with a lingering feeling of being an imposter or an escalating sense that they are facing demands beyond their abilities to cope. Some combination of environmental demands and emotional distress that do not respond to individuals' existing coping strategies may lead them to eventually seek help.

Most of the symptoms representative of ADHD and, by extension, executive dysfunction, concern behavioral dysregulation, such as difficulties related to impulse control and initiating and following through on planned actions. However, another important area for consideration, particularly in the clinical management of adult ADHD, is how the executive functions have an effect on—and are affected by—emotions.

Feelings of depression (for example, sadness, guilt, shame), anxiety (for example, worry, fear, dread), anger (for example, rage, annoyance), or any other distressing levels of emotion may interfere with higher order cognitive process. Conversely, ADHD may predispose individuals to have difficulties handling many tasks required of daily life, resulting in emotional distress. Of course, predisposition for both ADHD and emotional (for example, mood) difficulties may coexist.

Regardless of how these difficulties align, the fact that they co-occur for many adults with ADHD is an important part of the diagnostic picture and deserves attention. Many individuals with ADHD report bursts of relatively brief but upsetting emotional reactions to various internal triggers or environmental stimuli. Although not resulting in a more stable, enduring problematic mood state, such as a major depressive episode, such emotionality can be upsetting and disruptive in its own right. Our discussion below is meant to be applicable for both individuals with ADHD experiencing coexisting disorders and those who struggle with briefer episodes (for example, "shadow syndromes," [Ratey & Johnson, 1997]) in which they feel derailed by their emotional reactions.

Depression

Excessive feelings of sadness, physical feelings of fatigue or tearfulness, lack of enjoyment or pleasure (for example, anhedonia), and increased negative evaluations of oneself, the world, and the future experienced more often than not over at least a few weeks are some of the hallmarks of major depression. For adults with ADHD who may already struggle with procrastination and difficulty concentrating, symptoms of depression may magnify problems experienced in initiating behavior or sustaining attention. Some individuals who are depressed may mistakenly think they have ADHD because of their distractibility and poor follow-through. One key difference between depression and ADHD is that individuals who have experienced depression usually report that their symptoms (including concentration and restlessness) improve as their mood improves, even in cases of chronic depression. For individuals with ADHD, these functional problems persist regardless of their moods.

Of course, depression and ADHD may coexist, whether the depressed mood develops as a result of repeated life frustrations and demoralization or both disorders developed in a true case of co-occurrence. In our clinical experience, the combination of depression and ADHD leads individuals to be very sensitive to frustration and failure. Individuals with this comorbidity pattern seem to give up on tasks easily at the first sign of difficulty (or perceived difficulty). Thus, these patients may be significantly underfunctioning in life or have adopted a stoic attitude of settling for their circumstances, even if they express dissatisfaction with these circumstances.

Anxiety

Most forms of anxiety are associated with feeling on edge or keyed up, difficulty concentrating (including having your mind go blank), worry, and irritability. These feelings are associated with the perception of a threat, something that could potentially harm the individual. Such feelings can be very adaptive when individuals face situations involving a degree of risk, such as the approach of a strange dog or preparing to cross a busy city street. However, individuals with anxiety experience levels of arousal either out of proportion with the situation or resulting from a magnification of the appraisal of threat, leading them to avoid various situations. ADHD adults often describe similar patterns of avoidance regarding tasks they have found difficult or frustrating in the past, such as academics or demands of the workplace.

Not surprisingly, many individuals who are anxious may assume that they have ADHD because their performance and follow-through on tasks are inconsistent, and their worries interfere with their concentration. However, anxiety is usually associated with specific contexts and tasks that are associated with threat. Symptoms are not activated when anxious individuals are not faced with these stressors. Individuals with ADHD often report pervasive and enduring difficulties related to their symptoms (though they may be more pronounced when facing certain demands and settings).

Anxiety and ADHD commonly coexist (Biederman et al., 1993; Safren et al., 2001; Schatz & Rostain, 2006). Again, this may be the result of a true coincidence, the fact that some individuals develop symptoms of both disorders. In other cases, however, anxiety may develop secondary to the symptoms of ADHD. Because individuals with ADHD have faced greater difficulty and more setbacks when attempting to manage the demands of life, many seemingly simple tasks may have become perceived as threats insofar as they have been associated with embarrassment, shame, or other distressing feelings. Consequently, adults with ADHD may experience worry when facing these tasks, thus magnifying their attention problems and increasing the likelihood of downstream avoidance, procrastination, and other difficulties following through on tasks.

Bipolar Disorder

The quintessential feature of the bipolar spectrum disorders is significant fluctuation in mood states, most often swinging between an up mood (mania, hypomania) and a down mood (depression). Although full-blown mania may include psychotic symptoms or dangerous behaviors requiring hospitalization to stabilize, at lower points on the continuum, mania and hypomania are associated with varying degrees of decreased need for sleep, racing thoughts, impulsivity, increased activity level, and heightened confidence. Many of these complaints are similar to those of adults with ADHD. Adults with ADHD often describe a tendency to hyperfocus (which is more accurately described as perseveration) or to be particularly productive and energetic in brief bursts. However, these periods are very brief compared with mania or hypomania and do not last several days.

Although many adults with ADHD describe problems falling asleep because they "cannot turn off (their) thoughts," their sleep difficulties seem to be qualitatively different from those described by individuals with bipolar spectrum disorders. In the case of adults with ADHD, our experience has been that they describe feeling tired but that sleep difficulty results from resisting sleep due to perseveration (for example, playing computer games), lack of awareness of time, poor judgment about need for sleep, or sleep onset difficulties related to mental restlessness. Rather than having decreased need for sleep, individuals with ADHD usually end up feeling tired the next day or sleeping in. Individuals experiencing symptoms of hypomania or mania often describe not feeling tired and being able to seemingly function well with decreased sleep. Their activities during these mood periods seem to be more goal-directed and fall outside their typical behavioral pursuits, such as rearranging the furniture in a room late at night or engaging in excessive spending or risky behaviors.

Furthermore, bipolar spectrum disorders may also be associated with feelings of ongoing agitation or anger. Adults with ADHD often describe brief outbursts of anger or other emotions when upset, but then cool off afterwards and often recognize that they overreacted. Whereas individuals with bipolar disorder often describe a return to a semblance of normalcy between mood swings, individuals with ADHD struggle with their symptoms almost daily. Of course, individuals may manifest symptoms of both disorders, which creates a tricky combination both in terms of diagnosis and treatment (Nierenberg et al., 2005). While it is a tough differential diagnosis to make, our experience has been that it is more likely for ADHD to be misdiagnosed as bipolar disorder than vice versa. When they co-occur, it is our clinical experience that ADHD symptoms are more likely to be misattributed as solely the result of the bipolar symptoms rather than the converse.

Individuals with the comorbidity of ADHD and a bipolar spectrum disorder often experience extreme instability in functioning and, in turn, their sense of self (Nierenberg et al., 2005). Even if they have managed to avoid major disruptions in their lives, such as divorce or unanticipated job changes, they may be prone to reacting strongly to various stressors, such as disagreements with employers or coworkers, boredom, and stress associated with the demands and hassles of daily life. In some ways, many of these individuals may appear to prefer chaos in their lives and may be viewed as people who like to stir up trouble. However, these disruptive patterns usually leave individuals facing significant life stressors and feeling frustrated with themselves, angry with others, or a combination of the two.

Substance Abuse

Untreated ADHD is a risk factor for lifetime history of substance abuse. On the other hand, substance abuse is known to impair various cognitive functions and to create severe functional problems that may appear similar to the symptoms of ADHD. A good historical interview is usually sufficient for determining whether there were ADHD symptoms in childhood that predated the onset of substance use and eventual abuse. In fact, many clinicians subscribe to the self-medication hypothesis (for example, Khantzian, 1985; Whalen, Jamner, Henker, Gehricke, & King, 2003) in which it is posited that individuals use substances in an attempt to manage uncomfortable symptoms. In the case of ADHD, alcohol and marijuana are the most commonly reported substances of abuse (Barkley et al., 2002; Fischer et al., 2002; Wilens, 2004). Patients describe their effects as "quieting down" their brains or relieving associated stress and anxiety. However, it may also be that individuals who experience difficulties related to impulsivity and poor self-control may be at higher risk for engaging in risky behaviors such as substance abuse without considering the negative consequences and have greater difficulty changing their addictive behaviors.

In addition to the physiological cravings that contribute to the maintenance of ongoing substance abuse, there are many associated emotional, cognitive, and behavioral patterns that further maintain substance use. Emotional distress or physical discomfort may lead a person to use so as to gain relief (for example, drinking alcohol to reduce anxiety related to falling behind at work); beliefs about oneself and substance use may underlie rationalizations for ongoing abuse (for example, "Smoking pot opens up my creativity"); and behavioral habits may create automated patterns of substance use (for example, smoking marijuana after classes are done for the day).

Whether substance use develops as a form of self-medication for ADHD, because of poor self-regulation, or for some other reason, it becomes a key part of the diagnostic picture and treatment plan. It is important to assess patients for their substance use histories and current drug use. Although marijuana and alcohol are the most common drugs of abuse for adults with ADHD (Wilens, 2004), if an individual has tried cocaine, it is interesting to ask about her or his experience with the drug. Very often we hear individuals state that they recalled not euphoria or a high, but rather an ability to focus, though such evidence is not sufficient to confirm an ADHD diagnosis.

The concern about ongoing substance use/abuse is twofold: (a) the substance of abuse may interfere with the therapeutic effects of pharmacotherapy; and (b) the effects of substances may interfere with and undermine the development and use of adaptive coping skills. In our experience, current and severe substance dependence requires treatment and stabilization before adequate outpatient treatment for ADHD may begin, such as inpatient detoxification and rehabilitation. However, chronic substance abuse by patients who are otherwise able to function relatively adequately, substance use is considered an important part of the outpatient treatment plan. Substance use behaviors are conceptualized as ADHD-related issues and targeted in the therapeutic agenda. In cases in which patients say they do not wish to change their use, we ask that the patients be willing to discuss the issues openly in therapeutic and medication management meetings in order to keep open to the possibility of change or, at least, to make informed decisions about his or her well-being. Most patients find such agreements acceptable.

Regardless of how these difficulties develop and converge, emotions, executive functions, and environmental demands interweave to form a braided cord of experience from which we formulate our conceptualizations of ourselves, the world around us, and prospects for our possible futures. Identifying and understanding this connection is the first step in gaining control over and starting to change what had previously been thought to be uncontrollable impulses.

SUMMARY

ADHD is a valid and significant neurodevelopmental disorder of impaired executive functions that significantly affects self-control, behavior, and cognition and learning. It is apparent that symptoms persist into adulthood for well over half of children diagnosed with ADHD, but this may be an underestimation because there are currently no official diagnostic criteria designed specifically for the manifestation of symptoms of ADHD in adult patients. Thus, many individuals with ADHD go unidentified and untreated until adulthood.

In addition to the persistence of ADHD symptoms into adulthood, there are many potential negative outcomes associated with its course later in life. Among these life problems are fewer years of education, underemployment, more frequent job changes, interpersonal and marital discord, and higher than average risk for psychiatric and substance use problems.

ADHD appears to be the result of genetic predispositions and its symptoms are associated with the structure and neurobiological functioning of particular areas of the brain. ADHD is only weakly associated with environmental factors.

The first step in getting help for adult ADHD is to receive an adequate and comprehensive diagnostic assessment. The core components of such an evaluation are a comprehensive review of history, with an emphasis on academic and vocational functioning; review of presenting problems and current functioning; structured diagnostic interview to assess the presence of comorbid conditions or other conditions that could better explain the presenting problems; objective assessment of childhood and adult symptoms of ADHD; and a neurocognitive screen to get an overview of how patients handle different cognitive demands.

Once the diagnosis of adult ADHD has been confirmed and other relevant factors and diagnoses accounted for, attention can turn to developing a treatment plan for addressing the issues and symptoms associated with adult ADHD. The next chapter will describe a treatment model for adult ADHD, with an emphasis on the combination of cognitive behavior therapy and pharmacotherapy.

CHAPTER 2

Models of Treatment
Cognitive Behavioral Therapy and Pharmacotherapy for Adult ADHD

I have been searching for someone to help me with my ongoing and past issues related to my ADD. I was symptomatic but "got by" growing up, but then...college, marriage, career, a child...I am overwhelmed and feeling very bothered by what I'm doing to my family and co-workers. I am on a medication...and it helps...but, you know it doesn't make it go away... (Note from 32-year-old with ADHD)

We hope it is clear from the information presented in Chapter 1 that attention-deficit/hyperactivity disorder (ADHD) is a life span developmental neuropsychiatric disorder. The emerging evidence from longitudinal research of individuals with ADHD indicates that the diagnosis is associated with many negative life outcomes for those affected, including problems in work, school, and relationships and increased risk for coexisting psychiatric problems. What is more, adults with ADHD have been found to have significantly more negative thoughts, to be less hopeful about the future, and to be less accepting of themselves than are those not affected.

Because the symptoms of ADHD have pervasive effects on one's life, a multimodal treatment approach is most often recommended for ADHD patients of all ages (AACAP, 1997; Attention Deficit Disorder Association [ADDA], 2006; Murphy, 2005; The MTA Cooperative Group, 1999). *Multimodal treatment* refers to fashioning a collection of treatment modalities, such as pharmacotherapy, psychotherapy, ADHD coaching, academic accommodations and/or support, and vocational counseling, to name the most frequently cited components. Such an

39

approach is recommended in order to provide specialized support in the specific areas of life that are most problematic for an individual. Pharmacotherapy and psychotherapy form the foundation of treatment for most individuals (though academic accommodations and support would be included as the third common mode of treatment for most college students with ADHD).

Considering the effects of the core symptoms of ADHD on functioning and the high incidence of comorbidity, we recommend a combined treatment approach for most adults with ADHD that is comprised of pharmacotherapy and psychotherapy; namely, cognitive behavioral therapy (CBT) (e.g., Ramsay, 2005a; Ramsay & Rostain, 2003, 2004, 2005b, 2005c, in press; Rostain & Ramsay, 2006a, 2006c; Safren, 2006). The medications seem to work in a "bottom-up" fashion by intervening at the neurochemical level in the brain, thereby improving executive functioning and treating comorbid symptoms with additional medications, when indicated. CBT, on the other hand, works in a top-down fashion by helping patients become more aware of the behavioral and psychological effects of their ADHD symptoms in their lives. Understanding the effects of ADHD helps individuals to develop and implement strategies for changing these patterns, or at least to gain a measure of awareness and acceptance of those patterns that are not easily changed. Each component of treatment makes a unique and important contribution to improving the overall well-being of patients.

Pharmacotherapy is considered the first line of treatment for ADHD. Medications have been found to significantly improve ADHD symptoms in patients of all ages, though they are more widely studied in children than in adults. Medication management for adults with ADHD can be tricky due to a number of factors, such as the existence of comorbid medical or psychiatric conditions requiring additional medications, establishing a therapeutic dose, and so forth. That said, many individuals with relatively mild and uncomplicated symptoms (for example, no comorbidity) with stable life circumstances (for example, employed, strong support network) find that medications alone represent sufficient treatment. We will discuss our pharmacotherapy approach later in the chapter.

Despite the availability of medications that can be very effective for many ADHD adults, pharmacotherapy alone is insufficient treatment for an estimated 50% of these adult patients (Wilens, Spencer, & Biederman, 2000). Although the medications do their job well by reducing symptoms and improving executive functioning, these improvements may not be enough to improve the overall functioning of many adults with ADHD. That is, even though an individual with ADHD who is prescribed an appropriate dose of a psychostimulant is able to pay attention better, this improvement does not necessarily translate into less procrastination and greater confidence. Additional psychosocial intervention is often required to promote further clinical improvement. We have found that CBT can be a particularly helpful psychosocial treatment approach to achieve these improvements, which we describe in the next section.

COGNITIVE BEHAVIORAL THERAPY FOR ADULT ADHD

Said all too simply, CBT is a form of psychotherapy that focuses on cognitions (thoughts, images, beliefs) as a useful framework with which to understand and treat psychiatric disorders (Beck, 1976). More specifically, CBT involves helping individuals to recognize their existing cognitive patterns and belief structures in order to be able to modify them with alternative thoughts and beliefs. By considering alternative cognitions, individuals develop and experiment with new outlooks, which set the stage for novel behavioral and emotion experiences. These experiences provide the raw material for the modification of cognitions, behaviors, and emotions, thereby resulting in clinical improvements. CBT was originally designed as a treatment for depression (Beck, 1967; Beck et al., 1979) but has since been applied successfully to a number of different disorders, including anxiety and panic disorder, substance abuse, and bipolar disorder (see Beck, 2005, for a review).

Let us be crystal clear: ADHD is *not* caused by negative thinking. As we described in chapter 1, ADHD seems to be the result of a complex combination of genetic and neurobiological factors. However, the experience of going through life with ADHD, particularly when it has gone undiagnosed until adulthood, has potentially important consequences for the belief systems that develop about the self, the world, and the future—known as the *cognitive triad* (Beck, 1967). Thoughts and beliefs then interact with behaviors and emotions in an intricate web of experience. The CBT model does not maintain that thoughts and beliefs are necessarily the cause of all emotions and behaviors (in many cases, emotional processing occurs first and, besides, a hallmark symptom of ADHD—impulsivity—involves acting without thinking) but it has emerged as a very useful route of intervention to understand and modify these patterns.

Moreover, although identifying and changing the maladaptive thought patterns that are triggered in various situations is paramount in CBT for adult ADHD, it is important for clinicians to appreciate that these in-the-moment reactive thoughts may only be the tip of the iceberg. These reflexive cognitions may represent the culmination of many other cognitive and developmental processes that are important in constructing comprehensive and individualized treatment plans for patients. The case conceptualization offers a framework for understanding how living with ADHD has had a unique effect on each patient and, consequently, provides a personalized blueprint for how treatment should proceed. Thus, we will start our discussion of CBT for adult ADHD by introducing the case conceptualization that guides our psychosocial treatment approach.

CASE CONCEPTUALIZATION

The CBT case conceptualization is the integrated understanding of the patient's presenting problems, the relevant developmental history explaining the etiology of the clinical issues, and reasonable indications of future functioning (Beck, 1995; Persons, 1989, 2006; Ramsay & Rostain, 2003). As such, it often helps to clarify and prioritize the clinical issues for which patients seek help.

This framework helps clinicians and patients to "think like a cognitive behavioral therapist." In addition to guiding the treatment plan and selection of interventions, this conceptualization provides clinicians with a way to make sense of the myriad of clinical issues that may arise in the course of therapy, both the content of what is discussed and the process of therapy. The conceptualization is not designed to be stored in therapists' heads but rather is to be shared and discussed collaboratively with patients. The case conceptualization is an evolving formulation and is revised as new information comes to light. Various hypotheses are made regarding the contributing factors affecting the development and maintenance of the particular problems faced by individuals. Those hypotheses that do not seem to be supported by patients' experiences are set aside; those hypotheses that seem to accurately explain patients' experiences are maintained.

What is more, the CBT conceptualization is not only designed to improve insight and awareness but also to open up possibilities for new outlooks and experiences. Thus, the framework offered by the conceptualization provides patients with a system with which to make sense of and analyze problematic situations that arise in their lives and to figure out ways to change their long-standing patterns. The ultimate goal is to have patients become their own therapists. We will discuss the different components of the CBT case conceptualization for adult ADHD, which are illustrated in Figure 2.1.

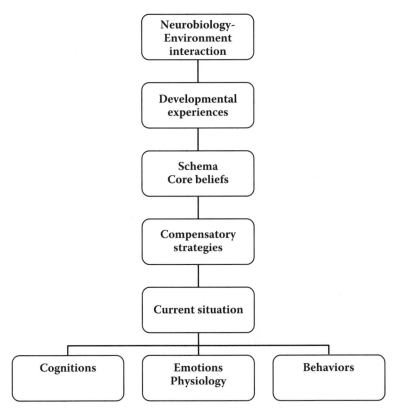

FIGURE 2.1   Diagram of CBT Case Conceptualization of Adult ADHD

Neurobiology and Environment Interaction

Our CBT conceptualization of adult ADHD begins with the awareness that ADHD is a highly heritable developmental disorder of impaired executive functions that probably influences one's functioning from a very early age. Even if the effects are relatively mild and are not diagnosed until later in life, because ADHD affects various aspects of attention, cognitive processing, and self-regulation, it likely plays a role in most situations and relationships encountered in life. Most individuals with ADHD, at some point in their lives, describe a realization that certain tasks or situations are more challenging for them than they are for others or that they "do things differently than other people." Thus, it is important to understand whether individuals were aware of these differences at an early age and how their ADHD affected their life experiences.

More specifically, ADHD symptoms have wide-ranging effects on various aspects of attention and focus, perception, and behavioral self-control. ADHD has likely influenced types of activities individuals pursued, their interpersonal styles, and their approaches to learning, resulting in there being stimuli to which the individual selectively paid attention to the exclusion of others. A highly relevant issue for most individuals with ADHD is inordinate difficulty inhibiting their responses (that is, prepotent response, Barkley, 1997a) and redirecting their attention away from these preferred stimuli when they must focus their attention and efforts on other salient tasks (Brown, 2005). These difficulties have a cumulative and corrosive effect for many individuals with ADHD as executive dysfunction conspires to make it difficult for them to keep up with many of the details and demands of life involved in school, work, and relationships.

Developmental Experiences

Because CBT is a here-and-now therapy approach, focused on measurable and observable symptom improvement and behavior change, it is often wrongly assumed that CBT does not place much emphasis on developmental experiences. On the contrary, these experiences are crucially important because they provide the raw material from which our deepest held beliefs are formed. Developmental experiences are particularly relevant for adults with ADHD because, as mentioned above, most individuals experience some degree of symptomatology in childhood and adolescence, even if it did not result in outright impairment at that time. The presenting problems that compel individuals to seek treatment as adults often represent the most recent manifestations of long-standing coping problems. Therefore, gaining insight about developmental influences is not an end in and of itself but rather a means to aid efforts to make changes in one's current and future life experience.

Growing up with ADHD affects how individuals interact with their environments and how they handle various demands in life. The difficulties associated with ADHD may lead to frustrations in various aspects of life that start to affect how individuals make sense of themselves and their place in the world. Of course, not all developmental experiences for individuals with ADHD are negative. There may be interactions with supportive family members or teachers and activities in which the individual was able to thrive. Special skills and aptitudes also may be discovered and cultivated. However, a diagnosis of ADHD is associated with many interpersonal, academic, and vocational problems that affect the areas of life from which we derive our sense of belonging and competence. Thus, it is important to understand the effects of these experiences.

It is useful to get a developmental picture of what patients were like at various points in their development and in various contexts. Actively inquiring about a patient's temperament, relationship with family, experience with teachers and peers in school, and significant developmental transitions (for example, transition from elementary school to middle school, middle school to high school, or high school to college or the work force) provides important background information. Further, retrospective accounts of how patients handled schoolwork, their hobbies and interests, their general sense of self-esteem, and other recollections of childhood are potentially informative; recent research has indicated that adults with ADHD recall having more difficulties and negative experiences in childhood than individuals without ADHD (Faraone & Biederman, 2005). Not surprisingly, these experiences affect the formation of individuals' views of themselves and their abilities.

Schema and Core Beliefs

The terms *schema* and *core beliefs* are often used interchangeably but are technically different (Beck, 1995; Young, 1999; Young, Klosko, & Weishaar, 2003). *Schemas* are cognitive structures or mental categories for assessing and interpreting the various stimuli that we encounter in life. There is a basic human propensity to make coherent sense of and find meaning in experience. This tendency has survival value because it allows people to catalog experiences and to develop a fund of information about the environment, thereby helping us to evaluate and handle new situations we encounter, often with the goal to avoid physical or emotional pain. Thus, schemas are primarily influenced by our developmental learning experiences. (See Table 2.1.)

Schemas could be seen of as CBT's version of Freud's notion of the unconscious because they operate nonconsciously and represent our absolute, unquestioned sense of how the world is and how it operates, including issues related to self-definition and identity. Schemas comprise our personal rule book for surviving in the world that is compiled from personal experiences and social learning. The different schema domains reflect categories of human experience, including disconnection and rejection, impaired autonomy and performance, impaired limits, other-directedness, and overvigilance and inhibition, that help orient us to how the world works. Schemas could be likened to the lenses through which we view the world. If someone peers through clear lenses and sees

TABLE 2.1   Common Schema and Core Beliefs Observed in Adult
ADHD Patients

Self-mistrust	"I cannot rely on myself to do what I need to do. I let myself down."
Failure	"I have not met expectations. I always have failed and always will fail at what I set out to do."
Incompetence	"I am too inept to handle the basic demands of life."
Inadequacy/incompetence	"I'm basically a bad, flawed person."
Instability	"My life will always be chaotic and in turmoil."

Note: From "A Cognitive Therapy Approach for Adult Attention-Deficit/Hyperactivity Disorder," by J. R. Ramsay and A. L. Rostain, 2003, *Journal of Cognitive Psychotherapy: An International Quarterly, 17*, pp. 319–334. Copyright; and "Adult with ADHD? Try Medication + Psychotherapy," by A. L. Rostain and J. R. Ramsay, 2006, *Current Psychiatry, 5*(2), pp. 13–16, 21–24, 27. Copyright. Adapted with permission of the author.

a small, slightly oblong yellow-skinned fruit, that person would easily identify it as a lemon. However, if that same fruit is viewed through blue lenses, the same person would identify the fruit incorrectly as a lime. Thus, our schemas significantly influence how we view the world and, consequently, our functioning. Schemas may exert influence on behavior as early as 8 years old (Taylor & Ingram, 1999), though they do not consolidate until adolescence (Hammen & Zupan, 1984).

Core beliefs, then, are the specific expressions of these schematic domains in the form of rules or conditional statements (for example, if–then) that are relevant and meaningful to individual patients in their daily lives. (See Table 2.2.) Hypotheses about potentially relevant schema can be formulated by observing how beliefs seem to cluster around the particular themes of the different schema domains. Because these schemas and beliefs are the result of personal experiences, they exert influence on behaviors, a significant category of which are the compensatory strategies, which we discuss next. It should be noted that healthy, adaptive schema and core beliefs also exist and play an important role in resilience and positive well-being. However, our focus here is to shed light on some of the maladaptive schema and beliefs we have identified in adult ADHD patients that undermine their well-being in the form of self-defeating behaviors, as we discuss in the next section.

TABLE 2.2   Common Cognitive Distortions Observed in Adults with ADHD

Overgeneralization	General conclusions are drawn from specific mistakes and these conclusions are applied to other situations, both related and unrelated to the original mistake. ("I cannot expect to get a job if I cannot remember to pick up my dry cleaning.")
Magical thinking	Overreliance on forces out of one's control (i.e., luck) to resolve problems. ("Once I get on the right dose of medication, all my problems will be solved.")
Comparative thinking	Basing one's sense of self in terms of how well an individual measures up against other people. ("I'm the only student in the class who needs extended time on my tests. I guess I do not really belong in college.")
Fallacy of fairness	The belief that life should be fair and equitable in all situations. ("It's not fair that it takes me longer to read a chapter than it does my roommate.")
All-or-nothing thinking	The tendency to view experience in dichotomous, black-or-white terms. ("My supervisor wrote 'needs improvement' for some items. I must not be any good at what I do.")
Mind-reading/ fortune-telling	Assumptions without sufficient evidence that others have negative opinions of an individual and that circumstances will turn out poorly. ("I just know that my coworkers think I'm unreliable.")
Should statements	Unrealistic and maladaptive imperatives regarding an aspect of one's self or behavior. ("I should be able to prioritize my schedule without having to sit down and think it over.")
Inappropriate blaming	Misattributing unfair amounts of blame to yourself or someone else for circumstances and overlooking other contributions. ("She should understand that I have ADHD and not be upset with me for forgetting our lunch date.")

Note: From *Feeling Good,* by D. D. Burns, 1980, New York: Signet. Copyright; and "Adult with ADHD? Try Medication + Psychotherapy," by A. L. Rostain and J. R. Ramsay, 2006, *Current Psychiatry, 5*(2), pp. 13–16, 21–24, 27. Copyright. Adapted with permission of the authors.

Compensatory Strategies

Compensatory strategies represent a crucial component of the CBT conceptualization and are an important level for therapeutic intervention.

These behaviors should not be confused with *compensations*, which are often discussed in the ADHD literature. *Compensations* refer to the ways in which individuals with ADHD learn to cope with and minimize the effects of the symptoms. So, for example, an individual with ADHD who regularly forgets to follow through when he has promised to do something for a coworker may learn to compensate by asking the person making the request to send a follow up e-mail reminder of their conversation. This strategy would improve the likelihood of the worker with ADHD fulfilling his promise by providing an important reminder. Compensations are viewed as positive coping efforts, though they may be vulnerable to disruptions, such as if the individual deletes the e-mail reminder before transferring the promised task to his to-do list and subsequently forgets about it.

Compensatory strategies in the CBT model, on the other hand, refer to the efforts to address the schema and core beliefs that may seem at first blush to be adaptive, but which ultimately and insidiously maintain and reinforce maladaptive beliefs. They could also be thought of as self-defeating behaviors. Procrastination is the most common compensatory strategy we have observed in adults with ADHD. (See Table 2.3.)

For example, Sarah, a college student with ADHD, has a long history of problems focusing on and comprehending reading material. She does not have a reading disability per se, but her attention drifts, she becomes bored and physically restless when reading, and she requires more time than her peers do to complete reading assignments. Sarah developed her dread of assigned reading early in high school when textbooks were longer and more difficult than they had been in previous years. In fact, she eventually stopped reading her textbooks altogether and, instead, relied upon studying her notes and what she heard in class.

Now in her first semester of college, Sarah tries to keep up with her assigned reading but has developed an emotional aversion to reading. Her current negative belief is, "I must be stupid because it takes me so long to read." This belief is, in turn, connected with an inadequacy schema with the theme "I'm not as smart as the other students." Thus, when faced with a highly technical reading assignment for biology class, she has the thought, "There's no way I can read this." This thought triggers physical feelings of stress, which magnifies her restlessness and distractibility. Sarah ends up procrastinating by doing something more pleasurable. In the short-term, Sarah's procrastination protected her from viewing herself as inadequate and circumvented uncomfortable feelings and frustrations. Moreover, when she shifted her attention away from the textbook, she immediately felt a visceral sense of relief from stress, promising herself, "I'll do this later." However, Sarah did not return to the reading assignment, eventually running out of time before her next

TABLE 2.3   Common Compensatory Strategies Observed in Adults with ADHD

Anticipatory avoidance/procrastination	Magnifying the difficulty of a pending task and doubting one's ability to complete it; results in rationalizations to justify procrastination behavior
Brinksmanship	The tendency to wait until the last moment to complete a task, often when compelled to do so by an impending deadline
Juggling	Taking on new, exciting projects and feeling "busy and productive" without making progress on projects already started
Pseudoefficiency	Completing several low-priority, manageable tasks (e.g., checking e-mail, cleaning desk) but avoiding high-priority, challenging tasks (e.g., completing report for work)
Stoicism	Impassively accepting one's circumstances due to excessive pessimism about the prospect of making desired changes in life

Note: From "A Cognitive Therapy Approach for Adult Attention-Deficit/Hyperactivity Disorder," by J. R. Ramsay and A. L. Rostain, 2003, *Journal of Cognitive Psychotherapy: An International Quarterly, 17*, pp. 319–334. Copyright; and "Adult with ADHD? Try Medication + Psychotherapy," by A. L. Rostain and J. R. Ramsay, 2006, *Current Psychiatry, 5*(2), pp. 13–16, 21–24, 27. Copyright. Adapted with permission of the author.

biology class. Consequently, Sarah was unprepared in class when the biology professor called on her to discuss the assigned reading, leaving her feeling embarrassed and with the devastating conclusion, "Now I know I'm stupid and can't handle college. I just knew I didn't belong here." Sarah's conclusion is unfair. She never even attempted the reading because she anticipated it would be overwhelming and she avoided it based on this assumption. However, because her experience was consistent with her belief system (schema congruent), it is assumed by Sarah to be a valid confirmation of her inadequacy belief, instead of attempting to explore an alternate possibility.

As you can see in this example, identifying compensatory strategies and using them to elicit the specific schema, core beliefs, and emotions attached to situations are crucial steps in developing a case conceptualization. Compensatory strategies also provide obvious targets for formulating personal experiments to embark on to promote behavior change. In Sarah's case, an early intervention in CBT involved setting up a personal experiment (aided by pharmacotherapy) in which she agreed to spend time reading a textbook to gather experiential information rather than relying solely on her anticipatory assumptions. Such specific situations yield important information about the in-the-moment experience of individuals, such as their automatic thoughts, emotions, and behavioral responses that help to shed more light on schemas and core beliefs, all of which are in the service of trying to see the world through the patient's eyes.

Automatic Thoughts, Emotions, and Behaviors

One of the hallmarks of CBT is the notion of *automatic thoughts*, those fleeting thoughts or images interposed between an event and our reaction to it. Automatic thoughts represent the ongoing flow of thoughts related to current experience. They occur quickly and just out of awareness, though they are easily recognized when someone is alerted to their importance, akin to Freud's notion of the preconscious. These thoughts often go unquestioned because they occur within the steady stream of thoughts, images, and other cognitions. Most automatic thoughts tend to be neutral in their emotional valence. However, because these thoughts occur rapidly and are often unquestioned, they can easily be distorted or based on incomplete information, especially when a situation is particularly meaningful to an individual and may activate a schema or strong emotions. For example, two coworkers pass in the hall and one says "hello" but the other person walks by without responding. The one who offered the greeting may think, "She must not have heard me" and is unaffected by the interaction. However, if the automatic thought in that situation is, "She ignored me on purpose," the individual may feel anger at being ignored. Left unchallenged, these automatic thoughts have the potential to alter mood, behavior, and subsequent cognitions in what can be a very vicious cycle.

Although emotions and reflexive actions may sometimes precede higher order cognitive processing, such as in the case of sympathetic nervous system arousal in response to seeing a snake (or the misperception of a garden hose), thoughts often play an influential role in mood shifts and behavioral choices and are always involved in how we make sense of experience. Even in the case of impulsive behaviors, it is often the after-the-fact realization that one's behavior was ill advised that contributes to the lingering feelings of guilt, negative thoughts, and self-criticism frequently reported by individuals with ADHD.

An important point could be made that there are times when an ADHD adult's negative thoughts are not distortions but instead reflect accurate interpretations of mistakes or negative outcomes. For example,

John, a man with ADHD who struggles with time management, ended up arriving 30 minutes late for a date with his girlfriend to see a movie. His initial automatic thoughts, "I'm late and the movie already started. My girlfriend is disappointed because she wanted to see this movie with me," are probably on the mark and not distorted. However, because such situations are common for adults with ADHD, secondary automatic thoughts likely draw conclusions that go beyond the experience of the situation and that might interfere with effective coping, such as, "I'm such a loser. I have nothing worthwhile to offer my girlfriend. She hates me now." CBT is not the power of positive thinking but rather the power of balanced thinking such that it allows us to find a balance between accepting things that cannot be changed and being resilient in making changes and exploring all possibilities regarding what can be changed. In John's case, he acknowledged his mistake, apologized to his girlfriend, and challenged his description of himself as a loser, reminding himself of the many ways he tries to be a good boyfriend. He was not happy that he had been late, but John did not let his mistake needlessly ruin his evening or his relationship.

As a case conceptualization takes form, even apparently self-defeating behaviors make perfect sense when viewed through the lens of the experiences and learning histories of ADHD adults. In the case of Sarah, the college student who is a slow reader, in view of her difficulties in high school it was no surprise that she had difficulty following through on her assignments in college and activated her sense of inadequacy. Her difficulties with reading created stress for her and undermined her confidence dating back to before high school, though she was able to get by. It made sense, then, that Sarah would avoid reading as it became more difficult in college. However, this belief system and resultant behaviors were at odds with Sarah's desire to further her education.

Progress in CBT requires being able to consider new ways of thinking about situations and the willingness to experiment with new behaviors and skills. In cases of mild ADHD, individuals may have had generally positive or uneventful experiences growing up and have predominantly adaptive belief systems. Thus, the focus of CBT for mild, uncomplicated ADHD may be devoted to modifying automatic thoughts and behaviors and developing coping skills without much need for an elaborate case conceptualization. However, in cases of moderate to severe ADHD, particularly when there are coexisting diagnoses and complicated developmental histories, the case conceptualization is pertinent because there is greater likelihood that negative beliefs and compensatory strategies influence the clinical picture.

CBT FOR ADULT ADHD IN CLINICAL PRACTICE

The case conceptualization serves as scaffolding for making sense of patients' experiences. It is a clinical heuristic used to identify the relevant clinical issues and potential interventions to help patients with ADHD to fulfill their treatment goals. This section provides an outline of various components of a CBT approach followed by sections devoted to specific cognitive and behavioral interventions for adults with ADHD. Several of the sections are not unique to CBT or to the treatment of ADHD, such as the importance of the therapeutic alliance. However, we emphasize how these therapeutic components can be utilized to further the case conceptualization and patients' understanding of the influence of their thoughts and beliefs related to the unique circumstances involved in living with ADHD. Likewise, some of the sections are not emphasized in traditional CBT, such as dealing with one's diagnosis, but they have special relevance for adults with ADHD.

Diagnosis of ADHD and Grief Reactions

Patients often express a sense of relief at learning that their chronic difficulties fit the ADHD symptom profile and that there is a coherent and nonblaming explanation of the chief source of many of their struggles. Several of our patients have been moved to tears as they gain an emergent understanding of how their long-standing troubles make sense because of having lived with undiagnosed ADHD. In fact, an accurate diagnosis provides the first cognitive reframe of their difficulties. To this point in their lives, most patients have viewed their difficulties as evidence of character flaws (for example, "I'm lazy" or "I'm stupid"). Many patients are further heartened to learn that they are not alone in their struggles, that there is hope for change, and they are in a hurry to get started with treatment.

In contrast, some patients remain skeptical of the diagnosis, particularly college-aged individuals who are already facing identity issues related to their transition to adulthood. These young adults may be overwhelmed by the unwelcome notion that ADHD is affecting their various life pursuits. Others in this age group may acknowledge the presence of ADHD but express a desire to handle it on their own rather than pursuing treatment. Older adults may react to the diagnosis with feelings of anger and/or sadness at the thought that their difficulties could have been identified earlier in their lives, perhaps resulting in much different life outcomes.

For some patients, the newfound awareness of the ADHD diagnosis triggers feelings of grief as they replay in their minds the many frustrations and lost opportunities in their lives with the sobering realization that there may have been help available. These reactions represent important issues to address in CBT. Grief issues are often not solvable but require emotional processing on the part of the patient and accurate empathy on the part of the therapist. The purpose of this processing is to allow patients to gain a measure of acceptance of their circumstances that allows them to move forward in their efforts to deal with their ADHD.

For example, Reggie was a 45-year-old biologist who worked for a chemical manufacturing company. He attended a feedback session during which he learned that the results of his initial evaluation confirmed that his symptoms fulfilled diagnostic criteria for ADHD. Upon hearing the impressions of the evaluators, he became tearful and shared his daily struggle with the sense that he was not as productive as his professional colleagues. Reggie could not understand the discrepancy between his intelligence and his inability to focus on and complete his work. He began to unload some memories about the emergence of his self-doubt during his school years. He recalled that his teachers' comments almost invariably suggested that Reggie understood the material better than was reflected in his grades and suggested that he was not working hard enough. For Reggie, as for most individuals, the assessment for and diagnosis of ADHD is much more than a perfunctory matter informing treatment choice. It is a deeply personal matter that has effects on one's self-definition and self-awareness.

Starting treatment for adult ADHD is not a matter of simply confirming the diagnosis, identifying treatment goals, and then beginning the business of imparting coping skills. When there is a relatively mild, uncomplicated case of ADHD, such as a patient who has a stable job, good social support network, and no psychiatric comorbidities, CBT is able to focus on identifying specific frustrations, introducing coping skills, and modifying the relatively circumscribed negative thoughts. In more complicated cases, however, individuals may require time to come to terms with the diagnosis, to think through how their difficulties may have affected various aspects of their lives, and to ponder their personal goals in light of this new information. Time spent discussing these issues with patients is time well spent in order to address and cultivate their motivations for participating in CBT.

Readiness for Change

Despite the nearly uniform sense of clarity and insight about the effects of ADHD symptoms provided by an accurate diagnostic assessment, patients differ in their commitment to treatment. Some patients respond to the diagnosis and newfound awareness of the effects of ADHD with eagerness to embark on a course of treatment and self-change. Other patients, however, may be more guarded of the diagnosis, about their abilities to change what seem to be uncontrollable cognitive and behavioral impulses, or about some aspect of treatment (that is, medications). Spending time addressing these issues and matching CBT to the patient's therapeutic pace helps to improve treatment compliance and effectiveness. (We discuss readiness for change in more detail in our discussion of complicating factors in Chapter 5.)

Psychoeducation

Hearing the results of an assessment for ADHD, including personalized information about one's neurocognitive profile and the effects of executive dysfunction on daily life, is an education for most patients. As was mentioned earlier, this information may be revelatory for some patients as they look back upon their past and review important life events with new insight about the contribution of ADHD symptoms on their functioning.

In addition to the self-awareness that occurs during the assessment process, explicitly providing psychoeducation about ADHD to the patient is one of the first steps of treatment (Ramsay & Rostain, 2005a, in press). The purpose of this component of treatment for adult ADHD is to demystify misconceptions about ADHD and treatment and to shed light on the nature of the syndrome insofar as it affects the patient's functioning. Information is not presented in a didactic fashion during sessions. Rather, answering patients' questions about their symptoms or descriptions of ADHD they have heard from friends or the media or about their treatment options are opportunities to provide information or, in some cases, to acknowledge where information might be lacking.

To encourage further self-awareness, we also encourage patients to engage in personal research into ADHD, such as reading about adult issues or exploring reputable online resources (see Appendix A). We caution that, while these resources can be very helpful and are useful adjuncts to treatment, they may not be as personalized to the patient's unique circumstances as treatment is meant to be. This is particularly true when the patient has significant comorbidities and functional problems that are often beyond the purview of most self-help books and websites for ADHD. Indeed, the purpose of our combined treatment is to focus on the individual patient's unique array of symptoms and strengths (for example, case conceptualization, medication response) to develop a treatment approach tailored to the unique needs of the individual patient.

Defining Treatment Goals

It may sound fundamental, but unclear treatment objectives lead to unclear treatment outcomes. This is not to say that the issues patients bring to therapy are always clear-cut and easily transformed into measurable objectives, but there should be discussion and mutual agreement about what the patient hopes to achieve by participating in treatment. Agreed-upon objectives allow both the patient and the therapist to monitor the progress of treatment and to clarify and modify its direction as needed.

Because the difficulties associated with ADHD are pervasive in patients' lives, it is easy to set broad, imprecise therapy goals (for example, "I want to procrastinate less," "I want to be better organized," or "I want to be able to fulfill my potential"). It is more prudent to identify specific problems encountered by patients in their day-to-day lives as a means to understand the effects of ADHD and to start exploring new coping strategies ("Can you describe a time in the past week or so when procrastination or disorganization caused a problem for you? What happened?"). This strategy increases the likelihood that the therapist and patient start treatment on the same page and helps the therapist to start to see the world through the patient's eyes.

For example, a college student with ADHD might set a goal of earning an "A" in a particular class (e.g., Ramsay & Rostain, 2004). This is a worthwhile aspiration but not a reasonable therapy goal. More reasonable therapy goals might include improving class attendance from the previous semester, experimenting with reasonable increments of time spent studying, spending adequate time and effort preparing for exams/projects, and making use of academic support resources, such as tutoring. Discussing these components of academic performance are more likely to yield clinically useful information, such as the student stating, "I always start the semester attending all my classes but then something eventually happens and I start missing too many." The therapist can inquire about what happens such that the patient misses a first class and how this can start a trend of being more likely to miss additional classes. Thus, the discussion of what is meaningful for the patient lends itself to the development of therapy objectives that will more likely lead to desired changes.

Another common example is when a patient says, "I want to be better organized." Again, this is a laudable and understandable goal, but, as worded above, it does not yet provide a clear picture of how treatment should proceed. Asking for examples from the previous week when the patient's disorganization proved problematic or a prospective inquiry such as "Two months from now, what would be a real-life example of being more organized that would signify to you that CBT was working?" Patients' answers usually shed light on specific areas of difficulty they commonly face that serve as useful treatment objectives, such as keeping track of and paying incoming monthly credit card bills.

On occasion, some patients might hesitate about mentioning a pressing goal for therapy or an agenda item for a session, stating, "I'm not sure this is an ADHD issue." We immediately clarify that we consider any life problem or issue as fair game for "ADHD therapy." Our rationale is that, as we have mentioned before, we consider ADHD to be a developmental disorder of impaired executive functions. As such, it plays a pervasive role in our developmental experiences, relationships, interactions with the world, and sense of self. Thus, it may affect, however subtly, even issues such as relationship problems and career planning that some patients may consider non-ADHD issues. Furthermore, considering that in a majority of adult ADHD cases there will be at least one comorbid psychiatric diagnosis (not to mention other complicating factors such as medical complications, relationship problems, etc.), patients should not feel limited in their freedom to raise concerns that might have implications for their overall well-being as part of the therapeutic agenda. Many of these patients have suffered because their ADHD symptoms had not been acknowledged and treated; the same error should not be made by trying to treat ADHD in CBT without recognizing other related problems.

Therapeutic Alliance

The importance of the therapeutic relationship is ubiquitous in the psychotherapy literature (Horvath, 2001; Lambert & Barley, 2001). It is considered a common factor that influences the outcome of all different forms of psychotherapy. Although it has received less attention in the ADHD literature, the importance of providing the patient with a safe environment in which to explore the nature of his or her difficulties, to develop new coping skills, and to discuss the range of emotions involved in this personal undertaking cannot be overstated.

The clinical consensus is that a therapist who works with adult ADHD patients cannot afford to adopt a passive role (Hallowell, 1995; Ramsay & Rostain, 2005a, in press). Rather than being a blank slate, the therapist actively inquires about patients' experiences, keeps sessions focused, and helps patients find a balance between accepting the effects of ADHD and working to make behavioral changes. This active therapeutic stance does not mean that there is no room for creativity in sessions but instead allows patients to receive valuable and timely behavioral feedback in a supportive context. For example, if the therapist observes that the session has deviated from the stated agenda, it would be appropriate to provide feedback to the patient and to collaboratively make a decision about whether to refocus on the agenda or to revise the agenda to focus on the new topic (for example, "I notice that we've gotten a bit off track from what you said you wanted to focus on today. Do we want to change our agenda for today or do we want to return to the original topic?").

Another common therapeutic issue is managing what would typically be deemed *therapy-interfering behaviors*. Tardiness to session and failure to complete therapeutic homework, actions traditionally thought to be signs of hostility or resistance, are better understood as manifestations of the executive dysfunction associated with ADHD. Framing these occurrences as opportunities to understand the effects of ADHD and to develop new coping strategies gently addresses both the core symptoms and the emotional frustration engendered by these sorts of recurring difficulties in a constructive, nonshaming way. In fact, it is often useful to predict that some or many of these sorts of behaviors will be encountered during the course of therapy and that they serve as grist for the mill in terms of ADHD issues.

The primary benefit a positive therapeutic relationship provides to ADHD adults, however, may well be the spirit of collaborative problem-solving it engenders for managing the symptoms of ADHD. Adults with ADHD frequently describe feeling ashamed of their recurring difficulties and demoralized by the criticisms they have heard in the course of their lives from parents, teachers, coworkers, and peers. It is common for ADHD patients to assume that their psychotherapists will be upset with them if their therapeutic homework is inadequate, incomplete, or forgotten. We often hear comments along the lines of "You must be frustrated with me," or "I bet no one else has this much trouble following through on homework." It is all too easy for the therapeutic relationship to become a reenactment of the patient's relationships outside of therapy. For example, a patient might assume that the therapist will be angry about slow progress or frequent tardiness for sessions. Consequently, the patient might respond either by being particularly accommodating and apologetic (for example, "I'm sorry I'm late. I'd understand it if you would want to reschedule. I don't want you to think this is not important to me") or by trying to circumvent the therapist's policies (for example, "I know I'm a little late, but can't we have a full session? This is what you're supposed to be helping me with anyway") (e.g., Bemporad, 2001; Bemporad & Zambenedetti, 1996).

Eliciting patients' thoughts about their behavior and their assumptions of the therapist's reactions (for example, "Do you have any thoughts about my reaction to this situation?") help to foster a collaborative conceptualization of the situation. Thus, unrealistic thoughts can be modified and specific behavior strategies for avoiding similar problems in the future can be discussed. More importantly, instead of repeating the all-too-familiar shame experiences of the ADHD adult, this approach provides a face-saving way to proactively address problems associated with ADHD as they arise in CBT. This problem-solving approach creates an environment in which patients feel comfortable exploring and changing problematic behavior patterns.

Session Structure

An immediate appeal of CBT approaches for adult ADHD is that sessions are more structured than in other therapy models. While the degree of structure may differ among individuals with various treatment objectives, with some patients requiring more structure than others, there is a common framework to each session.

Sessions generally start with a check-in of mood, current functioning, and a review of leftover issues from the previous meeting, including any medication issues (for example, compliance, side effects). Therapeutic homework from the previous session is reviewed. Homework compliance is an issue in CBT in general but even more so in the case of adult ADHD. However, when a patient has not completed a homework task it is viewed as an opportunity to gather important information. Identifying the factors that result in such a task not being done is just as informative as reviewing the results of completed homework tasks (for example, "Let's find out how you *don't* get things done"). Sometimes a review of homework experiences may constitute the primary or sole agenda item for an entire session.

The therapeutic agenda focuses on the main topic areas to be addressed during the session hour. The purpose of setting the agenda is to ensure that time will be spent productively and to decrease the likelihood that the patient and therapist will get to the end of the session and only then remember an important issue worthy of discussion. The structure of an agenda is not meant to curb creativity or the pursuit of insight. Rather, Socratic inquiry and pondering certain issues helps to draw connections of various patterns of thinking, feeling, and acting that are valuable to the case conceptualization and to the patient's personal development.

Once the agenda has been agreed upon, sessions focus on tackling each of the agenda topics, keeping in mind the overarching therapy goal for each patient. Change does not occur solely through the retelling and processing of events, though these are important steps in the process. The goal is to use examples of problematic situations in order to determine alternative ways to have handled these situations and potential barriers to their future implementation. This is accomplished by inquiring about the internal experience—thoughts and feelings—of the individual, and how these matched the context of the situation discussed and descriptions of the patient's behaviors and their outcomes. Using Socratic inquiry, in which therapists use questions to help patients discover their cognitive, emotional, and behavioral patterns, helps identify how particular interpretations of a situation may lead to limited coping options. Similar questions are used to explore other possible alternative interpretations and coping options and to anticipate how patients may use these insights to handle similar situations in the future.

Rather than operating on a conceptual level, discussing constructs such as automatic thoughts, organization, or attention, CBT therapists ask for explicit examples of problematic situations and, more specifically, cases highlighting the functional problems faced by ADHD adults in their daily lives. This approach helps to make these concepts real and relevant on an experiential level for both the patient and for the therapist. Further, they provide important information about the internal experience of patients, which may have connections with past developmental events. Thus, in addition to providing therapeutic material with which to develop possible interventions and homework tasks, such exploration of real examples helps therapists construct and refine their case conceptualizations.

It is equally important to review examples of situations handled effectively by patients. Highlighting the appropriate use of coping strategies and the avoidance of self-defeating patterns (for example, "Could you tell me how you were able to get started on that project without falling into the old procrastination pattern?") help to bolster adaptive coping skills and to lay the groundwork for revised beliefs. This is not to suggest that each agenda item raised in CBT can be neatly and effectively handled in each session. Much of CBT and psychotherapy in general deals with a patient's discomfort about the uncertainty of the future, such as important decisions about jobs or working toward long-range goals that may require numerous sessions to adequately address. However, by developing an awareness of their cognitive patterns and attributional styles, ADHD patients are better able to consider their options and make "informed" decisions about their options and choices rather than impulsive decisions.

Starting Small

Whether defining the treatment goals at the beginning of a course of CBT or setting agenda items at the start of a session, we prefer to err on the side of "starting small" and focusing on problems that are currently relevant and manageable rather than tackling the big issues right away. Our rationale for this approach is that individuals with ADHD often have problems prioritizing and facing tasks in their daily lives. Starting CBT by tackling big issues that may require ongoing time and effort to manage may result in frustration on the part of the patient, possibly leading to premature termination. Although it is important to acknowledge such large goals and to discuss how they will be addressed in CBT, it is useful to structure early sessions to examine smaller problems faced by patients that reflect the daily struggles of living with ADHD. Even important large goals can be pared down into smaller, manageable therapy objectives to decrease the likelihood of patients feeling unduly overwhelmed.

For example, Jeff is a 21-year-old college student who was diagnosed with ADHD and anxiety. He failed out of a 4-year college because he had difficulty concentrating in class and would procrastinate excessively on his coursework. He said he recognized the importance of an education but noted he could not follow through even when he knew he had to, which magnified his anxiety. At the time he started CBT, Jeff was working part-time and taking classes at a community college while living at home with his parents. He often skipped his college courses because he was not particularly interested in the classes, though he acknowledged the need to advance his education. He said the topics held some intellectual interest for him but Jeff much rather preferred tinkering with cars and electronic equipment. He had conflicts with his parents about his disregard for his schoolwork. Jeff's parent encouraged him to tough it out and to do enough to earn his associate's degree. Jeff, however, was unsure about whether to pursue his degree (for example, what he and others thought he should do) or to pursue his interest in mechanics and electronics in a technical school.

The question of whether to stay in community college or to pursue technical school was the central issue for Jeff. However, when asked for an immediate behavioral goal, Jeff sheepishly shared that he had several overdue rented videotapes under the seat in his car. The thought of making a special trip just to drop them off triggered thoughts that it would be a waste of time, though he also was bothered that he would appear irresponsible when he finally handed them in and faced the mounting late fees. Jeff said he often thought about returning the videos in the after-hours slot when he was out running errands but would simply forget. Jeff and his therapist agreed on the importance of making a decision about his future as a treatment goal, but dealing with the issue of the overdue videos became the first issue goal addressed in CBT. Although not a critical issue, the subsequent review of how he handled this problem, the role of his ADHD symptoms, and examples of his internal experience provided a template for understanding not only his difficulties returning the videos but also was generalized to the conceptualization of his decision-making difficulty about his future educational plans.

Once a shared understanding of the direction of CBT and specific problem list is established, attention turns to using specific cognitive and behavioral interventions to help individuals handle each of the problem areas. The goal for these interventions is to help patients adopt an expanded view of their situations, themselves, and ways for handling their lives. Although categorized as either behavioral or cognitive interventions below, we hope readers will understand that the influence of thoughts, emotions, and behaviors are inexorably interconnected throughout all experience and interventions.

Cognitive Interventions

> Think left and think right and think low and think high. Oh, the things you can think up if only you try. (Dr. Seuss, "Oh, The Thinks You Can Think!")

CBT therapists keep their ears attuned for examples of patients' cognitions throughout the process of reviewing past experiences, implementing behavioral interventions, and dealing with other clinical issues during sessions. Declarations made by patients such as, "I can't do that," "I just know that plan will not work for me," or "I'm a total failure" offer opportunities to explore how individuals came to those conclusions and to ferret out possible core beliefs and candidate schema. The cognitive interventions discussed below help patients to expand their interpretations and attributions of situations in order to maintain the potential for making constructive changes in their lives.

Cognitive Modification

Cognitive modification, or changing one's thoughts, starts at the level of the automatic thoughts. Drawing attention to these thoughts and learning to monitor their effects is often novel for many patients and helps them to recognize the influence of their cognitive style. A useful starting point is simply catching and describing these thoughts, with later attention focused on developing alternative thoughts.

A useful tool toward this end is the Daily Thought Record (DTR) (Beck et al., 1979). It is a simple form that helps individuals to record problematic situations and to draw connections between their thoughts, feelings, and outcomes. The first column is used to write down the relevant details about situations or events associated with a change in mood, though it can also be used to record problematic situations related more specifically to ADHD, such as procrastination. The second column is used to note the specific automatic thoughts (or images) that went through their mind during the situation. The third column is devoted to recording the resulting emotions. When first introducing the DTR in CBT, patients are encouraged to use the form to simply record examples of their thoughts and feelings in commonly encountered problematic situations in order to become familiar with the form. Examples may be reviewed in session to illustrate how the form is used and to start considering alternative interpretations of those situations.

The fourth column of the DTR is where alternative thoughts are developed. First, automatic thoughts can be classified based on the type of cognitive distortion they represent. The list of cognitive distortions reflects some common systematic ways that our reflexive thoughts can be skewed either by ignoring or exaggerating information. In addition to identifying the distortion, respondents are encouraged to consider alternative ways of construing the original situation. Questions listed at the bottom of the form help guide this process, such as "If a friend of yours was in the same situation and had this thought, how would you tell him/her?" and "What's the best that could happen? What's the worst that could happen? Could you handle it? What's the most likely outcome?" A final column is available to make a note of the outcome of this process. In addition to monitoring the effects on emotions, which are relevant for many ADHD adults, the DTR can be adapted to record ADHD-related behaviors, such as ratings of distractibility, time spent procrastinating, and so forth.

It is not surprising that the automatic thoughts of adults with ADHD tend to cluster around notions of self-criticism related to difficulties managing situations at hand (for example, "I forgot to pay my credit card bill again. I'm such a loser"). Left unchallenged, these negative thoughts can trigger a cascade of further self-criticism, emotional distress, and avoidant behavior. The therapist and patient can work together to develop an alternative interpretation of the situation (for example, "How would you advise a friend who was in the same situation?") that maintains the patient's esteem and leaves room for coping and problem management (for example, "I'm frustrated with myself that I forgot to pay the bill, but I'm not the only person who's ever done that. I'm going to try writing the next due date on my calendar as a reminder").

Of course, using a paper-and-pencil self-monitoring tool may create some obvious problems for adults with ADHD. It is not uncommon for patients to lose their forms or forget to use them in the course of the week between CBT sessions. Rather than engaging in all-or-nothing thinking and colluding with the notion that these problems indicate that the DTR does not work, creative solutions such as setting up a computerized version of the form or making do by drawing several columns on any available piece of paper are reasonable alternatives. The important issue is that patients exhibit an understanding of the influence of their thoughts on their experience. Thus, if a patient does not produce a completed DTR form but is able to identify his or her automatic thoughts in different situations and to develop alternative thoughts, it is evidence that the patient understands and is able to use this strategy. On the other hand, if a patient has difficulty implementing the DTR and seems unable to recognize the effects of her or his thought processes, the therapist and patient could take time to complete a DTR during session to illustrate its relevance and usefulness.

Personal Experiments and Skill Practice

Though recognizing and modifying distorted automatic thoughts is a crucial skill and one that can be enlightening for many patients, it is not an end in and of itself. The goal is to be able to implement these skills in order to change and improve personal experience. Thus, another strategy for modifying cognitions is to engage in difficult life situations in new ways in order to experience new outcomes. These personal experiments also provide opportunities for practicing new skills and often constitute the homework tasks that create continuity across sessions. Although a case could be made that skill practice and experiments constitute behavioral interventions, we include them in the cognitive section because, paired with developing alternative thoughts about situations, having novel experiences is another way to change one's outlook, particularly when dealing with compensatory strategies, which are strongly linked to core beliefs and schemas.

For example, Sarah, the college student mentioned earlier, concluded that she was inadequate when she was caught unprepared in class. She ended up in this situation because she had an aversion to reading because it took her a long time to complete assigned readings. Her thought about reading is, "I must be stupid because it takes me so long. I can't do this." Considering Sarah's ADHD symptoms and their effect on her reading, it is likely that reading will be difficult for her and it will take her a longer time than her peers to complete it, which would not be a distorted thought. However, her subsequent conclusion that being a slow reader meant she was incapable of completing reading assignments was likely a distortion. Thus, similar to conducting a scientific experiment, she subjected her automatic thought to a test.

Sarah's task was to attempt to spend shorter amounts of time reading a textbook to compare her negative automatic thought ("I can't do this") with her actual experience when reading. After experimenting with briefer periods of reading, Sarah found that she was able to retain more information than she predicted she would, though she learned that she required about 10 minutes to warm up before she could get focused on the text. By going through this process, she set more realistic expectations for how long she could read at one sitting (for example, "I can stay focused for about half-an-hour before I need a break") and, consequently, she could budget her time in order to keep up with her reading assignments, thereby gaining confidence in herself as opposed to concluding that she was "stupid."

The development and implementation of new coping skills is important in CBT for adult ADHD. Adults with ADHD, many of whom have gone undiagnosed most of their lives, very often have unsuccessfully tried to adopt coping strategies used by individuals without ADHD and have not developed a set of coping skills tailored for their symptoms. Consequently, many facets of daily life such as time management, organization, and distractions have become associated with pessimistic thoughts: "I can't do that. It doesn't work for me." When asked for the evidence to support that thought, individuals often say that they have repeatedly tried to implement specific coping skills. What we find, however, is that they often have been unaware of the effects of their ADHD and have repeatedly tried to use coping skills that work for other people. In addition, they use the first sign of difficulty as evidence that the skill does not work. We use CBT as a laboratory for researching different coping strategies to find what works for the individual. The cognitive element of this process involves monitoring patients' attributions about the effectiveness of the coping strategies. Individuals with ADHD are often quick to become frustrated and to abandon a project when it appears to not be working out well. Reframing these difficulties as normal and as an essential component of trial-and-error learning helps foster a sense of resilience and sticking with a plan to gain an adequate assessment of its usefulness before deciding to abandon it and try something else.

Problem-Management and Decision-Making

Most forms of psychotherapy address problem-solving and decision-making in some manner. Problem-solving involves defining in specific terms the problem or problems being faced by the patient, determining the possible outcomes, considering the available resources, brainstorming various possible solutions, determining the best course of action, and following through on the chosen course of action and assessing the outcome of this choice. In fact, the term *problem-management* reflects that there are some problems for which there may not be idyllic solutions but rather ways to cope with situations to minimize their negative effects. In a similar manner, decision-making involves clarifying the decision to be made, assessing the different choices available, assessing the pros and cons and potential implications of each option, selecting the best option based on the available information, implementing this decision, and assessing the outcome.

The first step in each of these processes, defining the problem to be addressed or decision to be made, is an important step because there may be multiple issues involved that become conflated and interfere with developing a resolution. For example, Jeff, the college student who was not sure whether he wanted to earn a college degree or pursue his interest in mechanics, faced both a decision and a problem when dealing with this issue. He faced the decision of which educational course to follow (for example, community college or technical school) and the problem of how to manage the fact that his parents might disagree with his choice. Teasing apart these different issues was helpful for him as he sorted through his options and clarified how he wanted to handle his life.

Individuals with ADHD may have particular difficulties related to problem management and decision-making that are associated with their chronic symptoms. That is, ADHD adults often have had greater difficulty than non-ADHD adults in navigating the typical business of daily life. These difficulties may stem, in part, from inefficiencies in processing and synthesizing the trial-and-error lessons learned in work, school, or relationships. Subsequently, individuals with ADHD might have problems drawing from past experiences and applying these insights to current situations. Consequently, patients with ADHD may now doubt their judgment when handling new situations that arise. Many ADHD adults must exert tremendous effort to manage many tasks, such as time management or organization, which non-ADHD individuals take for granted, further undermining their confidence in their judgment.

The knowledge that someone has ADHD neither clarifies the steps needed to manage various life problems nor spells out right decisions, such as the right job choice for someone with ADHD. These decisions remain individualized issues that are contingent upon a number of unique factors. However, we have observed that problem management and decision-making can be very stressful propositions for adults with ADHD, perhaps based on negative experiences related to past misjudgments. Thus, there is a tendency for decisions to be delayed until the last minute or for handling problems hastily and unthinkingly to avoid the stress associated with facing choices and taking time to consider all options.

In the case of many important life decisions, such as job choice or the decision to get married or to have children, there is a large degree of uncertainty about the long-range effects of choices made that weigh on the decision-making process; that is, "Will I still want to be married to this person in 10 years," "Will I be happy in this job 5 years from now," or "Will I be a good parent if my child has ADHD?" In such cases, we differentiate between two aspects of decision-making. First, there is making the choice of the best option with the information at hand. At some point in the process, however, there is no more information to gather (for example, available jobs in a particular field within a desired salary range) or the desired information is unavailable (for example, "What will our marriage be like in 20 years?").

Thus, the second part of decision-making is following through on one's choice and living into a good decision. The manner in which a person follows through on a decision may affect the eventual outcome. Individuals may underestimate their potential influence on outcomes, such as taking steps to be a good employee or an active partner in a marriage.

CBT cannot offer easy answers to problems and decisions faced by patients, though it offers a process and a supportive environment in which to thoroughly consider all options in order for patients to make fully informed decisions. Rather than settling on the first reasonable option or making a quick decision to avoid the stress of facing a problem, CBT focuses on systematically thinking through issues important to the individual and coping with stress-inducing situations by facing them, and in doing so fostering tolerance for accepting and handling discomfort (for example, "selective *solution* reuptake inhibitor") (Ramsay & Rostain, 2003). The ultimate goal for this process is for the individual to develop more confidence in his or her coping skills. This process includes recognizing when the first choice or plan is not working out and going back to the drawing board rather than giving up and sidestepping such issues out of frustration.

Resilience

Embedded in each of the aforementioned cognitive interventions is the notion of fostering resilience: maintaining a focus on and pursuit of personal goals in the face of surmountable difficulties and setbacks. In some cases, of course, it may be reasonable to reassess and revise personal goals as new information and experiences are gathered. However, individuals with ADHD may be particularly sensitive to frustration from a combination of low frustration tolerance and past disappointments, leading to overgeneralized beliefs, such as "I cannot do it" and "Nothing works out for me." While these outlooks might make sense based on ADHD patients' experiences, these beliefs very often were shaped without the individual (or others) recognizing the effects of ADHD.

Spending time during goal-setting for CBT to ensure that treatment objectives reflect valued personal goals for patients increases the likelihood that they are invested in the change process and are willing to see it through the rough spots.

Implementation Focus versus Goal Focus

As we have attempted to emphasize in this section on cognitive interventions, the cognitive framework held by individuals greatly affects how they experience and handle various situations. It is not that there is a preordained correct way to interpret events, but rather it is adaptive to be flexible and constructive when understanding and handling various circumstances. In this vein, we have increasingly found it useful to differentiate between a *goal focus* and an *implementation focus* for behavioral objectives. Having these two mindsets with which to approach behavior modification plans may help overcome barriers to change.

A *goal-focused* orientation is probably already a familiar and intuitive approach for achieving desired behavioral outcomes. There is a specific desired outcome or product that an individual hopes to achieve. This superordinate goal helps clarify and guide specific subordinate behavioral steps required to achieve it. For example, an individual may have the goal to keep up with paying bills and other household paperwork (for example, renewing automobile insurance). This overarching goal helps her to review her incoming mail on a regular basis and to devote time to paying bills as they arrive. Such an outcome-driven goal is prudent and can be helpful for carrying out proactive behaviors.

However, such long-term outcome goals may be too distal and weak for some individuals, such as many adults with ADHD, and, thus, they exert little influence on behavior. For example, an adult with ADHD has the goal to keep up with household bills and paperwork but feels overwhelmed when facing a stack of incoming mail (for example, "I cannot deal with this right now"). Paperwork to renew insurance or to complete quarterly tax payments appears confusing at first glance and is likewise set aside, either to be forgotten or only to be dealt with when the person faces an impending deadline. The goal of keeping up with paperwork remains important but seems increasingly unrealistic to the ADHD adult.

In such cases, a reformulation of behavior change from an outcome focus to a proximal, process focus may be useful. More specifically, adopting an *implementation-focused* orientation may foster improved behavioral follow-through (e.g., Gollwitzer, 1999; Gollwitzer & Schaal, 1998). Such an orientation involves identifying pivotal decision-making points or high-risk situations that interfere with performing the desired behavioral steps. For example, in the case of the individual with ADHD who has difficulty keeping up with bills and other household paperwork, there may be specific high-risk tasks that interfere with attaining the goal, such as sorting through the daily mail. Exclusive attention is paid to the relevant issues (for example, automatic thoughts, avoidant behaviors) that may interfere with execution of that task and an alternative plan is developed (for example, "What thoughts go through your mind when you see the pile of the day's mail? What do you end up doing?"). Thus, rather than focusing on a large goal (for example, keeping up with bills and paperwork), the patient focused on the steps required to initiate sorting through that day's mail (for example, "Let me first go through each piece of mail and discard the unnecessary items. I'll then open the envelope that seems most important and deal with it"). Eventually, steps toward fulfilling the original goal are achieved as a side effect of progressively implementing small, manageable changes for these sorts of pivotal behaviors.

Changing Core Beliefs and Schema

Because schema and core beliefs develop as part of the process of making sense of experience, not exclusively but primarily during childhood, revision of maladaptive beliefs usually requires both (a) an experiential component of assimilating novel experiences that are incongruent with existing negative beliefs and (b) a cognitive component of accommodating the belief system to account for these new experiences. The person with a failure schema, for example, who assumes axiomatically that he will ruin any important undertaking, may be asked to reassess his belief when he finds himself making progress in CBT on his goal of completing work projects on time. Furthermore, negative belief systems can be challenged by encouraging patients to identify, emphasize, and utilize their personal strengths and abilities, thereby fostering strengths-based beliefs as a counterpoint to the existing negative beliefs.

These deeper level schemas and beliefs are not as easily accessed and modified as are automatic thoughts. An effective strategy for drawing them out is the *downward arrow* technique (Burns, 1980). In this exercise, a patient is encouraged to consider the connection of a seemingly superficial automatic thought to more deeply held, underlying beliefs. When an automatic thought has been identified, the patient is then asked, "Assuming for a moment that your thought is true, what would be the meaning of it for you?" Subsequent thoughts are progressively met with the same question until the relevant underlying belief is revealed.

For example, John, a 41-year-old graphic artist, had not filed his federal income taxes in 3 years. He hired an accountant to help him and was asked to submit personal financial information in order to complete his tardy tax returns. However, John continued to procrastinate on sending the forms. This issue was placed on the agenda for one of his early sessions of CBT:

Therapist (T): So, let's address the issue of procrastination regarding your financial paperwork. What is the issue you are facing?

John (J): My accountant needs my receipts, W-2 forms and other paperwork from the past three years and I still haven't started to get it together for him.

T: What would be the first step?

J: I have to find a lot of these papers, though I generally try to shove most tax papers into the same drawer in a filing cabinet. I guess I could open that drawer and sort through the papers in there.

T: What is your automatic thought about taking that first step?

J: There will be a mound of confusing papers. I will be overwhelmed.

T: For the moment, let's assume that this is the case, that you are overwhelmed when you open the drawer. What would that mean to you?

J: That I really messed up this situation and I should be more responsible about these sorts of things.

T: And what is the implication of these thoughts?

J: I'll probably have to pay some sort of tax penalty for my irresponsibility and now my family will have to suffer financially for my mistakes.

T: Again, without yet questioning the accuracy of this thought, what does that thought mean to you?

J: That I'm not doing a good job taking care of things that affect my wife and children. And that I'm not smart enough to just give this stuff right away to an accountant who can take care of it for me before the tax deadline.

T: What does that conclusion mean to you?

J: I'm not a good husband or a good father. I'm incompetent when it comes to handling things that are important.

As we can see, though procrastination is a common problem for ADHD adults, John's avoidant behaviors and incompetency beliefs reciprocally compound each other, resulting in his continued delay in dealing with his taxes and his negative view of himself as a poor provider for his family. Thus, behavioral experiments related to reducing procrastination and handling problems in a timely manner represent not only coping skills for ADHD but also experiential exercises to help John challenge his negative beliefs. Additional cognitive intervention would help John to identify positive ways in which he fulfills his roles as father and husband that have nothing to do with whether or not he procrastinates.

As mentioned earlier, individuals with mild, uncomplicated cases of ADHD may not exhibit maladaptive schema, and CBT for these individuals helps them to learn to cope better in their current environments, such as improving their organizational skills at work. In many other cases, the various cognitive and behavioral interventions hopefully provide ways to modify the belief system (Freeman, 1993). Because schemas and core beliefs are so entrenched, wholesale *schema reconstruction*, building new adaptive, foundational beliefs, though possible, may not occur within a relatively brief course of CBT for adult ADHD, though it may be the focus of longer term CBT. *Schema modification*, or making the necessary changes to certain aspects of the belief system without a complete overhaul, may be more feasible. When therapeutic efforts focus on finding adaptive ways to understand and manage their belief system, *schema reinterpretation* is the desired outcome. Finally, *schema camouflage* refers to efforts to change observable behaviors without necessarily having yet achieved or even striving for belief change. This level of schema intervention reflects a fake-it-until-you-make-it approach to deal with ambivalence about change that hopefully allows an individual to experience what it would be like to have a different belief system.

CBT is not often thought of as an experiential form of psychotherapy, despite its emphasis on exposure to various situations and testing out new thoughts and beliefs in real-life settings to modify one's identity and ways of viewing the world. Therefore, the behavioral interventions discussed in the next section are important companions to the aforementioned cognitive interventions.

Behavioral Interventions

The aim of behavioral interventions is to help patients gain new coping skills and have novel experiences in domains of their lives that heretofore have proven difficult to manage. The dual purpose is to improve functioning and, consequently, to have new experiences from which to revise one's belief system. The particular behavioral targets chosen by patients represent areas of importance in their respective lives. In addition to setting up new contingencies, the very choice of the behaviors on which to focus can be important to discuss.

CBT for adult ADHD does not involve simply teaching a disembodied assortment of coping skills to patients, though certain skill areas may be standard for most adults with ADHD, such as time management, organization, and behavioral activation. The particular interventions and manner in which they are implemented are influenced by individuals' particular troubles, treatment goals, and case conceptualization. For a patient who struggles with running late for appointments and running out of time when working on projects, it would make sense for time management to be a focus. On the other hand, for a patient who is generally punctual but has significant difficulties related to activation and putting off tasks, issues related to procrastination offer a good starting point for sessions. Furthermore, the delivery of these interventions requires good clinical skill and tact in order to determine the specific behavior plan the patient is ready to undertake. What seems to the therapist to be a reasonable behavioral task may seem overwhelming to the patient, thus decreasing the likelihood of follow-through and increasing the likelihood that the patient will feel frustrated. Finally, assessing the usefulness of these interventions requires collaboration and negotiation by the patient and therapist. What follow are some of the more common behavioral interventions in the treatment of adult ADHD.

Behavioral Activation to Reduce Procrastination

Among the compensatory strategies that function as self-defeating behaviors, we find procrastination to be the most common (Ramsay, 2002; Rostain & Ramsay, 2006a). From a conceptualization standpoint, procrastination among adults with ADHD makes sense: tasks that are not immediately compelling or seemingly manageable are harder for adults with ADHD to initiate and to complete. Everyone procrastinates at times, and there is a body of research on adaptive procrastination, how it may serve a function in getting a task done in some circumstances (see Ferrari, Johnson, & McCown, 1995, for a review). However, procrastination is particularly maladaptive for ADHD adults.

A problem that starts as one related to self-management (Barkley, 1997a, 1997b; Brown, 2005) is often compounded by a learned aversion to facing certain jobs stemming from a history of frustrations related to the effects of ADHD symptoms. We have used the analogy that ADHD adults' responses to mundane, though necessary, everyday responsibilities is similar to what happens in cases of food poisoning. That is, a food that is typically enjoyed becomes associated with feeling physically ill, which is the body's adaptive response to toxins. Consequently, the next time that same food item is offered, despite the logical recognition that it is safe, the body responds to the sight, smell, and thought of eating the food item with feelings of nausea. It is nature's version of "fool me once, shame on you; fool me twice, shame on me."

In the case of task procrastination, individuals with ADHD have often had negative experiences with academic assignments, work projects, or other tasks requiring sustained commitment of time, effort, or concentration. Although ADHD adults recognize the importance of and incentives for completing such tasks, their aversion to facing such tasks overwhelms them and they often end up avoiding them. Of course, as the amount of work that needs to be done increases and the time before the deadline decreases, individuals feel increasingly overwhelmed at the thought of starting the projects and have stronger negative thoughts about them. This procrastination pattern sets up a vicious cycle in which avoidance of tasks becomes associated with short-term relief from having to face a stressful task, but these feelings of relief insidiously negatively reinforce (that is, increase the likelihood of performing a behavior by removing an aversive stimuli associated with it) avoidant behavior. Procrastination obstructs opportunities for gaining a sense of competence and mastery from facing and handling various everyday chores of adult life (Ramsay & Rostain, 2003). Thus, tasks are avoided until the stress associated with looming deadline pressure outweighs that associated with the task itself.

Behavioral activation strategies are crucially important for overcoming procrastination. Cognitive interventions set the stage for action, such as identifying negative thoughts about the task (for example, magnification of difficulty and minimization of one's ability to face it), recognizing the influence of past frustrations on current avoidance, and developing more realistic expectations for the task, including potential positive outcomes. However, hands-on experience usually provides ADHD adults with the most convincing evidence that they can handle various tasks. More specifically, we have found that individuals start tasks thinking about all that must be done to complete them. While this is an important part of a work plan, thinking about the totality of a task can be overwhelming. We encourage individuals to shrink the focus to the steps necessary to get started on a task, akin to an implementation focus.

Though the strategy of breaking down a large task into smaller, more manageable steps is a familiar one, we have called our emphasis on the steps required to get started on a previously avoided tasks the *10-minute rule* (Ramsay & Rostain, 2003). ADHD adults often have unrealistic expectations for how long they hope to perform a task and subsequently procrastinate because they feel overwhelmed by their own expectations. For example, a college student may expect to be able to research and write a 10-page essay in 6 hours on a day he does not have classes. As we point out, we often do not do tasks we enjoy for 6 hours, much less a task as difficult as researching, organizing, and writing a long essay. What often happens is the student keeps putting off starting the task because the timeframe is too overwhelming (for example, "I'll watch this TV show, then I'll be in the mood to write" or "I'll take a nap first. I'll feel rested and still have plenty of time to write") and ends up not working on it at all and consequently feeling frustrated.

Instead, we ask, "What is the amount of time you could work on this task even if it ends up being as difficult and uncomfortable (for example, distracted, cannot organize thoughts) as you anticipate it might be?" Usually the answer is somewhere around 10 minutes—hence our nickname for the intervention. The behavioral (or, implementation) task is to start work on the task for a full 10 minutes, such as sitting in front of the computer with the essay file open. After those 10 minutes, the individual is encouraged to reassess the task. If the task is, in fact, overwhelming or the individual is unable to focus on it, the person is permitted to stop working on it and to do something else without feeling guilty. We consider that an informed decision made by gathering information about the task and not the result of procrastination. More often, however, after 10 minutes, individuals have overcome their initial aversion to the task and are able to work relatively productively. Though not spending as much time on the task as they originally (and unrealistically) planned, individuals find that they are able to make reasonable headway on projects and gain satisfaction from staying on task. Adults with ADHD gain confidence based on their hands-on experience once they get started working on tasks. Moreover, they are more likely to be able to return to the task at another time to continue working on it because it is less threatening once that they have been able to face it effectively. However, should they find themselves again mired in the procrastination cycle, the 10-minute rule provides a useful heuristic for getting back on task.

Time Management

Poor time management among adults with ADHD is the result of some combination of having a poor sense of the passage of time (Barkley, Murphy, & Bush, 2001), inaccurately assessing how long various tasks will take to complete, and poor scheduling and prioritization skills. Consequently, individuals with ADHD arrive late for appointments (or forget them altogether), become overwhelmed by the number of things they have to do, or have the sense that they have mismanaged their time and energy.

When patients with ADHD cite time management as a therapeutic issue, we ask them how they keep track of their schedules (see Safren et al., 2005). Very often, these patients do not have a preferred schedule management system. The individuals with ADHD who own appointment books or electronic organizers (for example, a personal digital assistant, or PDA) commonly report that they do not use them or use them inconsistently. Patients who fit this description often report thoughts such as, "Other people seem to get by all right without writing everything down," "I don't have so many scheduled activities that I need to write them down," or "I've tried those scheduling tools but they don't work for me." These thoughts reflect the tendency for adults with ADHD to underestimate the potential benefit of such coping strategies based on the fact that others do not seem to need them. However, we encourage patients to experiment with a scheduling system. It serves to both keep track of scheduled appointments and to record how one's time and effort is spent. Most people would agree that it is prudent to keep track of how money is spent in order to improve their efforts to manage their finances; similarly, schedules help to keep track of how we spend our time and our effort.

We also encourage individuals to find a scheduling system that fits their personal style. Some individuals respond well to handheld PDA's and make use of various functions offered by them, such as alarms or the ability to automatically schedule a standing appointment far into the future. For other people, however, such technology is not convenient or the gadget goes in their pockets and they do not subsequently take it out and review the information they entered, thus resulting in frustration. Paper-and-pencil appointment books that are easily opened may be preferred by many ADHD adults. The act of writing down appointments, personal notes, and the convenience of glancing at the schedule book throughout the day help to increase its usefulness and the likelihood that information is more effectively encoded and ultimately remembered.

Some individuals with ADHD, such as stay-at-home parents or students, may claim to have few official appointments and, therefore, feel ambivalent or skeptical about implementing such scheduling tools. However, review of time management frustrations may reveal inefficiencies in their budgeting of time and energy for various tasks, chores, and even recreational activities (for example, exercise). Individuals are encouraged to experiment with the use of a scheduling book as an all-purpose strategy for managing time and activities. We use the guidelines for the recommended daily allowance of various vitamins and minerals to draw the analogy that time management strategies help to ensure individuals fulfill their daily allowance of work tasks, recreational tasks, and other important pursuits in a well-balanced manner. Thus, patients are encouraged to start using the scheduling book in a specific, limited way in order to experiment with its usefulness, such as monitoring exercise, social engagements, or recreational pursuits (for example, scheduling to watch favorite TV programs). Such preferred tasks provide reasonable starting points to allow individuals to gain experience with time management and scheduling that may be applied to other areas of their lives.

Organization Skills

In addition to organizing one's schedule, many adults with ADHD have problems organizing paperwork, objects (for example, tools, books), and other items associated with the business of daily living. There are many tried-and-true organizational techniques that are very useful for adults with ADHD and many available resources for how to implement those techniques (Kolberg & Nadeau, 2002).

Discussion of specific organizational skills is appropriate for CBT for adult ADHD, though it is important to continue to use the CBT model to identify difficulties individuals may have in implementing the behavioral strategies. Most adults with ADHD make statements akin to "I know what I'm supposed to do to get organized but I do not do it" or "I could advise someone else about how to get organized but I cannot follow my own advice." Thus, there are usually some negative thoughts about the process that interfere with effective follow-through (Ramsay, 2005b).

A problem we frequently encounter is that individuals with ADHD often view organization in all-or-nothing terms. They have an understandable desire to get organized but the task soon becomes overwhelming and is abandoned with the conclusion "I'll never get organized." We encourage starting small and focusing on a single task in which to gain mastery; for example, finding a predictable place for items used everyday, such as books for school or car keys, or dealing with bills in a more systematic manner.

Another common problem for ADHD adults is underestimating the effectiveness of simple solutions. Color-coded filing systems and other strategies are helpful for many ADHD adults but, similar to time management systems, individuals must find strategies that work for them and are sustainable. It is a significant step forward for some individuals with ADHD to simply be able to sort through their daily mail in order to discard junk mail or to have a plain cardboard box that is devoted to storing incoming tax-related paperwork.

Finally, the standard organizational strategies are proven effective. However, it is easy to drift away from using them. People forget to put a bill where it belongs and end up paying it late or put their keys in a coat pocket and toss the coat on a chair, only to later forget where they put their keys. Adults with ADHD often respond to such mistakes by magnifying them into evidence of personal failure and concluding that the organization strategies themselves are ineffective. A task in CBT for adult ADHD is to normalize such setbacks as par for the course in skill development. Thus, organizational problems are collaboratively reviewed with a problem management mindset to determine potential difficulties related to implementing the strategies. This corrective process is further normalized as an expected feature of the ongoing effort required to maintain organizational skills. Patients' automatic thoughts and other reactions to these setbacks are identified to determine their influence. Modifying these thoughts and recommitting to using the coping strategies fosters the resilience needed for the long-term management of ADHD symptoms.

Environmental Engineering

A closely related topic to organization is for ADHD adults to understand the influence of their surroundings on their functioning. Individuals with ADHD may be particularly sensitive to visual, auditory, or even tactile distractions. Someone with poor impulse control may sit down to do some work or chores but soon find himself turning on the television or checking e-mail. While it is impossible to eliminate all distractions at home, in a dorm room, or at an office, it may be possible to reduce them and to make certain settings more ADHD friendly.

As with previous suggestions, there is no one-size-fits-all approach to environmental engineering. It must be personalized to a patient's surroundings and particular vulnerabilities for distraction. Spending time discussing the details of what the patient has tried, his or her particular sensitivities (for example, sounds, visual distractions), and the reasonableness of different possibilities increases the likelihood of determining a reasonable option.

For example, one of our patients described spending about 30 minutes each day looking for his car keys, which often left him running late and feeling frustrated with himself. He jokingly said that he should hammer a nail in the wall next to his front door and hang them up whenever he entered his house. He laughed at his idea but his therapist asked if he would be willing to experiment with his solution. The patient's initial thoughts were, "I should not have to resort to that" and "It's a stupid idea." However, he agreed to give it a try and it ended up being a simple, effective, and sustainable environmental modification that greatly reduced his daily frustration.

In addition to modifying the physical layout of a workstation or study space, there are various organization, time management, and other coping tools and gadgets that are available specifically for adults with ADHD. The choice of specific tools to be used is an individualized decision based on the unique circumstances of each patient. We adopt a pragmatic view of using whatever works for individuals. However, we caution that these items are coping tools, as are the components of our combined treatment approach (for example, medications, CBT strategies). There is no magic solution and their strength lies in their appropriate and continued use.

Assertiveness

The behavioral strategy of assertiveness may seem out of place in a discussion of CBT for adult ADHD. However, in addition to the effects of ADHD on managing many of the tasks of daily life, its symptoms also affect interpersonal functioning. Individuals with ADHD, particularly those who grew up without being diagnosed, often had the sense that they were disappointing others (for example, parents, teachers, coaches) and were not fulfilling their potential. Many ADHD adults also tend to act impulsively and may have issues related to anger management, thus possibly alienating friends, family, and coworkers. Such experiences may result in a tendency to assume too much personal blame for creating problematic situations. The result is that many patients find themselves reluctant to stand up for personal needs or boundaries out of a sense of operating from a deficit in their relationships (for example, "I cannot ask my professor to review a draft of my essay because I show up late for every class").

Assertiveness is not the same as aggressiveness, nor does it mean that someone is entitled to get their way in all situations. It refers to the skill of being able to share one's opinion, state one's needs, and request help in a forthright manner. It also involves the ability to apologize after making a mistake and to adopt a nondefensive approach to dealing with some recurring problems related to ADHD (for example, "I'm sorry, but could you tell me your name again? Sometimes I forget names right after I've been introduced to someone new"). In terms of managing ADHD, assertive communication provides a model for handling frustration in a way that reduces the likelihood of unnecessary conflict. It also serves to remind individuals with ADHD that it is acceptable to speak out and request help from others when needed. Assertiveness also includes acting as one's own advocate and making use of available resources and supports in order to optimize one's ability to cope.

CBT Summary

CBT provides a clinically useful, evidence-supported framework for understanding the interaction of attitudes and behaviors commonly experienced by adults with ADHD. The basic tenets of CBT—that thoughts and beliefs exert significant influence on and are influenced by emotions, actions, and experiences and that modification of these thoughts and beliefs leads to clinical improvements—are elegant in their simplicity, which leads most people to respond to descriptions of the CBT model by saying, "Of course." However, the identification and disentangling of the candidate thoughts and beliefs and their influence on emotions and behaviors, and then the structuring of interventions that allow patients to develop new outlooks represent the crucial intersection of the science and craft of CBT.

Likewise, pharmacotherapy for adult ADHD can appear to be a straightforward undertaking, simply matching the correct medication at the right dose to treat the symptoms described by patients. However, issues of compliance, side effects, tolerance, and psychiatric and medical comorbidity complicate the practice of pharmacotherapy, as will be discussed in the next section.

PHARMACOTHERAPY FOR ADULT ADHD

The most important step before starting pharmacotherapy for ADHD adults is thorough education. To begin with, the purposes for using medications need to be clarified. This involves delineating the target symptoms that are the focus of treatment (for example, inattention, distractibility, restlessness, and impulsivity). Next, a method for measuring and keeping track of symptom improvement needs to be agreed upon. We have found it useful to employ a medication log for this purpose in addition to standardized instruments like the Barkley Symptom Checklist, the CAARS, or the BADDS described in Chapter 1 (see Figure 2.2). Finally, a medication regimen needs to be chosen in keeping with patients' individualized treatment goals, personal preferences, prior and current experiences with psychotropic medications, family members' responses to medications, and comorbid psychiatric conditions.

Once a medication is selected, both written and oral information is provided to patients, and specific plans are discussed for starting the medication. Typically this means starting at a relatively low dose, observing initial clinical effects, noting side effects, and setting a schedule for increasing the dosage to appropriate levels. Frequent follow-up visits are scheduled at first to insure that the patient has ample opportunity to discuss the positive and negative effects observed and to address any questions or concerns. Further adjustments to the regimen are made in accordance with patients' reports, although it is highly recommended to solicit input from significant others regarding the impact of the medication.

MEDICATION RESPONSE FORM   Patient Name _____

Medication _____   Dose, Schedule _____

Instructions: Please rate the following factors on a scale of 1 - 10 where 1 = poor, 5 = average, and 10 = excellent. Please write comments in the appropriate column.

Day	Time	Dose	Concentration Attention span	Task Completion	Mood	Comments

FIGURE 2.2 Medication Response Form

In most cases, a stimulant medication is prescribed as the first line of treatment. If a patient has had prior experience with a particular medication and found it to be helpful, we will start with that class of compound. If a negative response was obtained from one type of stimulant, we will try another variety of stimulant. With the immediate release preparations, we will start at the lowest recommended doses and titrate upward on a weekly basis to the maximum recommended levels unless negative side effects are encountered. We prefer to start with the immediate-release form of stimulants in order to help the patient to recognize the onset and duration of action of the medication. Once it is determined that the medication is working properly and that an optimal dose has been reached, we will switch the patient to a longer acting preparation. If the patient experiences serious side effects such as cardiac symptoms, tics, mood instability, or severe insomnia, we will discontinue the medication. Mild side effects can be addressed either with dose reduction or with the introduction of adjunctive medications (for example, mirtazapine or clonidine for stimulant-associated insomnia). Close monitoring of cardiovascular status and weight is mandatory. Finally, failure of adequate treatment response or any evidence of inappropriate use (or abuse) are indicators to switch the patient to another medication.

Atomoxetine is a reasonable alternative to the stimulants, particularly for patients who have a high level of anxiety, who are not comfortable with taking stimulants, and/or who report emotional dysregulation as a major target symptom. As with the stimulants, it is best to start at a low dose (for example, 25 mg daily) and to increase slowly up to the target range of 80 to 120 mg daily. Taking the medication with meals reduces the occurrence of gastrointestinal (GI) side effects, and taking it at night minimizes the sedating effects. Unlike the stimulants, this medication takes up to 8 to 12 weeks to reach full effect, so patients need to be told not to expect rapid symptom improvement. If partial response is seen with atomoxetine, it is safe to add low-dose stimulant medication, particularly for daytime activities requiring greater concentration and freedom from distractibility.

When patients fail to respond to either stimulants or atomoxetine, we generally turn to the second-line medications: bupropion, tricyclic antidepressants, or modafanil. We generally start bupropion XL at 150 mg daily and increase after 2 weeks to 300 mg daily if initial response is suboptimal. Headache, dry mouth, insomnia, and nausea are the most common adverse effects. Agitation or irritability are sometimes serious enough to warrant stopping bupropion. We usually use desipramine or imipramine at doses ranging from 150 to 300 mg daily or nortriptyline 50 to 150 mg daily, with good results. If the patient reports excessive fatigue or other intolerable side effects, we will lower the dose before stopping the medication altogether. Close monitoring of EKG is mandatory, and any sign of cardiac rhythm disturbances is an indication to stop the medication. Modafanil can be used in doses from 100 to 400 mg, once or twice daily, as needed. We generally titrate upward on a weekly basis until a positive response is recorded. We will discontinue the medication if no positive results are seen at the maximum dose of 400 mg twice daily.

Combining selective serotonin reuptake inhibitors (SSRI) with stimulants has shown to be useful for adults with ADHD and comorbid anxiety or depression. While any of the SSRIs can be combined safely with either methylphenidate or amphetamine, we tend to select the more sedating agents (for example, paroxetine or sertraline) when patients report difficulty with insomnia or overactivation and the less sedating compounds (for example, fluoxetine or citalopram) when they complain of being too tired or underactive. In cases where patients already taking an SSRI are looking for additional help with ADHD symptoms, adding a stimulant usually proves successful in reducing inattention, distractibility, impulsivity, and/or subjective feelings of restlessness. Since there is no interference with hepatic metabolism or any interaction between stimulants and SSRIs, we usually prescribe these at usual dosage strengths. To date, we have not observed any serious side effects from combined medication treatment, although occasionally patients will report feeling overly sedated.

Another useful medication for patients with ADHD comorbid with anxiety and/or depression is venlafaxine. We generally start with 37.5 mg of the extended-release preparation and increase in increments of 37.5 mg every week or every other week up to a maximum of 225 mg daily. This gradual titration schedule is generally well tolerated and enables the patient to observe effects on both mood/anxiety and on ADHD symptoms. In cases where patients are already prescribed venlafaxine but are complaining of difficulties with concentration or impulse control, we will start low-dose stimulant medication as an adjunctive treatment. It is vital that the patient be monitored for potential cardiovascular side effects (especially hypertension) and for signs of overactivation or agitation.

Another class of medications that are potentially helpful for ADHD symptoms is known as alpha-2 adrenergic agonists. These include clonidine and guanfacine, which are similar in mechanism of action but different with respect to duration of effect and side effects. Clonidine tends to be more sedating and shorter acting than guanfacine (approximately 4 hours versus 12 hours), but they both can cause sleepiness and fatigue. Originally developed as antihypertensive agents, and not yet FDA (U.S. Food and Drug Administration) approved for ADHD, these medications tend to reduce hyperactivity, restlessness, impulsivity, and anxiety. We generally use the alpha-2 adrenergic agonists in combination with stimulants, particularly with patients who are experiencing rebound phenomena (that is, becoming very restless and hyperactive when the stimulants wear off). They are also helpful to induce sleep in patients with ADHD and insomnia, regardless of whether the sleeplessness is related to taking stimulant medication or is simply a feature of the patient's basic clinical presentation. With clonidine, we usually start with 0.1 mg at bedtime and increase weekly in 0.1-mg increments to a maximum of 0.4 mg, usually on a b.i.d. or t.i.d. schedule. With guanfacine we begin with 1 mg at bedtime and increase by 1-mg increments (either once or twice daily) on a weekly basis to a maximum of 4 mg daily. Besides sedation, the most common side effects of these medications are dry mouth, headache, dizziness, and irritability. Furthermore, it is not advisable to stop the alpha adrenergic agonists suddenly, since abrupt cessation can lead to serious hypertension, tachycardia, agitation, and excessive sweating.

Conversely, it is not uncommon for patients with partially treated mood or anxiety disorders to seek additional medical treatment for ADHD symptoms. In these circumstances, we try to maintain the patient's current medication regimen while introducing an attention-promoting medication. For example, if the patient is being managed with an SSRI, it is our customary practice to initiate a trial of stimulant medication at the usual doses used for uncomplicated ADHD. If the patient is taking venlafaxine or duloxetine (so-called combined norepinephrine-serotonin reuptake inhibitors), a trial of low-dose stimulants might be attempted with cautious monitoring of cardiovascular effects. Stimulants can also be added to bupropion with the similar cautions. In all of these situations, changes in both attentional measures and mood or anxiety levels should be monitored. If stimulants prove too difficult for the patient to tolerate, we often suggest a trial of modafanil. If these steps do not provide sufficient relief for ADHD symptoms, we generally recommend starting the patient on a tricyclic antidepressant medication. Despite concerns about potential side effects, the tricyclic antidepressants are actually very effective for depression and anxiety as well as for ADHD. Many patients come to appreciate the advantages of being on a single medication with multiple clinical effects. Lastly, when there is evidence of treatment resistant depression along with prominent ADHD, a trial of an MAO inhibitor is certainly warranted.

Special care should be taken with patients suffering from comorbid bipolar disorder. It is critical that effective mood stabilization is achieved prior to introducing a stimulant medication. If the patient has been free of any manic or hypomanic symptoms for at least 3 months, it is reasonable to start the patient on a low dose of methylphenidate and observe the response. While many clinicians express a fear that stimulants can trigger a manic episode, this is actually a relatively uncommon occurrence, and when it does it occur, it is often triggered by disturbances of the sleep–wake cycle. Cooperative patients can be instructed to watch for signs of insomnia, irritability, or impending hypomania and to contact the physician if any serious mood shifts occur.

With respect to patients with substance abuse disorders, we usually initiate treatment with atomoxetine or buproprion and avoid prescribing stimulants. Once a therapeutic alliance has been established, and the patient is reporting successful abstinence (backed up by clean urine tests), it is permissible to introduce stimulant medication into the equation.

Patients with comorbid sleep disorder, chronic pain syndrome, Tourette's syndrome, or autistic spectrum disorders require special pharmacotherapeutic approaches that are beyond the scope of this book.

While there very few long-term studies of pharmacotherapy for adult ADHD, we have found that for most of our patients, medication effects remain evident for as long as they are prescribed. Of course, there are times when the dosage needs to be adjusted upwards or when a previously effective medication seems to stop working. In these cases, it is important to help the patient to understand that alternative treatments are still available and that loss of efficacy is not a sign that the patient is becoming too dependent or addicted to the medication. As before, the choice of using other medications must be approached using a cost/benefit analysis.

Despite periodic controversies that surface regarding use of medications, pharmacotherapy remains the most effective treatment for ADHD that is available, regardless of the age of patients. Stimulant medications stand out as the first line treatment option. Other classes of medications, including the nonstimulant atomoxetine, may be effective for individuals who do not respond to or cannot tolerate the side effects of stimulants. Furthermore, cases that involve comorbid and/or complex psychiatric symptoms may require the choreography of several different medications for adequate treatment.

SUMMARY

In this chapter we have provided detailed descriptions of both psychosocial, namely CBT, and pharmacotherapy approaches for the treatment of adult ADHD. Each treatment makes a unique contribution to symptom reduction and improving the overall well-being of patients. Hopefully this chapter has provided clinically useful models for handling the craft of CBT and pharmacotherapy of adult ADHD. The next chapter is devoted to describing the current scientific evidence that forms the basis for recommending this integrative treatment approach.

CHAPTER 3

Research Evidence for Cognitive Behavioral Therapy (CBT) and Medications for Adult Attention-Deficit/Hyperactivity Disorder (ADHD)

If we knew what we were doing, it would not be called research, would it? (Albert Einstein)

ADHD has wide-ranging effects on cognition, behavior, self-control, and learning, which have important downstream consequences for individuals' abilities to manage many of the important demands of life. Consequently, *multimodal treatment*, combining medications, counseling, and other therapeutic services (for example, academic support, vocational counseling, support groups, and so forth), is widely endorsed as the treatment of choice for ADHD individuals of all ages to address its many effects, though it has only been systematically studied in childhood samples (AACAP, 1997; ADDA, 2006; Robin, 1998; The MTA Cooperative Group, 1999; Weiss et al., 2002). Medications provide the foundation of most treatment plans, with psychosocial treatments being the next most widely used treatment. Regardless of the constellation of treatment approaches used, it is clear that managing the symptoms of ADHD requires a truly bio-psycho-social approach to conceptualization and treatment.

Empirical support for pharmacotherapy, particularly the use of psychostimulants, has established medications as the first line of treatment to be considered for ADHD patients of all ages (AACAP, 1997, 2002; Spencer et al., 1996; Weiss & Murray, 2003; Wilens et al., 2000). The stimulant medications are the most thoroughly researched medications (not just psychiatric) prescribed to children. Although not as widely studied among adults, the use of stimulant medications for ADHD is well supported by research as the most efficacious treatment available for adult patients with ADHD. Other classes of medications have been found to be beneficial for individuals who do not respond to or who cannot tolerate the side effects of the stimulants (Dodson, 2005; Spencer, Biederman, & Wilens, 2004a, 2004b; Weiss et al., 2002).

There are currently three medications approved by the U.S. Food and Drug Administration (FDA) specifically for the treatment of adult ADHD—mixed salts of a single-entity amphetamine product (Adderall XR®), dexmethylphenidate hydrochloride (Focalin XR®), and atomoxetine hydrochloride (Strattera®)—though many others have been subject to research and are prescribed for off-label use for adults with ADHD. Medication management for adult patients with ADHD is complicated by a number of factors, including the need to treat comorbid psychiatric and medical problems, effective dosing, and treatment compliance issues.

While many patients respond well to pharmacotherapy alone and may not require additional modes of treatment, mental health professionals often encounter cases that are more challenging and less responsive to medication management alone. In particular, adult patients whose symptoms of ADHD have gone on mis- or undiagnosed until adulthood may present for treatment with severe functional problems affecting their well-being, complicated psychiatric comorbidities, and a complex assortment of ADHD symptoms, clinical problems, and executive dysfunction that add several degrees of difficulty to treatment (Adler & Chua, 2002; Spencer et al., 2002; Weiss et al., 1999).

Even with the positive effects associated with medication treatment, it has been estimated that pharmacotherapy alone is insufficient for upwards of 50% of adult patients (Wilens et al., 2000). Moreover, improvements on measures of core symptoms offered by medications do not always translate into satisfactory functional improvements (for example, time management, organization, self-control, anger management) in the daily lives of patients (Weiss et al., 1999). The findings from studies of the effectiveness of medications are often based on responses to symptom questionnaires and neuropsychological testing results. Although these are crucial clinical data, improvements on these sorts of measures do not necessarily mean that the day-to-day well-being of these patients has adequately improved or that they will be able to carry out the necessary coping skills to manage their ADHD over the long haul.

The promise of psychosocial treatments for adult ADHD is indeed appealing. These treatments target the very areas of functioning that are relevant to each patient and, hopefully, provide useful coping skills and problem-solving strategies. Said differently, these treatments pick up where medication treatment leaves off to relieve residual symptoms (e.g., Safren et al., 2005). Psychosocial treatments also may be beneficial for treating comorbid mood and anxiety disorders and other secondary effects of ADHD, such as relationship problems and low self-esteem, the latter issue being particularly relevant for women with ADHD (Gaub & Carlson, 1997; Rucklidge & Kaplan, 1997; Solden, 1995). Finally, with all the focus on coping skills and ADHD symptoms, it is important to acknowledge the potential restorative benefits of the therapeutic relationship, which provides a safe environment in which adults with ADHD can focus on the difficult task of making changes in their lives (Ramsay & Rostain, 2005a, in press).

Despite their promise, the benefits of psychosocial treatments for adults with ADHD remain sorely understudied. As recently as 1997, a review of treatment recommendations for professionals treating ADHD summarized the state of affairs for psychosocial interventions for ADHD adults as follows: "The data on psychosocial interventions in the treatment of adults with ADHD are entirely anecdotal" (AACAP, 1997, p. 107S). Scientific research on psychosocial treatments still lags far behind the research base justifying pharmacotherapy, but there have been several studies in recent years that have provided guidance in developing and implementing treatments for adults with ADHD.

In this chapter, we will review the published research on both psychosocial treatments and pharmacotherapy for adult ADHD in order to provide the evidence base for our integrative treatment approach. We begin with a review of the psychosocial treatment literature.

REVIEW OF RESEARCH EVIDENCE FOR PSYCHOSOCIAL TREATMENTS FOR ADULTS WITH ADHD

A few years ago, a panel of experts in the field of ADHD research and clinical practice were surveyed in order to establish treatment guidelines for ADHD (Conners et al., 2001). One of the questions posed to the panel of experts was: "In what ways do you feel that the current quality of ADHD (psychosocial) treatment in the United States could be improved? Give your highest rankings to the most important problems in the way that ADHD is currently being treated" (Conners et al., 2001,

p. S-115). The experts' four highest ranked responses were, in descending order, "inadequate training in appropriate psychosocial strategies," "inappropriate choice of psychosocial interventions," "inappropriate duration of psychosocial interventions," and "too little psychosocial treatment is being used." These responses bring to mind Woody Allen's monologue at the beginning of the film *Annie Hall* during which he tells of two women eating dinner at a Catskills mountain resort. The first woman complains that the food there is terrible and the second responds, "Yeah, I know, and such small portions." So it is also for the experts' opinion regarding the state of affairs of psychosocial treatments for adult ADHD: It is not being done well and there is too little of it.

A computerized search of several psychological and biomedical research databases revealed that there are currently eight published outcome studies of psychosocial treatments for adults with ADHD (see Ramsay & Rostain, 2005a, in press, for a comprehensive review of these studies and ways to adapt psychotherapy based on these studies) and one additional study slated for publication in 2007. Thus, we are certainly not at a point at which there is sufficient empirical evidence to propose a set of empirically validated psychosocial treatment guidelines for adult ADHD. That said, the extant psychosocial treatment literature provides important insight about treatment approaches and directions for future research.

All studies of psychosocial treatments reviewed focused on adult patients with ADHD, though they varied in the assessment procedures used to confirm the diagnosis and outcome measures used to assess treatment effects. Most researchers, however, employed strategies and objective assessments to retrospectively confirm the presence of ADHD symptoms in childhood and to confirm the presence of current, clinically significant symptoms. Outcome measures frequently included ADHD symptom assessments, measures of problems commonly associated with ADHD (though not necessarily included in official diagnostic criteria; for example, anger, organization, self-esteem), mood and anxiety ratings, and ratings of overall functioning. Almost all of the participants in the studies were on a stable medication regimen when they were in therapy, though a small number were medication free. There were no differences in results reported for those on medications and those who were medication free, though the available data are insufficient to draw any conclusions about the effectiveness of psychosocial treatments delivered without concurrent pharmacotherapy.

The psychosocial studies reviewed also employed a variety of research designs. Several studies used open clinical study designs (including chart review) in which participants were assessed at both the beginning and end of treatment to determine whether treatment was associated with clinical improvements (Ratey et al.,1992; Rostain & Ramsay, 2006c;

Solanto et al., in press; Wilens et al., 1999). Such exploratory designs provide preliminary information about the clinical usefulness of a treatment. The findings provide information regarding whether or not the treatment studied was associated with clinical improvement. However, without comparing the treatment group to a control group, it is impossible to assess whether the treatment benefits obtained are greater than would be obtained by the spontaneous improvement of symptoms or from other factors.

Nonrandomized control studies compare a group of participants receiving treatment with a similar clinical group that is not receiving treatment (for example, wait list control, Hesslinger et al., 2002; Wiggins et al., 1999). The use of a control group provides a comparison against which to judge the outcomes obtained from a particular treatment. However, without using random assignment to the respective groups, there is the possibility that extratherapeutic factors influenced the treatment outcomes, such as those participants agreeing to be placed in the treatment group being especially motivated to follow treatment recommendations.

Finally, randomized control studies provide the highest level of quality assurance of the studies reviewed. In these studies, a treatment group is compared with a control group, and participants are randomly assigned to these groups (e.g., Safren, Otto, et al., 2005; Stevenson, Stevenson, & Whitmont, 2003; Stevenson et al., 2002). Consequently, it can be inferred with greater confidence that differences obtained between groups are the result of treatment interventions and are less likely the result of other factors.

The purpose of this part of the chapter is to provide the empirical basis for the CBT component of our combined treatment approach. Consequently, although all of the interventions reviewed are compatible with a CBT framework and could be considered part of the CBT family of psychotherapy approaches, for the purposes of review we have separated the three studies that focused on psychoeducation/cognitive remediation from the six studies that explicitly described a CBT-oriented approach. (See Table 3.1.)

Psychoeducational and Cognitive Remediation Treatment Approaches

Three of the outcome studies involved psychosocial treatment approaches that identified the different problem areas commonly reported by ADHD adults and focused on targeted skill development to address these problems. Ratey et al. (1992) published the first study to systematically document the clinical challenges of diagnosis and treatment in adults with ADHD, although this was not a treatment effectiveness study per se.

TABLE 3.1   Outcome Studies of Psychosocial Treatments for Adult ADHD

Reassessment of treatment failures with untreated ADHD	Ratey et al. (1992)
Psychoeducational group for adult ADHD	Wiggins et al. (1999)
Chart review of CBT and medications	Wilens et al. (1999)
Dialectical behavior therapy-modular group treatment	Hesslinger et al. (2002)
CRP group treatment	Stevenson et al. (2002)
Self-directed CRP with minimal therapeutic contact	Stevenson et al. (2003)
Randomized control trial of CBT and meds vs. meds only	Safren et al. (2005)
Combination of CBT and meds	Rostain & Ramsay (2006)
CBT group treatment	Solanto et al. (in press)

Note. CBT = Cognitive Behavioral Therapy; CRP = Cognitive Remediation Programme.

The authors examined 60 adult patients who had been deemed treatment failures by their previous psychotherapists. None of the patients had been diagnosed with ADHD in childhood but all exhibited chronic symptoms sufficient to fulfill diagnostic criteria when reassessed by clinicians experienced with ADHD. Thus, all these newly diagnosed adult ADHD patients were prescribed a very low dose of the tricyclic antidepressant desipramine (10 to 30 mg), a commonly prescribed medication for ADHD at that time, for a 1-month period. Increasing doses of the psychostimulant methylphenidate (range 10 to 60 mg/day) were used if the initial clinical response was not adequate.

These 60 patients had been previously given a number of different diagnoses and had diverse developmental histories, backgrounds, and clinical problems. The authors found that traditional conceptualizations of patients' presenting symptoms, such as resistance, defense mechanisms, or low self-esteem, provided little benefit in terms of treatment formulation and more often served to lower patients' already fragile self-images. Ratey and colleagues (1992) instead employed a coping model of therapy, including psychoeducation about the symptoms of ADHD, emphasizing the neurobiological nature of ADHD (versus it being the result of a character flaw); a focus on developing coping skills; and building up patients' existing strengths and capabilities. All patients were judged as being significantly improved by the end of treatment, though these improvements were based on clinical impressions without the use of formal outcome measures. However, the study shed light on the issue of unrecognized adult ADHD in clinical practice.

More recently, Stevenson et al. (2002) performed a systematic evaluation of the efficacy of their cognitive remediation programme (CRP). The CRP specifically targeted problems commonly associated with ADHD in adulthood: attention problems, poor motivation, disorganization, impulsivity, anger management, and low self-esteem. Subjects were assigned to either a CRP group (*n* = 22) or a wait list control group (*n* = 21). Medication status remained stable throughout the study, with participants being either unmedicated or on a stable, effective dose. CRP was provided in eight weekly 2-hour group sessions. A clinical psychologist facilitated the groups with the assistance of coaches, who helped participants complete various exercises. The results indicated that, after treatment, participants reported improvements on ADHD symptom checklists, organizational skills, self-esteem, and anger management skills. These treatment gains were either maintained or continued to improve at 2-month follow-up. Significant treatment gains in ADHD symptoms and organization were maintained at 1-year follow-up. Despite the impressive improvements, the authors hypothesized that additional interventions might be necessary to garner more substantial and sustainable improvements in self-esteem and anger.

Stevenson and colleagues (2003) conducted a follow-up randomized control study of a self-directed version of their CRP for patients, with minimal therapist contact. Participants in the study were randomly assigned to either the CRP group (*n* = 17) or wait list control group (*n* = 18) and there were no significant differences between groups on pretreatment clinical measures. Medication status again remained stable throughout the study, with participants being either unmedicated or on a stable, effective dose. As in the previous study, participants were paired with coaches, but this time the coaches' role was to contact participants weekly by telephone and remind them to keep up with the therapeutic assignments and to use the CRP self-help book they had been given. Coaches also monitored compliance with the program. There were three therapist-led sessions at the start, middle, and end of treatment to monitor progress. Outcome measures were obtained at baseline, end of treatment, and 2-month follow-up.

All outcome measures (for example, ADHD symptoms, organizational skills, self-esteem, and both state and trait anger) showed significant improvements for participants completing CRP treatment when compared with pretreatment scores and with controls. At 2-month follow-up, CRP-related treatment gains were maintained for ADHD symptoms, organizational skills, and trait anger. Forty-seven percent of CRP participants were considered treatment responders in terms of ADHD symptom reduction at the end of treatment and 36% were responders at 2-month follow-up. Analyses of treatment compliance revealed that participants generally followed the program outline and there was a significant and positive correlation between compliance and treatment outcome. Thus, not surprisingly, participants who followed the CRP treatment program experienced greater improvements than participants who did not.

CBT-Oriented Psychosocial Treatments

Although the three aforementioned treatment approaches are compatible with CBT approaches, particularly Stevenson and colleagues' model, they did not emphasize cognitive modification interventions in the form of targeting the influence of negative and self-defeating thoughts and beliefs on behaviors and coping. The remaining six studies used psychosocial treatments that are either explicitly CBT or are primarily CBT oriented.

Wiggins et al. (1999) examined the effectiveness of a four-session psychoeducational group composed of nine adults diagnosed with ADHD. A group of eight adults with ADHD who did not receive group treatment served as the control group. The authors described the theoretical approach of the group as focused on the reciprocal relationships of thoughts, feelings, and actions (TFA). The goal of this paradigm is to help participants to more systematically and effectively implement behavioral changes in targeted skill domains pertinent for managing ADHD symptoms, consistent with a standard CBT treatment model.

Pre- and posttreatment measures included an unpublished 68-item instrument (Adult ADHD Checklist) (Wiggins, 1995, as cited in Wiggins et al., 1999) that concentrates on seven problem areas commonly associated with ADHD: self-esteem, hyperactivity, interpersonal difficulties, disorganization, impulsivity, emotional lability, and inattention. The groups were conducted in four 90-minute sessions that focused on participants' difficulties related to setting realistic goals, organization/time management, task completion, and managing their environments.

Results indicated that there were statistically significant decreases on three of the seven domains of the Adult ADHD Checklist: disorganization, inattention, and, interestingly, self-esteem. These results suggest that subjects who completed the group treatment reported improved organization, improved attention, and, counterintuitively, lower self-confidence. The authors interpreted the latter finding by suggesting that adults who experienced long-standing functional difficulties associated with ADHD might experience transitory lowered self-esteem when finally facing the magnitude of their symptoms in treatment. This interpretation is consistent with our clinical observation, although this hypothesis was not examined using follow-up measures to confirm that participants' self-esteem did, in fact, later rebound.

Significant differences also emerged between the treatment and control groups on posttest scores, indicating that group treatment had significantly better clinical outcomes than did the control group. The treatment group's scores on subscales measuring disorganization, inattention, emotional lability, and self-esteem were significantly lower than were those for the control group, indicating that participation in group treatment was associated with improvements on measures of organization, attention, and emotional stability, but also lowered self-esteem.

Hesslinger et al. (2002) examined a structured skills training program in a group format adapted from the dialectical behavior therapy (DBT) for borderline personality disorder (Linehan, 1993). The modified DBT approach involves breaking down treatment for ADHD into specific skill-based modules, such as neurobiology and mindfulness, chaos and control, impulse control, and relationships/self-respect, among the 13 modules. The groups were conducted in weekly 2-hour meetings for 13 consecutive weeks, each session devoted to a single module. Written materials and daily exercises were part of the treatment regimen. A total of 15 patients were selected based on meeting *DSM-IV* (APA, 1994) diagnostic criteria for ADHD. Childhood onset of ADHD was confirmed using the Wender Utah Rating Scale (WURS) (Ward et al., 1993), and persistence of symptoms into adulthood was confirmed using a self-rating ADHD Check List (ADHD-CL). Eight patients agreed to participate in the group. Seven adults who were placed on a wait list for the group served as the control group. However, these individuals in the control group were referred elsewhere for regular outpatient medical management of ADHD and were recommended to seek behavior therapy. There were no significant differences between the treatment and control groups with regard to age and gender, and their pretreatment clinical measures were described as being well-matched. Only three of these controls were available for follow-up, however, and all of them had started some form of medication treatment by that time, compromising any reasonable interpretation of group differences with the treatment group.

The results indicated statistically significant improvement on the Beck Depression Inventory (BDI) (Beck & Steer, 1987), ADHD-CL, Symptom Check List (SCL-16) (an adapted version of the SCL-90-R containing elements relevant for ADHD) (Derogatis, 1977, as cited in Hesslinger et al., 2002), and self-ratings of overall personal health status. Furthermore, patients who completed the group showed improvements on neuropsychological tests measuring selective and split attention.

Patients' evaluations of treatment were generally positive, and the group format was rated as being the most helpful aspect of treatment, followed by psychoeducation, the therapists, and the skill-building exercises, in descending order. There were no changes in the medication management of ADHD in the treatment group; thus, the treatment effects are not attributable to medication effects. The researchers suggested that the DBT approach struck an effective balance between accepting and validating the symptoms of ADHD and challenging these symptoms by teaching patients specific skills and coping strategies with which to manage them. The Hesslinger study is also notable because it integrated mindfulness and neurobiology as a discrete treatment module. Researchers are starting to investigate the effectiveness of mindfulness-based relaxation strategies in the treatment of ADHD.

Wilens et al. (1999) used a systematic chart review to study the effectiveness of an adaptation of CBT for adults with ADHD. The CBT approach was adapted from the traditional cognitive modification approach for depression (e.g., Beck et al., 1979) and was tailored to the difficulties encountered by adults with ADHD and the types of negative thought patterns that were observed to interfere with functioning and coping efforts (see McDermott, 2000). The participants in the study were 26 patients who met *DSM-III-R* (APA, 1987) diagnostic criteria for ADHD. All of the patients had received previous psychotherapy and 96% had some sort of lifetime psychiatric comorbidity. Of the patients included in the study, 85% received medications and CBT concurrently. The length of CBT averaged 36 (+24) sessions over 11.7 (+8) months. The investigators obtained clinical measures at three time points: at baseline, at the point at which medications were stabilized (for those on medications), and at the final clinical appointment.

Wilens and colleagues' (1999) results indicated that ADHD adults respond well to CBT and that psychosocial treatment augments the positive response obtained from medication stabilization alone. At the point at which medications were stabilized (and before CBT was introduced), participants had significant improvements on measures of ADHD symptom severity, depression, anxiety, and ratings of overall functioning when compared with pretreatment scores. The combination of CBT and medications was associated with statistically significant improvements on measures of Clinical Global Impression of Severity (CGIS) for anxiety symptoms; Clinical Global Impression of Improvements (CGII) for both ADHD and anxiety symptoms; the BDI (Beck & Steer, 1987) for depressive symptoms; the Global Assessment of Functioning (GAF); and on an ADHD symptom checklist (administered to 12 subjects) when compared with pretreatment scores. What is more, there was statistically significant improvement on the CGIS for ADHD symptoms associated with the completion of CBT (with medications) when compared with the point of medication stabilization. The addition of CBT was also associated with significant improvements on the other previously cited clinical measures when compared with the point of medication stabilization. Overall, 69% of the patients completing treatment had *much* to *very much* improvement in their ADHD symptoms based on clinician ratings. These findings suggest that CBT and medications form an effective combined treatment for adulthood ADHD that improves both core symptoms and overall functioning.

Drawing from McDermott's (2000) CBT for adult ADHD, Safren, Otto et al. (2005) conducted a randomized control trial of a modular CBT approach (Safren, Perlman et al., 2005) for adults with ADHD on stabilized medication regimens but who report the presence of significant residual symptoms. Safren and colleagues' CBT approach is composed of three core modules, with sessions dedicated to organizational, planning, and problem-solving skills (module one), reducing distractibility (module two), and cognitive modification (module three). Optional modules are available to address anger management, relationship issues, and procrastination.

Participants were randomized to either CBT (with ongoing medication management, $n = 16$) or continued medication management only ($n = 15$). Participants completing CBT had improvements on ratings (using both self-rating and independent raters) of ADHD symptoms, depression, anxiety, and global functioning and were four times more likely than those receiving pharmacotherapy alone to be full treatment responders (56 vs. 13%), further suggesting that CBT makes a distinct contribution to the treatment of adult ADHD.

Rostain and Ramsay (2006c) conducted a prospective study of an individual psychotherapy approach for adult ADHD. They combined a CBT approach for adult ADHD with medications (Ramsay & Rostain, 2003, 2005b, 2005c). Their sample was composed of 64 adult patients who underwent an extensive diagnostic assessment and who completed a course of combined treatment. The clinical measures obtained at the diagnostic assessment served as baseline data, and clinical measures were obtained again at the end of treatment, around the sixteenth session of CBT.

The results indicated that the combined treatment was associated with statistically significant improvements on scores on the Brown Attention Deficit Disorders Scale (BADDS) total score and all five subscale scores (Brown, 1996), Beck Depression Inventory-II (BDI-II) (Beck, Steer, & Brown, 1996), Beck Anxiety Inventory (BAI) (Beck & Steer, 1990), Beck Hopelessness Scale (BHS) (Beck & Steer, 1989), and Clinical Global Impressions (CGI) of ADHD severity and of overall functioning. Overall, more than 67% of participants reported at least moderate improvement in ADHD symptoms and 56% were at least much improved in their overall level of functioning. Thus, the combined treatment approach was associated with improvements in ADHD symptoms, depressive symptoms, anxiety symptoms, hopefulness, and overall functioning. Because the order of treatments was not controlled for, no conclusions regarding the relative contribution of the individual treatments could be made from the data.

Most recently, Solanto et al. (in press) assessed the effectiveness of a manualized group CBT program for ADHD adults. The explicit targets for the intervention approach were various areas of impairment associated with executive dysfunction, namely time management, organization, and planning. Thirty adults (18 women; 12 men) completed either an 8- or 12-week versions of a weekly, 2-hour CBT group program and completed both pre- and posttreatment measures. The majority of treatment completers met diagnostic criteria for ADHD predominantly inattentive type (70 vs. 30% combined type) based on clinical interview and responses to the Conners' Adult ADHD Rating Scale (CAARS). Coexisting psychiatric diagnoses were common, with 63.3% presenting with comorbid depression and 43.3% presenting with comorbid anxiety. Medication status remained stable during the study and there were no outcome differences among participants who were or were not medicated or based on treatment duration.

Solanto and colleagues' (in press) results indicated that treatment completers exhibited significant improvements on the CAARS subscale measuring *DSM-IV* Inattentive Symptoms (with nearly half of the sample reporting posttreatment scores below clinical threshold), BADDS total scores, and the On Time Management, Organization, and Planning Scale (ON-TOP), a 24-item self-report questionnaire developed by the researchers as a functional measure of various executive function skills. There was no statistically significant improvement on the CAARS subscale score measuring *DSM-IV* Hyperactive–Impulsive Symptoms, though this result may be an artifact of the overrepresentation of participants with predominantly inattentive type ADHD. These findings lend further support to results obtained by aforementioned clinical researchers that CBT-oriented approaches, in either individual or group settings, represent a useful psychosocial treatment for adult ADHD, particularly in combination with pharmacotherapy.

ADHD Coaching

Although not a psychosocial treatment for adult ADHD insofar as it is not a comprehensive treatment approach, adult ADHD coaching is a newly emerging field that may serve as an adjunct to counseling and psychotherapy or, for some individuals, may be an effective level of intervention by itself. While different from psychotherapy, its similarity to some aspects of CBT for adult ADHD, not to mention its increasing popularity, warrants a brief review of ADHD coaching and preliminary research of its effectiveness.

Coaching is based on a wellness model, and interventions are aimed at supporting individuals in their efforts to achieve specific task-based goals (Ratey, 2002). More specifically, adult ADHD coaching focuses on the areas of life in which individuals' ADHD symptoms and executive dysfunction interfere with academic and vocational functioning (Swartz, Prevatt, & Proctor, 2005). Coaching is different from psychotherapy insofar as coaching is predominantly focused on helping individuals achieve specific action goals (that is, organizing and completing a work project) and does not emphasize comprehensive assessment, diagnosis, or the assorted developmental, social–emotional, or medical issues that may affect an individual's well-being. Furthermore, coaching does not include explicit cognitive modification interventions, though increasing self-awareness about the effects of one's attitudes on task completion and the role of observational learning could be considered a cognitive component of ADHD coaching (Swartz et al., 2005). Coaches provide timely reminders and feedback to their clients, often by phone or e-mail, in addition to face-to-face meetings, and the regular accountability seems to be helpful for many adults with ADHD.

Swartz et al. (2005), though a single case study, published one of the first efforts to gather evidence about the potential benefits of ADHD coaching. Swartz and colleagues followed a student who completed their 8-week coaching program for college students diagnosed with ADHD. The authors gathered pre- and postintervention data from the student's responses to the Learning and Study Strategies Inventory (LASSI) (Weinstein, Palmer, & Schulte, 2002) and The Coaching Topics Survey, a self-assessment that is comprised of five-point Likert ratings of the respondent's judgment of how much work is required in various domains of personal and academic life. The student who was the focus of the study exhibited improvements on eight out of nine Coaching Topics goals (for example, time management, organization, planning), had improvements on four of seven goals (in addition to one goal with no change and two other goals on which the student's performance worsened) measured by the LASSI, and exceeded her study hour goals for 4 out of 7 weeks. Thus, ADHD coaching was considered helpful for this college student with ADHD.

Allsopp, Minskoff, and Bolt (2005) examined their individualized course-specific strategy instruction approach for college students with ADHD and other learning disabilities (LD). Forty-six subjects from three different colleges who had been identified with a learning disability and/or ADHD participated in the study, with nearly half starting the intervention while on academic probation or suspension. There was variability in assessment measures used to document LD and ADHD owing to different requirements for documentation at different institutions.

Individualized strategy instruction was provided over the course of a semester, and its frequency was adapted to the needs of each student. Treatment goals and progress were assessed using the Learning Needs Questionnaire (targeting problem areas), instructor and participant evaluation forms (rating effectiveness of each session), and session logs (brief instructor summaries), each developed by the authors. Strategy instruction sessions focused on introducing various academic strategies designed to improve participants' academic skills in problematic domains identified by them. Results indicated that completion of a semester of instruction was associated with significant improvements on overall grade point average (GPA) when compared with overall GPA before treatment. There were also significant improvements when comparing the GPA of the semester immediately prior to instruction with the GPA of the semester during which participants received instruction. Participants maintained these gains for at least a semester after instruction. Further analyses indicated that participants who independently employed the academic strategies taught to them (as measured by instructor evaluations) significantly improved their GPAs, whereas participants who did not use the academic strategies, not surprisingly, did not improve their GPAs. Thus, factors related to improvement were (a) the independent use of academic strategies and (b) a supportive relationship with the instructor, as measured by participant evaluations.

Taken together, these two limited coaching studies suggest that ADHD coaching, particularly for college students, may be helpful, particularly for managing the academic demands. The benefits of coaching for vocational functioning and for managing the demands of daily life remain untested. However, although there is not sufficient empirical evidence with which to recommend ADHD coaching (Goldstein, 2005), it appears to be a potentially useful adjunctive intervention worthy of further research.

Psychosocial Treatment Summary

There are important limitations to the extant outcome studies of psychosocial treatments for adults with ADHD. They generally utilized small samples, which greatly reduces the power of the statistical analyses. Further, only three of the eight studies employed a randomized control design to control for extratherapeutic influences, and only one study

(Safren, Otto et al., 2005) used blind raters to reduce potential experimenter rating bias. Stevenson and colleagues (2002, 2003) performed follow-up assessments of the maintenance of treatment gains, which is an important variable considering that ADHD is considered a chronic syndrome that will require ongoing coping to manage. Furthermore, the studies reporting the ethnicity of participants revealed that samples were predominantly Caucasian, and most participants were employed or at least had completed high school, indicating that there is the need for more research about the effectiveness of these psychosocial treatment approaches for minority individuals and those with severe symptoms that significantly interfere with academic and occupational functioning.

Despite these drawbacks, the treatment studies reviewed above indicate that psychosocial treatment is associated with clinical improvements beyond those offered by pharmacotherapy alone. Psychosocial treatments appear to contribute to ADHD symptom improvement as well as improvements on measures of mood, anxiety, and overall functioning and can be considered as an evidence-based treatment for adult ADHD in combination with medications. In the next section of this chapter, we review the research evidence for different pharmacotherapy approaches for treating adult ADHD and commonly encountered comorbidities.

REVIEW OF RESEARCH EVIDENCE FOR PHARMACOTHERAPY FOR ADULTS WITH ADHD

Empirical studies of pharmacotherapy for adults with ADHD are not as numerous as those for children and adolescents; however, there is now a growing consensus regarding practice parameters to assist clinicians in prescribing medications. AACAP (2002) guidelines as well as other reviewers (Dodson, 2005; Spencer et al., 2004a, 2004b; Weiss et al., 2002; Wilens, 2003) all recommend the use of stimulant (that is, methylphenidate and amphetamine-based compounds) and certain nonstimulant medications (for example, atomoxetine, buproprion, desipramine, nortriptyline). The particular choice of initial medication depends on numerous factors including the patient's clinical profile (especially the presence of comorbid conditions), physical health, current and past medication use, treatment goals, and patient preferences for medication effects and dosing patterns. In this section, we will present an overview of the most commonly used and best studied medications for adult ADHD.

Stimulant Medications

It has been documented for more than 40 years, in hundreds of published papers, that stimulant medications are effective for children and adolescents with ADHD. More recently, a growing number of well-controlled studies in adults with ADHD indicate that stimulants are highly effective in reducing the core symptoms of ADHD, with an overall effect size of 0.9 (highly significant) (Cohen, 1992) and with response rates of 80 to 90%. In general, the stimulants are immediately effective, well tolerated, cause few side effects, and can be adjusted quite easily to suit patients' needs.

While different in their mechanisms of action and duration of effects, methylphenidate and amphetamine-derived compounds work by enhancing monoamine transmission (norephinephrine [NE] and dopamine [DA]) at the synaptic level. Methylphenidate (MPH) reversibly blocks the reuptake of DA and NE, thereby increasing the presence of these neurotransmitters in the synapse. Amphetamine (AMP) similarly blocks reuptake of these transmitters but also increases the rate of their release into the synapse through various mechanisms. The efficacy of these compounds is similar; however, certain patients respond preferentially to one versus the other, and certain preparations (immediate release vs. extended release) are differentially tolerated by patients. Greenhill et al. (1996) conducted a meta-analysis of five studies of children comparing the efficacy of AMP versus MPH and found that 37% of patients had a better outcome on AMP, 26% had a better response to MPH, and 37% had an equal response to both medications.

Although there are no large-scale head-to-head studies of AMP versus MPH in adults with ADHD, patients show similar patterns of preference to one over another stimulant preparation. Given that there is currently no evidence to suggest the superiority of one type of stimulant over the other, it can be left up to the discretion of the practitioner and the patient to decide which one to initiate first. There are several products to choose from (see Appendix D) that differ primarily in terms of their delivery mechanisms and duration of action. For instance, OROS methylphenidate (Concerta®) uses an osmotic pump mechanism to slowly release ever increasing concentrations of MPH in a continuous fashion over 10 to 12 hours. By contrast, the beaded long-acting preparations (for example, ADDerall XR®, Metadate CD®, Ritalin LA®) release the stimulant in two pulses: one shortly after ingestion and the other approximately 4 hours later).

Patients will describe differential preference for these preparations, although there is little published data to support the superiority of one versus another. The most common side effects seen with stimulants are appetite suppression, gastrointestiral (GI) upset, insomnia, nervousness, and slight increases in heart rate and blood pressure. Less common but critically important adverse events include irritability, mood instability, dysphoria, tics (involuntary movements), and potentially harmful cardiovascular effects such as hypertension or cardiac arrhythmias. The onset of these symptoms may warrant discontinuation of the medication.

Nonstimulant Medications

Atomoxetine is a norepinephrine reuptake inhibitor that is FDA approved for ADHD in adults (see Michelson, Adler, & Spencer, 2003; Reimherr et al., 2005; Simpson & Plosker, 2004). By reducing the presynaptic reuptake of norepinephrine from the synapse, both NE and DA neurotransmission in the prefrontal cortex is increased, leading to the positive effects reported on attention span and impulse control. Atomoxetine has a long duration of action (longer than 12 hours) but works with gradual onset (4 to 6 weeks), so that positive effects emerge over a longer time period than with stimulants. The response rate to atomoxetine is 60% and the effect size of 0.4 is considered moderate.

Atomoxetine is most helpful for patients who do not tolerate stimulants, who are highly anxious, and/or who express a preference for a medication that works "around the clock." The most common side effects from atomoxetine are nausea, GI upset, headache, sedation, fatigue, reduced sexual drive, and difficulty with urination. Mild increases in heart rate and blood pressure have also been reported, but rarely are these significant enough to require discontinuation.

Bupropion, a dopamine reuptake inhibitor with slight norepinephrine reuptake activity, is a widely used antidepressant that has been shown to have beneficial effects on ADHD symptoms in adult patients. Its efficacy in smoking cessation provides an added value for ADHD adults who are dependent on nicotine. While it is not FDA approved for ADHD, two controlled studies by Wilens et al. (2005) and Wilens, Spencer, and Biederman (2001) found response rates of slightly over 50% and a treatment effect size of 0.6 (significant). Common side effects of bupropion include headache, dry mouth, insomnia, nausea, dizziness, irritability and constipation. Seizures can occur in 0.4% of patients on the short-acting form of the medication but lower rates occur with the extended-release preparations.

Tricyclic antidepressants, especially desipramine and nortriptyline, have been shown to be highly effective for adults with ADHD (see Wilens et al., 1995; Wilens et al., 1996) with response rates reported in the range of 65 to 68%. These medications work by inhibiting the reuptake of NE, DA, and serotonin to varying degrees, which results in improved attention span and impulse control over periods of 2 to 6 weeks. A major drawback of the tricyclics is their side effects profile. Of greatest concern is the potential for cardiac arrhythmias, necessitating close electrocardiogram (EKG) monitoring. Other problems include somnolence, constipation, urinary retention, dry mouth, and headache. Moreover, they are not FDA approved for the treatment of ADHD.

Modafanil, a wakefulness agent approved for treatment of narcolepsy, was reported to be effective for ADHD in adults in two studies (Taylor & Russo, 2000; Turner et al., 2004); however, a more recent double-blind, placebo-controlled study of 113 adults found that it had no advantage over placebo for ADHD symptoms (Cephalon Inc., 2006). While modafanil is well tolerated and has fewer side effects compared to stimulant medications, its usefulness as monotherapy for ADHD is still questionable. At present, this agent is not FDA approved for ADHD, and it does not appear likely to receive approval in the near future.

One hypothesis regarding the pathophysiology of ADHD is that it results from dysregulation of the central noradrenergic system. Alpha adrenergic agonists work by modulating noradrenergic activity, both at the level of the locus ceruleus (with downstream cortical effects) and by directly acting on receptors in the prefrontal cortex. There is increasing evidence to suggest that attention regulation in the prefrontal cortex, and its enhancement by psychostimulants and other medications, is primarily mediated via these alpha adrenergic receptors (for an excellent review of this subject, see Arnsten & Li, 2005).

Most of the published literature on the efficacy of alpha adrenergic agonists for ADHD is based on studies of children and adolescents, particularly those with ADHD and comorbid Tourette's syndrome and/or tic disorders (Scahill, et al., 2001; Singer et al., 1995; The Tourette's Syndrome Study Group, 2002). For instance, The Tourette's Syndrome Study Group multicenter clinical trial of methylphenidate versus clonidine found that clonidine was most helpful for symptoms of hyperactivity and impulsivity, whereas methylphenidate seemed to be more effective for symptoms of inattention and distractibility.

There is some evidence that the alpha adrenergic agonists can improve symptoms of adults with ADHD. A double-blind, placebo-controlled study comparing guanfacine to dextroamphetamine in adults with ADHD found that each were comparable in their clinical effects as well as in their impact on neuropsychological measures (Taylor & Russo, 2001). Clinical trials of long-acting guanfacine are now underway under the sponsorship of Shire Pharmaceuticals, which expects to receive FDA approval in the near future. A recent study of 345 children and adolescents showed significant improvement in ADHD symptoms on both impulsivity–hyperactivity and inattention domains (Shire Pharmaceutical, 2006).

Controlled studies of combination medication treatment of adults with ADHD are surprisingly quite scarce. Hornig-Rohan and Amsterdam (2002) compared patients taking venlafaxine, bupropion, or tricyclic antidepressant monotherapy with patients taking the combination of stimulant plus antidepressant and with patients taking stimulants only. They found that the combination treatment was highly effective in 88% of patients and was superior to either stimulant alone or antidepressant alone, although patients taking venlafaxine alone had an 80% response rate. Weiss, Hechtman, and the Adult ADHD Research Group (2006) studied the combination of paroxetine and dextroamphetamine in 98 adults with ADHD. They found that internalizing symptoms, but not ADHD symptoms, were improved with the combination approach. Adler et al. (2006) studied the combination of d-MPH and mirtazapine for the treatment of stimulant-associated insomnia and found that this combination was very helpful in reducing sleep problems. There are numerous case series of other combination regimens for adult ADHD with comorbid disorders (for example, atomoxetine and stimulants, stimulants and serotonin reuptake inhibitors, stimulants and mood stabilizers), but given the current limited state of published studies, it would be premature to advance guidelines for combining medications besides suggesting that this be done with caution and careful monitoring.

Pharmacotherapy Summary

There are many medication options for adults with ADHD, though they have not been as widely studied as in children with ADHD. Stimulants emerge as the most effective class of medications for reducing symptoms and improving executive functioning. However, there are secondary, nonstimulant options for patients who do not respond to or cannot tolerate stimulants. Likewise, there are tertiary medications with more limited effectiveness in the treatment of ADHD, though these agents may be useful in cases of comorbidity and/or nonresponse to other medications.

SUMMARY

The combination of pharmacotherapy and specialized psychosocial treatment, namely CBT, seems to be emerging as the foundation of treatment for the wide ranging effects of ADHD symptoms for adult patients based on the findings from many studies. Medications alone may be very beneficial for patients with relatively mild impairment, and stimulants, in particular, continue to stand out as the first line of treatment to be considered. However, in complex cases involving greater functional impairment and comorbid difficulties, a comprehensive treatment plan including psychosocial treatment may be indicated. In the next chapter we will provide case illustrations of the application of our combined treatment approach with adult patients with ADHD.

CHAPTER 4

Clinical Case Examples

> One of the most serious problems confronting psychology is that of connecting itself with life....Theory that does not someway affect life has no meaning. (Lewis M. Terman)

The previous chapter provided empirical evidence that the combination of cognitive behavioral therapy (CBT) and pharmacotherapy is an effective treatment approach for adults with attention-deficit hyperactivity disorder (ADHD). However, very often, practicing clinicians do not find such evidence compelling, not because they doubt the veracity of research findings, but rather because it is difficult to translate findings from research protocols into clinically useful procedures to be used with "free range" patients in day-to-day clinical practice. Thus, our goal for this chapter is to provide case examples that illustrate our combined treatment model "in action." While we cannot cover all manifestations of ADHD and patterns of comorbidity, we have selected case examples that address a range of clinical issues commonly faced by clinicians treating ADHD. All case illustrations are composed of genuine clinical material, though identifying information and other details have been changed and/or combined in order to safeguard confidentiality.

CASE EXAMPLE 1: WILLIAM

William is a 51-year-old married father of two adult sons. He works two part-time jobs as a personal health care worker and as a bartender. His wife of 30 years works as an upper level executive for a major corporation.

William contacted our program to schedule an initial evaluation for adult ADHD after his younger son was diagnosed with ADHD a few months before, during his senior year of college. William said that as he read more about adult ADHD and looked through some of the questionnaires he was asked to fill out for his son's evaluation, he recognized his own behavior patterns as fitting the ADHD profile. The family had briefly been in family counseling several years before and he remembered that the counselor had offhandedly observed that William "sounded ADHD" but he never pursued the issue. However, seeing his son's positive response to treatment, he considered the possibility that some of the recurring difficulties in his life might have an explanation other than his being "lazy" or "irresponsible."

Assessment

Presenting Problems

William said that main reason he decided to schedule an evaluation was in preparation for the possibility of returning to school. In particular, he was considering applying for an emergency medical technician (EMT) training program in hopes of finding a stable, better paying job. However, he was concerned about his ability to keep up with the demands of the certification program. His goal for the evaluation was to confirm the diagnosis of ADHD and, if appropriate, consider treatment options that might help improve his symptoms and provide support in his career aspirations.

Diagnostic Interview

A structured diagnostic interview indicated that William was not suffering from significant mood or anxiety problems. He denied history of substance abuse problems and was in excellent overall health. However, he reported that he was easily and noticeably frustrated with himself and experienced brief, though upsetting periods of worry and self-recrimination when his disorganization or poor attention caused problems at work or at home. For example, he frequently confused his schedule and assignments for the home healthcare agency for which he worked and had difficulties keeping track of his sons' various school and extracurricular activities when they were younger. He described such episodes as being frustrating for him (and for him family) and that he considers his current difficulties following through with pursuit of the EMT program as creating significant stress and interfering with his well-being, thus warranting a diagnosis of an adjustment disorder.

ADHD Assessment

William completed several self-report symptom questionnaires regarding past and current ADHD symptoms. He also recruited his older brother and his wife to complete observer ratings of his past and current ADHD symptoms. These same symptoms were also assessed in the course of

the clinical interview. Regarding childhood symptoms, there was corroboration between William and his brother that he exhibited symptoms
of both inattention and hyperactivity/impulsivity in sufficient number
and severity to indicate that he fulfilled diagnostic criteria for ADHD,
combined type as a child. His brother remembered that William was
never considered to be a behavior problem, but teachers reportedly complained that he had difficulty completing work and tended to be fidgety
and talkative during class. Review of current symptoms also revealed
corroboration between William and his wife that he continues to experience diagnostic levels of these symptoms as an adult. However, William
and his wife had slightly different ratings of his hyperactivity–impulsivity symptoms, with his wife rating them as exceeding the diagnostic threshold (for example, saying things without thinking, impulsive)
and William reporting slightly subclinical levels. However, considering
that such symptoms persisted into middle age and the convergence of
other observations, clinical assessment indicated an ongoing diagnosis
of ADHD, combined type.

Review of standardized adult ADHD questionnaires provided further corroboration of the diagnosis. His total score on both the Brown
Attention Deficit Disorder Scale (BADDS) and Conners' Adult ADHD
Rating Scale (CAARS) well exceeded the threshold for clinical significance. Problems with inattention, memory, activation, and sustained
effort emerged as areas of executive dysfunction. Measures of hyperactivity were on the border of being clinically elevated but, combined
with behavioral observations, were viewed as confirmatory evidence of
ADHD, combined type.

Neuropsychological Screening

William's performance on each of the four Wechsler Adult Intelligence
Score (WAIS) substests administered to him—Vocabulary, Block Design,
Digit Symbol Coding, and Digit Span—fell in the average range. In particular, Digit Span is used to assess auditory working memory for numbers. William said he was used to dealing with numbers in his head in
his work as a bartender. However, he said he often forgot drink orders
during busy times and would have to get reminders from customers or
waitresses, an observation that made sense considering his performance
on the Selective Reminding Task (SRT), a test of auditory working
memory for words. His total recall of words fell one standard deviation
below the mean when compared with other men his age. However, his
performance on measures of the efficiency of his information encoding (long-term storage) and consistent information retrieval (continuous
long-term retrieval) fell significantly below average, indicating an inef-
ficiency in his auditory verbal working memory.

Computerized tests of continuous performance, inhibition, and working memory further indicated slow cognitive processing speed, a tendency to make impulsive mistakes, and an inconsistent style of responding to stimuli. As has been found in many reviews of neuropsychological measures of ADHD, his overall neuropsychological profile would be considered normal and not indicative of abnormal functioning, but there were areas of cognitive functioning that showed relative inefficiencies that could explain some of his functional difficulties.

Medical and Psychiatric History

William's personal and family medical histories were unremarkable. There was no reported history of complications during his mother's pregnancy with him and no past head injuries or medical conditions that could mimic ADHD symptoms. Likewise, there was no family history of psychiatric problems, though William noted that he remembered his father exhibited many of the same characteristics as William and his younger son. His father had worked as a self-employed neighborhood handyman. He had his own business, reportedly out of necessity because William's father had been fired from various employers in the carpentry and construction business for being late to work or for mistakes on the job (for example, misreading blueprints and doing a job incorrectly). Even so, he had difficulty keeping up with appointments and managing his affairs, jobs that eventually fell to William's mother to manage.

As was mentioned earlier, William, his wife, and their sons participated in a brief course of family counseling to help manage some parenting issues they faced as their sons became teenagers. There was no other history of therapy and no past psychiatric treatment.

Developmental History

William grew up in a stable, intact family and described his childhood experiences as generally positive. He was the middle brother and said he had good relationships with his siblings and parents.

He said he had never been identified as having ADHD as a child but noted that teachers consistently observed that he was "always on the go" in elementary school. Poor handwriting was a common complaint by his teachers. William said he frequently lost things, such as regularly forgetting his lunch box or a jacket on the school bus or leaving a completed assignment at home on the day it was due. He also noted often getting reprimanded by his parents for being noisy and excessive squirming during Sunday church services. However, William was well liked and not considered a "behavior problem," instead viewed as "energetic."

William encountered increasing academic difficulties in junior high and high school. He said that he "did enough to get by" and often put off difficult assignments "until the last minute." William tried to keep up with assigned readings but often did not finish them, instead relying on notes from classes or, more often, the notes he could get from friends. He said it was difficult for him to pay attention in class. He said he would feel restless and, not infrequently, a teacher or other student would comment on his bouncing leg or tapping pencil. He said there were occasional instances of impulsivity in class, usually along the lines of speaking out of turn or cracking a joke, but nothing that ever got him in trouble. There were a few difficult classes in which he failed big tests and received a low grade for a marking period, sometimes benefiting from extra credit work granted by the teacher, but he never failed an entire course and was graduated on time, describing himself as an average student, though he felt he could have done better.

William entered the local community college after high school and said it was very difficult for him. The academic work was more difficult and required a more organized approach to stay on top of it. He said he felt greater stress in school and his tendency to procrastinate worsened. In fact, he frequently missed deadlines for papers and would plead with instructors for extra time. In one case, the teacher was unyielding and William failed a course for the first time in his life. He took an incomplete in one class in order to finish a project and dropped another course altogether because he fell too far behind. He said he eventually "squeaked by," earning his two-year degree in 3½ years.

Although he had originally planned to transfer to a 4-year college to earn a bachelor's degree in business, the difficulties William encountered in community college shook his confidence about school. Instead, he entered the workforce. He found a job in construction while continuing to explore longer term career paths. However, he was fired because he had difficulty getting to work sites on time. Over the next decade he found himself regularly starting new jobs, becoming bored with them or having difficulty keeping up with the expectations of the employer, and then leaving for another job. He met his wife and they got married during his stay at one company and as they started a family. However, William's erratic employment record started to have financial and emotional consequences on their relationship.

He eventually found a job he enjoyed working as a nursing assistant in a geriatric nursing home. William worked the overnight shift so that he could be a stay-at-home father while his wife worked during the day and took MBA classes in the evening. William described himself as a combination of "Mr. Mom" and "Mr. Fix It." He enjoyed the hands-on aspect of the nursing job and being able to help people. William took some health care certification courses to improve his credentials. Of course, there were periodic problems related to forgetting to make entries in patient charts and misplacing important objects, but he was well regarded. Working the overnight shift was difficult and, after a few years, he left to take a part-time position as a home health care worker, which allowed him to have a flexible schedule while his sons were in school and his wife worked. He also found another job as a bartender in a local tavern with similar scheduling flexibility.

William reported that he encountered problems related to poor time management and disorganization at home. He said it took him several months each school year to develop a system for getting his sons off to school in the morning. Although he had enough time to take care of various chores, errands, and home repairs, he often found himself rushing to get things done or forgetting about promises he had made to his wife. William's wife had hoped that he could take charge on monitoring family finances and balancing the checkbook but he found this responsibility overwhelming. After a few months of bounced checks and late payment fees, she assumed responsibility for money matters. However, William was by all accounts a good father and supportive husband, which allowed his wife to focus on her career and her movement "up the corporate ladder." The issues related to the effects of William's ADHD symptoms would trigger brief arguments and create stress but generally the family was stable and got along well.

As the second of his sons completed college and prepared to move out on his own, William sought to extend his interest in health care and to pursue work as an EMT/paramedic. He learned from a friend in the field that there would be openings in a local agency in the near future and that he would recommend William for a position, but he would have to complete the requisite training. Thus, as he learned about his son's diagnosis of ADHD and considered it as a possible source of his chronic struggles, he thought that treatment might provide the support he would need to pursue this goal.

Assessment Conclusions and Treatment Plan

It soon became clear that William's situation was a classic example of someone with ADHD whose symptoms were undiagnosed until adulthood. In addition to his self-report of past and current symptoms, reliable observers provided corroborative evidence of the presence of diagnostic levels of symptoms in both childhood and adulthood. Consequently, there was sufficient evidence of childhood onset and chronicity of symptoms. Adult ADHD questionnaires revealed clinically significant levels of current symptoms. To his credit, William managed to gain a measure of interpersonal and occupational stability in his life despite moderate to severe symptomatology. He benefited from having consistent family support and the absence of psychiatric comorbidity. However, beneath his generally sanguine temperament were descriptions of recurring frustrations, job losses, and the sense that he had not been able to follow through on reasonable personal goals because of what was now understood to be ADHD.

William was an excellent candidate for combined treatment, and his prognosis for improvement was very good. In fact, his presentation was somewhat atypical for our clinic because patients usually enter experiencing greater levels of impairment or are facing significant problems, such as academic suspension or falling behind at work. William's life situation was stable and the main reason he sought help was in anticipation of returning to school. However, William's case represents an example of impairment in the form of underfunctioning and withdrawing from the pursuit of personal goals (e.g., McGough & Barkley, 2004). Nonetheless, our recommendation was for William to begin a course of pharmacotherapy, starting with a low dose of a psychostimulant to determine whether he experienced improved executive functioning and a reduction in symptoms. We also recommended concurrent CBT to clarify his plan for returning to school, anticipating potential difficulties, and to develop coping skills and explore other changes he could make in how he handles issues in his current daily life (for example, time management). William agreed with the treatment recommendations and was eager to schedule his first meetings with his psychiatrist and with his therapist.

Course of Treatment

Medication

Because his son had found methylphenidate (MPH) to be effective for his symptoms of ADHD, William was started on a daily regimen of long-acting immediate-release Oros® MPH (Concerta®). He was titrated upwards from 36 mg daily to 54 mg and then to 72 mg and reported optimal response at the higher dose, which he continued for about 6 months. At a later follow-up visit, he described that he was noticing decreased efficacy of the medication, so he was increased to 90 mg with good response over the ensuing time period. His ADHD symptoms remain markedly improved and he has had no side effects from this regimen. It should be noted that while his final dose is higher than current (U.S. Food & Drug Administration) FDA recommendations, we have found that many patients require these dosage strengths to achieve an optimal response.

CBT

In a way, the start of William's CBT was trickier than usual. Most adults with ADHD present for treatment in the midst of a pressing situation for which they want help, be it a relatively recent development (for example, "I've been written up at work for being late and I need to get there on time") or an ongoing issue (for example, "I always put off projects until the last minute and I'm getting tired of the stress of always going up against the deadline"). William, on the other hand, hoped to enter an EMT/paramedic training program in the near future but was not yet enrolled. Consequently, it would be important to spend time in the first session of CBT identifying some immediately relevant goals that would also be applicable for his overarching goal to complete an EMT program.

After about 10 minutes, however, William's first session seemed directionless. A friendly inquiry about how he had been doing since his evaluation led to a lengthy description of various family affairs. It had been somewhat apparent during the evaluation that William tended to be talkative and would go off on tangents unless the clinician kept the interview on track, which is a tendency exhibited by some adults with ADHD. The therapist gently redirected William to the task of discussing possible goals for therapy. It continued to be difficult to find an area that William viewed as being particularly problematic. Even when the therapist suggested possible areas of focus drawn from comments made by William during his assessment, such as remembering drink orders in his bartending job, William seemed to downplay their severity, suggesting to the therapist that William's sanguine demeanor might also serve to avoid facing potential problems, a hypothesis for a possible compensatory strategy for the case conceptualization.

After a few more minutes of discussion the therapist said, "William, I know the long-term objective for therapy is to help you manage the demands of the EMT certification course. Without your being enrolled in a course right now, however, are there any challenges coming up in the next month or so that are important for you and, that if you handle them well, would let you know that therapy was working?" William hedged for a moment before saying, "Well, a prerequisite for EMT training is that I must have up-to-date CPR certification. I have to renew my CPR certification soon and I've been putting off signing up for a class." Although it did not seem to be a major issue, it fit with the idea of "starting small" in CBT for adult ADHD and the assumption that such problems will likely provide illustrations of the cognitive and behavioral patterns that are activated in other problematic situations.

What follows is a transcript of a portion of William's first session of CBT in which the therapist explores the effects of ADHD symptoms on William's cognitive and behavioral patterns with regard to signing up for a CPR course.

Therapist (T): Okay. Can you tell me specifically what you have to do to enroll in a CPR course?

William (W): It's simple. I just have to call and enroll for the course I need. They offer it at a variety of times and days so I should be able to find one that works.

T: What thoughts do you have about the course that might contribute to your putting off signing up?

W: I'm not sure whether I need to sign up for a 3-hour refresher course, or if I need the 8-hour CPR course for health care professionals.

T: Do you have any thoughts about the different length of the courses?

W: I'm worried that they might require the longer course.

T: What are your thoughts about the longer course?

W: I've done a 3-hour course in the past and by the end it was hard to pay attention. You have to remember a lot of complex sequences of compressions and breaths. I don't know how I would do in an 8-hour course. I'd be worried I might make some mistakes, especially when I'm working in a group with others. That might be why I'm putting it off. I imagine they would have breaks, so I guess it would be all right.

T: Any other differences between the courses that might be of concern?

W: The longer course is usually especially for people who work in health care, including other paramedics, nurses, and doctors.

T: What thoughts do you have about that?

W: These are the people who'd be coworkers, who I'd be working with and interacting with. I'd be worried about messing up in front of them. They might not think I'm up to their standards. That makes me a little apprehensive.

T: Can you describe your apprehension in more detail, what specifically makes you feel that way?

W: Well, you get tested on your own for the procedures in front of everybody and then you have to work in teams. I'm worried about the team effort and my not holding up my end of the bargain. I could see myself losing my concentration and doing a compression or a breath out of sequence.

T: And what would the consequence of that be?

W: We'd have to start over from the beginning and get retested because of me and I'd hold up the entire class.

T: If, by chance, that did happen, what thoughts would you have about that?

W: Other people might say, "He's not cut out for this work." How could I be a paramedic and handle real emergencies if I cannot even handle a CPR class with no pressure?

T: William, you're giving me a lot of good information about how your thoughts and your ADHD interact to make you procrastinate on the seemingly simple task of calling to schedule a CPR class. It really shows the power of our thoughts. Before we continue to look at how your thoughts affect your procrastination, I'd like to ask if you remember having had any experiences in your life in which the worries you've described—making mistakes in front of others or holding up a group—actually happened?

W: I don't know. It hasn't happened a lot. I've been able to avoid big embarrassments. [William grimaces.]

T: [Noticing William's grimace] Any "little" embarrassments?

W: Well, in one of the 3-hour CPR courses I made a mistake on the compressions during one of the team exercises. It was toward the end of the class and everyone wanted to leave. I was tired and I lost my focus on what I was doing. I had made some mistakes earlier in the day, too.

T: What happened next?

W: We had to be retested and had to start over from the beginning.

T: When you realized you made a mistake, what thoughts did you have?

W: "What's wrong with me? Why can't I do this right?"

T: Usually when we have negative automatic thoughts in the form of questions, they usually function as statements, such as "There is something wrong with me."

W: Yeah, that's what it felt like.

T: Okay. So there was a situation in your past that is similar to what you're concerned might happen in a longer CPR course. Recognizing you made a mistake is not a distorted thought. In this case, it was accurate—you made an error during the compressions. However, it sounds as though the conclusions you drew that something was "wrong" with you and that you "could not" do the task right may have been distorted. Another concern you have about the possibility of taking a course with health care workers is that they might think negatively of you if you should make a mistake. What was the reaction of your teammates in the class in which you had to redo the CPR sequence?

W: Nobody laughed, but I could see it in their faces that they were upset and that they were annoyed at me.

T: What did you see in their faces that was evidence that they were annoyed?

W: One lady rolled her eyes.

T: What happened then?

W: We redid the sequence correctly and had a few minutes of wrapping up before class ended.

T: How long after the course do you think the lady thought about your mistake? Do you think she went home and told her family, "You won't believe what happened in CPR class today? This guy made a mistake during our final test?"

W: (Laughing) No. She probably didn't give it much thought.

T: How long did it take you to redo it correctly?

W: Not long. I got it right the next try. It took about a minute, maybe.

T: How did you feel when you were done?

W: Fine. I was happy to be done.

T: How did the others on the team react to you, especially the woman who rolled her eyes?

W: They were fine. We all said goodbye to each other. The woman talked to me as we left the room to go to our cars.

T: So it seems there were no hard feelings. During the class, did you notice if any other people had to redo their sequences?

W: Oh, sure. There's a lot you have to learn and practice. A lot of people had to redo things.

T: What thoughts did you have about those people?

W: Nothing much. I was glad it wasn't me but I just thought, "They'll do it and we'll move on."

T: How long did it bother you right after you made the mistake? Did it keep you up that night?

W: (Laughs) No. Once we had the sequence done right I forgot about it and was looking forward to going home. I was able to handle it.

T: When you or someone else learns something difficult, such as CPR, how common do you think it is to have to redo things or to practice something more than once?

W: Very common. That's how you learn and remember over the long term. You have to practice to learn.

T: So how do you reconcile that conclusion, which seems reasonable to me, with the automatic thoughts you had after your previous mistake and your anticipations of taking another CPR course?

W: Hmm. I hadn't really put it all together in that way. I guess I'm being a little unfair to myself. I should give myself credit for finishing the course. But this sort of thing seems to happen to me more than it does to other people, so I guess I'm pretty sensitive to it.

T: I think you just summarized how CBT can be helpful for you. Let me summarize what I've heard you describe. Using the example of the CPR course, you had a real-life experience of making a mistake in front of others and feeling bad about it. It makes perfect sense that when you think about signing up for another CPR course it triggers your concern, particularly with the possibility of being in a class with health care professionals. However, I think you also described how your thoughts affect your outlook and that some of your thoughts might be unfair and contribute to your procrastination about signing up for the CPR class. Usually these sorts of patterns come up in other areas of life. By understanding the patterns, we can focus on changing your thoughts and looking at new behaviors you could experiment with in order to make changes in your life. Does that make sense to you?

W: Sure does. I didn't realize procrastination was this complex.

T: So, that brings us back to the phone call. What do you think might be a reasonable first step in changing your procrastination pattern in terms of the CPR class?

The rest of the first session focused on developing William's first homework task of finding out which length CPR course was required of him. He and his therapist identified the negative automatic thoughts that might interfere with his follow through (for example, "I cannot handle it if an 8-hour course is required") and developing alternative thoughts to increase the likelihood of his follow-through (for example, "I may have to do some exercises more than once, but I can do well enough to get by and to pass").

Many of William's difficulties followed a similar pattern of procrastination and avoidance fueled by automatic thoughts that ADHD symptoms would undermine him. His case conceptualization was straightforward and his negative core beliefs, though influential, were relatively modifiable as he experienced the positive effect of pharmacotherapy and an increasing sense of competence in handling various personal affairs. William attended 18 sessions over the course of 6 months. He eventually followed through on the phone call to schedule the CPR class and learned that the long version was required. He took the class and passed it but later recognized that he was unsure if he wanted to work as a paramedic. Sessions focused on dealing with his uncertainty about leaving his current jobs that had provided a sense of stability. An ongoing theme for him was challenging procrastination by being proactive and assertive. He eventually found a career path in health care he thought would be a better fit for him. It required him to complete a different certification process. He continued to attend CBT sessions during the first term and, though it was difficult, he was able to keep up with the work and earn passing marks. He continued with booster sessions during the second term and eventually discontinued sessions as he felt confident he could continue his progress with ongoing pharmacotherapy.

CASE EXAMPLE 2: JACK

College represents an opportunity for early intervention for ADHD adults whose symptoms may have glided underneath the radar screen to this point in their lives (Ramsay & Rostain, 2005d, 2006b; Rostain & Ramsay, 2006b). Many previously undiagnosed young adults who immediately enter the work force after high school may also experience difficulties keeping up with the demands of attendance, productivity, and organization in the real world, though it may take more time for deficits to become apparent than in college. The adjustment to college is uniquely frustrating for first-year students with ADHD because the academic habits and coping skills that had seemed to work well enough in high school may no longer be as effective. Moreover, students may be unprepared for assuming many adult role responsibilities, such as prioritizing a schedule, keeping up with the business of adult life (for example, registering for classes, scheduling car maintenance), and being able to defer immediate gratification in the service of long-term payoffs.

Jack is a 20-year-old college sophomore who sought an evaluation and treatment for ADHD. Unlike our typical college student referral, who seeks an evaluation for ADHD as a last resort to understand significant functional difficulties, Jack reported that he had been diagnosed with ADHD in elementary school and had since received ongoing treatment, primarily with medications. However, he sought help because he was finding it increasingly difficult to keep up with the demands of college and felt that he was quickly "falling apart." In fact, it turned out that Jack's medication treatment had reached a point of diminishing returns and was no longer sufficient by itself to help him manage the demands of college and young adulthood. Jack faced the prospect of making some difficult changes in his attitudes and his behavior patterns.

Assessment

Presenting Problems

Jack reported that he had been diagnosed with ADHD in elementary school. Consequently, he learned that he had to work harder than his peers to achieve the same amount and quality of work as them. In high school he set his sights on attending a prestigious college near his home and he was thrilled when he was accepted into this school.

When asked about his grade point average during his first year of college, Jack proudly reported that he had earned a 4.0 grade point average (GPA). When asked how he achieved that high average—the story behind the number—Jack's countenance became distressed. He said, "I worked all the time just to keep up." As he reviewed his schedule from his freshman year, the use of the phrase *all the time* seemed to be closer to an apt description of his college life rather than an exaggeration.

It was only a few weeks into his first semester when Jack stopped participating in intramural sports and dropped out of a campus choral group. He found himself staying up progressively later in the evening to complete work and setting his alarm earlier in order to wake up and make use of study time before attending classes. Weekends initially provided a brief respite, as he would socialize with his roommate and other friends from his dorm floor. After facing his first set of mid-term exams, however, Jack started to decline social invitations in order to spend the time necessary to keep up with his work. His efforts seemingly paid off as he earned straight A's his first semester.

During the break between semesters, however, he felt increasing dread about the upcoming second semester. He continued to take introductory courses but found it increasingly difficult to keep up the same study pace he had set the semester before. Jack continued to get his stimulant prescription filled by the family physician familiar with him. Jack's dosing had remained consistent throughout high school. He had always handled his medication treatment responsibly, the only deviations from his regular dosing schedule occurring when he took an agreed-upon extra dose during final exams or the night before a project was due and "drug holidays" when he chose not to take his medication, such as during summer vacation or breaks from school. However, during his second semester, Jack started to take an extra dose of medication in the morning in order to "get focused" so he could wake up and start working. Further along during his second semester he found himself requiring another extra dose later in the day in order to stay alert and focused during the evening when he was studying. This later dose interfered with his sleep and Jack sometimes further increased his dose in the morning to get started, the beginning of a vicious cycle.

In terms of maintaining a high GPA, Jack's coping strategies seemed successful, though he was disappointed that despite his efforts, his grades went down slightly. However, just as disturbing was that when it came time for applying for next year's housing assignments, Jack learned that his roommate and friends on his dorm floor had worked out a plan to get an off-campus apartment but had not invited him. He recognized that he had virtually become an academic recluse in order to keep up with his schoolwork. Furthermore, rather than drawing confidence from his ability to earn high grades, Jack was left feeling anxious and overwhelmed by his anticipation of the effort he would have to expend to get through the next semester, much less the rest of his college career. Thus, Jack recognized the need for help.

Diagnostic Interview

A structured diagnostic interview indicated that Jack reported significant symptoms of anxiety during the previous semester at school that went beyond a simple adjustment reaction to the demands of school, warranting a diagnosis of generalized anxiety disorder. Although not meeting the threshold for major depression, he also described increased feelings of depressed mood that fulfilled the criteria for depressive disorder not otherwise specified. Finally, Jack's level of prescription medication misuse was sufficiently problematic to be identified as abuse. He also reported increased marijuana use as a means for managing his mood and attempting to counteract the effects of his medications at night. Although not apparently interfering with his academic or social functioning, he noted that he was smoking more often and more regularly than he had intended, bordering on abuse.

ADHD Assessment

Jack completed several self-report symptom questionnaires and recruited his parents for their impressions of him both in childhood and recently. Ideally, though we would have preferred to have obtained the observations of one of his college friends on a current symptom questionnaire, we certainly understood and respected Jack's desire to keep his assessment private from them.

There was agreement between Jack and his parents that he had exhibited clinically significant symptoms of both hyperactivity–impulsivity and inattention during childhood that fulfilled diagnostic criteria for child-hood ADHD, also corroborated by past psychological assessment reports. Regarding current symptoms, Jack endorsed enough symptoms of each subtype to warrant a diagnosis of ADHD, combined type. His parents' ratings of current symptoms were somewhat lower (though they still exceeded diagnostic threshold), but this was attributed to the fact that they saw him in high school and on break from college when there were fewer demands on him.

Review of standardized adult ADHD questionnaires provided further confirmation of his current symptoms and difficulties. Both his BADDS and CAARS total scores were clinically elevated, though some of Jack's subscales scores, while elevated, did not reflect the level of impairment we expected based on his day-to-day functioning. Upon reflection, however, we recognized that Jack's assessment of his functioning was based on what had been, until recently, effective treatment. That is, until he reached college, his pharmacotherapy regimen had sufficiently managed his symptoms. Thus, there was currently adequate clinical evidence of severity, pervasiveness, and chronicity of symptoms and resulting impairment.

Neuropsychological Screening

We asked Jack to not take his medication on the day of his evaluation in order to assess his executive functioning without the benefit of pharmacotherapy. His score on the Vocabulary subtest of the WAIS fell in the superior range. His Block Design score was much lower but fell in the average range. His scores on measures of auditory working memory for numbers (for example, Digit Span) and cognitive processing speed (Digit Symbol Coding) both fell in the low average range.

Similarly, his performance on the three subtests of the SRT each fell well below the average score for males his age. The Penn Abstraction, Inhibition, and Working Memory Task (AIM) indicated that he was more accurate than other individuals who completed the same task but took significantly longer than average to make a correct response. Thus, our observation was that Jack was intelligent and had the capacity to do work but that he had slow cognitive processing, at least without medications. (Note: While adjusting his medication early in pharmacotherapy, Jack was asked to retake an alternate version of the SRT as a measure of medication response. His scores were at least one standard deviation above the mean on each subtest.)

Medical and Psychiatric History

Jack's family had been in family counseling when he was first diagnosed with ADHD to learn appropriate behavior management strategies. Jack said his father seemed to have many of the same behavioral symptoms as he and had dropped out of college due in large part to these difficulties. He said his father joked that he gave Jack his "ADHD genes." Jack said that there had been some mention of anxiety on his mother's side of the family and that his mother tended to be "high strung" when under pressure, but that there was no other history of notable medical or psychiatric problems.

Jack said that he also underwent some individual counseling in conjunction with some family sessions in early high school to address the pressure associated with the increased work load. He said he did not find it helpful just to "talk about" his problems. He said that adjusting his medication dosage was then the more helpful intervention.

Developmental History

Jack was the younger of two children born to his parents. His older sister, 5 years his senior, was reportedly an "all-star" in everything she did. She was well liked, was considered a good student, and was athletic. His parents were each career-minded professionals who made sure they were involved with their children's lives. They each earned a good living and Jack said his upbringing was comfortable, both financially and emotionally.

Jack said that his parents could tell he was different than his sister. He was much more restless and had difficulty sitting still as a child. He learned to read at an early age but was a slow reader thereafter. Babysitters reportedly said that Jack tired them out by the end of an evening. Likewise, his elementary school teachers said he was restless, easily distractible, and that his behaviors could at times be disruptive, though they also noted that he was bright and did not seem to be intentionally defiant. After mentioning the comments made by Jack's teachers to the family pediatrician, they were given a referral for an assessment, at which time Jack was diagnosed with ADHD. He was started on a stimulant medication and his behavior and grades improved quickly and markedly.

Jack experienced some difficulties with the increased amount and complexity of schoolwork involved with the transition to middle school. There were also increased social pressures. During this time Jack entered brief counseling, which he did not find helpful, and his psychiatrist adjusted his medications, which he did find helpful.

Jack sought additional academic support for some subjects in which he was having some difficulties. Math was always a difficult subject for him and he received some specialized help after school from his teacher. In the course of a tutoring session in which Jack was having a difficult time understanding an equation, the math teacher reportedly said, "Well, you might just have to face that you're not college material."

Jack was petrified by this statement because his sister was in the midst of applying to colleges and his parents made allusions to Jack's future college plans. He said he feared failing by not going to college and he devoted himself to making sure he worked hard and gained admission to college. In fact, he remembered the math teacher's statement throughout high school and the drive to get into college motivated him to sacrifice many social and recreational activities in order to improve his grades, thereby improving his application packet.

He eventually gained entrance to his first choice school, a prestigious local university. He steeled himself to face a more difficult, competitive academic setting from high school, but he also looked forward to the total college experience. However, although his GPA did not indicate that he was having problems, Jack felt as though he was falling apart and was ready for help by the time he sought his assessment.

Assessment Conclusions and Treatment Plan

Jack's situation is a fairly common one among the college students with ADHD whom we see in our program. The transition to college proves to be more difficult than originally anticipated and attempts at making the necessary adjustments to the increased academic and social demands prove insufficient in light of the severity of ADHD symptoms.

We liken the adjustment to college life for students with ADHD to the tectonic plate shift that results in an earthquake. The earth is comprised of a series of plates that push up against each other. As long as the plates are in line and stable, the ground is solid. However, if there is a tectonic shift and the plates are moved out of line with each other, the ground shifts and there is a destructive earthquake. Going to college, especially if it involves moving away from home, results in a complete overhaul of students' lives, with a new geographic environment, living situation, social network, and academic environment. College also requires the assumption of increased responsibilities for self-care and self-management. This can be very challenging for young adults with ADHD, particularly if it has gone undiagnosed.

Jack entered college already aware of his ADHD diagnosis. He recognized the need to spend more time than his peers on his studies and started school with an effective, stable medication regimen. However, Jack responded to the increased pressure of school by adopting a more-of-the-same coping approach by spending inordinate amounts of time studying and increasing his medication dosage until he reached a point of diminishing returns; in fact, his solution had become part of his problem.

We met with Jack and confirmed his diagnosis of ADHD, combined type. His comorbid anxiety, depressive symptoms, and substance use (including overuse of his ADHD medications) appeared to us to be a consequence of his primary ADHD symptoms insofar as his previous coping strategies were no longer effective. We recommended our combined treatment approach. Jack's overall goals for treatment were to manage his college life more effectively, to find an effective medication regimen, and to repair his social life. We noted that his substance use was a concern and he said he would be willing to monitor and discuss his use during treatment.

However, Jack was disturbed to hear that the initial focus of pharmacotherapy involved a *reduction* in his medication dosage and a more conservative approach to the guidelines for adding an extra dose. This plan worried Jack, as he said, "Medications are the only reason I have gotten this far. I need to find something else that works." He was encouraged to address these concerns in the course of CBT and to also explore cognitive and behavioral strategies that might be helpful in meeting his treatment goals.

Course of Treatment

Medication

The first issue to be addressed in treatment was Jack's pattern of overusing his stimulant medication. Upon reflection, he was able to recognize that increasing the dose and frequency of the stimulant was not improving his performance. The decreased effectiveness was most likely due to several factors including habituation of his brain to the medication, lack of sufficient sleep (which eventually causes worsening concentration), rising anxiety levels, and concomitant increase in marijuana usage. Furthermore, it was explained to Jack that raising the dose of stimulant beyond a certain point can lead to worsening rather than improved concentration (that is, the *optimal dose* concept). All of these factors were interacting in such a fashion to greatly reduce the effectiveness of the medication, which Jack readily acknowledged.

The next step was to begin a course of atomoxetine, which was selected because it would address Jack's anxiety as well as his ADHD symptoms. He was titrated upward over a 2-week period to a daily dose of 80 mg, with simultaneous reduction of the stimulant. At a follow-up visit, Jack reported noticing less anxiety, better sleep patterns, and improved focusing despite reducing his stimulant dose to minimal levels. It was agreed that he would remain on atomoxetine as his primary treatment and that he would use the stimulant only at times when he needed to sharpen his focus for a brief period of time.

At a subsequent visit, Jack reported that he was taking the atom-oxetine during the week but was skipping it altogether on Fridays and Saturdays and taking half the dose on Sundays. His purpose for doing this was to make it possible "to relax" with his friends, another way of stating that he wanted to indulge in using marijuana and drinking. It was explained to Jack that given its pharmacologic profile, stopping atomoxetine for several days at a time was reducing the efficacy of the medication. His pattern of marijuana use and drinking was discussed, and it was pointed out that while he might be experiencing some imme-diate gratification from using these substances, in the long run it was working against his goals of doing well in school and reducing his anxi-ety level. With some reluctance, Jack agreed to continue his atomoxetine dose during weekends, albeit at a reduced dose. He also agreed to reduce the frequency and amount of his marijuana usage and drinking on a "limited trial basis" and to observe its effects on his ability to study and get schoolwork done. Eventually, he was able to see the benefits of atomoxetine when using it in a more sustained fashion and was able to selectively make use of the stimulant for times of intensive studying.

CBT

Unlike most college students, who start ADHD treatment at the urging of others and are ambivalent about its usefulness, Jack was clearly pre-pared for action. In fact, he had already attempted to make many changes in his study schedule in the previous semester. However, his strategy of using his prescription medications to fuel marathon study sessions was unsustainable, unhealthy, and, in the end, unsatisfying for him.

Jack's treatment goals were amenable to specific behavioral objec-tives, though his initial academic goal was to maintain his perfect GPA. We reformulated this goal to focus on behaviors to improve his studying efficiency and to allow time for his desire to improve social relationships. Early sessions were devoted to understanding the specific effects of his ADHD symptoms on his ability to carry out his goals. We performed behavioral analyses on various specific examples of problematic situa-tions he described in order to gather clinical information about the inter-play of his ADHD, thoughts, emotions, and behaviors. This information provides ideas for potential homework experiments and provides data for the case conceptualization.

Because Jack started CBT at the beginning of a semester, early homework experiments focused on his academic strategies (e.g., Ramsay & Rostain, 2006b). We agreed to the notion of starting small on behav-iors such as taking the prescribed dose of his stimulant medication, to practice a task-focused study approach (for example, "I'll read 20 pages of the text") instead of a time-based study approach (for example, "I'm going to study for 6 hours"), and following a reasonable plan of self-care (for example, Stop studying at 1 a.m. at the latest).

Jack's initial response to several of the homework tasks was "It does not work." He agreed that it would be useful to explore his apparently unsuccessful experiences in order to understand whether we needed to revise our behavioral plan or whether there were problems with the plan we set out. For example, he reported that the task-based approach to studying was not working.

Therapist (T): Describe a time when you attempted the task-based study approach.

Jack (J): I started with something simple, an introductory chapter for my psychology class. I remembered what you said about focusing on a specific chunk of work rather than focusing on studying for a certain number of hours. I tried it for a little while but it didn't work.

T: Let me ask a specific question: Did the plan not work or was it difficult to carry out the plan we discussed?

J: I could just tell that it would not work.

T: How could you tell? How far did you get in the chapter?

J: I read for about 5 minutes but I couldn't focus on the words.

T: As you were getting your book to start reading, what thoughts were going through your mind, what was it like to be in your skin?

J: I had taken my medications [the nonstimulant, atomoxetine] as my psychiatrist had prescribed. But I did not feel the intense focus I felt when I took a stimulant last semester.

T: So, your thought was, "I'm not focused." Any other thoughts as you started to read?

J: Reading one chapter will not do anything. I have to get a lot more done.

T: Any other thoughts?

J: Those are the main ones.

T: Let's do an exercise called the "downward arrow" to see the effects of these thoughts. Suppose for a moment, those two thoughts are true—"I'm not focused" and "Reading one chapter is not enough"—what would the implication of these thoughts be for you? What would they mean to you?

J: I'm going to fall behind in my work.

T: If that would be true, what would that mean to you?

J: I'm going to fail the class or not do well.

T: If that were true, what would it mean to you?

J: I'm not working hard enough. I'm a slacker.

T: Assuming again that was true, what would that mean for you?

J: It would show that I'm really stupid and don't belong here. I'd be ashamed.

T: What about the possibility that the plan we're working on might help you in the long run?

J: It makes sense but I don't trust that it will work for me.

T: How well was the plan you used last year working for you?

J: Not great, but at least I could be a good student and get my work done if I had enough time and felt focused.

T: Let me summarize what I'm hearing. You did not feel focused on your work right away. You had the thought "I'm not focused...this won't work...one chapter is not enough" after about 5 minutes of reading. The implication of these thoughts is that you assume you will fall behind in your work and fail the class, or at least not do as well as you expect. Consequently, this would indicate that you are a "slacker" and prove that you are, to use your term, "stupid" and do not belong in college, which would leave you feeling ashamed. Further, although the plan we discussed seems feasible to you, you did not trust that it would work for you. It seems that you associate taking excess stimulant medications and having marathon study sessions to the exclusion of your social life with being a "good student," and, conversely, taking a prescribed dose of a different medication and shorter study session with being "a slacker." Does what I said fit with how you feel?

J: Yeah, it sounds a little extreme when you put it that way but my study approach works for me. That is how I work best.

T: Compared with what? What I mean is that your old way of studying with the long hours and needing to feel focused seemed to reach a point of diminishing returns, if not being downright detrimental to your social life and your health. You must ultimately make the final decision about how you want to manage your studies. What I'm proposing is finding a way to experiment with a different approach to balancing school, your social life, and any other important aspects of your life in order for you to make an informed decision about what you do. Does that make sense?

J: Yes, but how do I start doing that?

T: Should we spend some time talking about that now?

The rest of the session focused on identifying Jack's tendency to engage in all-or-nothing thinking and that unless an approach was perfect, he considered it to be not working. Consequently, he would feel anxious based on the thought he was failing, which would further interfere with his ability to concentrate. His reflex reaction would be to return to his habitual strategy of taking a higher dose of a stimulant medication and studying until he could not stay awake. Although, as Jack noted, this approach was not effective, it was familiar and resulted in a short-term decrease of his anxiety but at the cost of his long-range well-being and ability to cope. An ongoing theme in his CBT was developing greater tolerance of initial discomfort in order to be able to experiment with new behaviors and to consider new meanings of what it means to succeed or fail.

Considering his ambivalence about employing new coping strategies, early sessions focused on periodic analysis of the costs and benefits of making change (for example, readiness for change) and helping him to see the potential long-range benefits of investing in the change process. The willingness of the therapist to accurately empathize with Jack's concerns but to also develop alternative possibilities seemed to contribute to the development of a positive therapeutic relationship. Although Jack was skeptical of his ability to change during these first several sessions, the behavioral analysis of one of his failed homework tasks revealed that Jack underestimated the influence of the distractions in his dorm room. The goal for him had been to spend a minimum amount of time reading a chapter he had been avoiding. His roommate was in the room listening to music and a friend stopped by a few minutes later, interfering with Jack's concentration. Rather than assuming that the plan does not work, Jack agreed to retry the experiment during a time he knew his roommate was in class and took steps to minimize distractions (for example, turn off the phone and computer). Making these simple changes resulted in somewhat improved ability to focus, which provided Jack with evidence that there were some behavioral (that is, nonmedication) changes he could make to improve his work efficiency.

Jack completed his mid-term exams and projects and, though he did not have straight A's, he was doing well in his classes with a stable dose of his nonstimulant medication. In a session soon thereafter, he reported that his anxiety seemed to have recently increased despite things seeming to be progressing well in CBT and in his efforts to change his study behaviors. He and his therapist agreed to put the issue on the therapeutic agenda.

Jack reported that he had finished studying and was relaxing in his dorm room, reflecting on the fact that he was much less stressed than when he started the semester and had more time for recreation. He said he recognized that he was feeling uncharacteristically low key. Soon thereafter, he felt much more anxious and questioned whether he had put forth his best effort on his mid-term projects. He began to worry about the rest of the semester, eventually taking some leftover stimulant pills and staying up until the next morning studying. Jack expressed concerns that CBT was not working for him.

Reviewing Jack's recent bout of anxiety provided an opportunity to review and discuss his CBT case conceptualization. He had a long history of recognizing the effects of his ADHD and that school required more time and effort for him than it did for his peers. What is more, his math teacher's comment that he was not "college material" crystallized his *inadequacy* schema ("I'm inherently less intelligent than others"). Consequently, he also developed a schema of *mistrust* ("I cannot trust myself") related to school. A related conditional belief was "If I work harder than everyone else, I'll be okay; but if I slack off even a little, I'll lose everything I've worked for and be found out to be stupid." His *compensatory strategy* was working harder and doing more. However, he reached the point in college at which he could do no more. Due to his inherent lack of confidence in his abilities and effort, he also developed a schema of *social undesirability* ("Others will not like me"), which was magnified when he was not asked to live in the off-campus apartment. He compensated through people-pleasing and assuming that if he let someone down or made a choice based on his own well-being, then others would not like him.

His observation that he felt anxious in response to feeling relaxed was actually a sign that he was starting to make changes in his life. Feeling relaxed activated his old concerns that he was slacking. The conceptualization laid bare his conundrum of feeling that he did not have enough of himself to give to either his schoolwork or his friends. The case conceptualization also provided Jack with a framework with which to understand the meaning of his anxiety, particularly when triggered by his distractibility or procrastination. By reducing his anxiety, he was better able to direct his energy to refocusing his attention or effort to the task at hand or recognize when he needed to take a break from his work.

Thus, middle sessions of CBT focused on continued development of a healthy middle ground in most areas of his life. In his schoolwork he was discovering that he could continue to be a good student without necessarily getting perfect grades or devoting all his time to work. As he focused on expanding his social and recreational life, Jack initially erred on the side of going with the crowd in an effort to not disappoint others (for example, to appear socially desirable). However, at times this approach caused some problems. By this point in therapy, Jack developed trust in his therapist and in the collaborative empiricism of CBT. He was able to identify his automatic thoughts that were triggered in social situations and to determine different courses of action he could have tried. These ideas became his homework experiments, such as declining invitations the night before a test or setting limits about how much he would drink at a party. Jack found that with reasonable give-and-take he was able to foster new friendships and to reconnect with old friends who he thought no longer liked him.

Jack's desire to resume use of stimulant medications decreased in the course of CBT. Again, he previously associated the feeling of being medicated with the notion of productivity. On the other hand, taking a nonstimulant medication that improved his cognitive skills but allowed him greater flexibility in his choice of activities had been associated with being a "slacker and a failure" and a presumed inability to work. His recognition that he could no longer maintain his old study strategies helped Jack to make the investment in facing short-term anxiety related to modifying his behaviors and to start to have new experiences in school and in relationships—in effect moving from contemplation/preparation into the action stage (e.g., Prochaska, DiClemente, & Norcross, 1992). Rather than needing his medications to study "perfectly," he found a reasonable dose (in addition to new study behaviors) could help him to study "well enough." By the end of the semester, Jack was doing well in all his classes, had developed a fulfilling social and recreational life, and was generally more relaxed.

Jack continued to meet with his therapist during his second semester of his sophomore year, though less frequently. Sessions focused on reviewing and reinforcing his more adaptive belief systems, ongoing situational problem-management, and helping him to maintain a balanced life. His ongoing marijuana use was the focus of several sessions to discuss his ambivalence about reducing it. On the one hand, he recognized that it was not a healthy habit but, on the other hand, he liked how it made him feel and he often smoked in social situations. He reported that he smoked less than he had during his freshman year when he would use it primarily to "chill out" and reduce his anxiety.

Jack experienced a slip during his second semester. He received a low passing grade in a difficult class. He admitted the exam was harder than he expected and that he had not managed his time well, being further distracted by making plans for spring break. He described some worry about the possibility that his balanced approach might not work as classes became more difficult and some of the old concerns about whether or not he was college material. After spending some time discussing his reactions, he and his therapist slowly reviewed the factors contributing to the low grade. Jack said it was helpful to reevaluate the circumstances in this way because he recognized specific behaviors he could change in preparation for the next exam in the class, identified ways his negative thoughts were exaggerated, and was able to draw some measure of comfort from the experience (for example, "I didn't study enough and I still passed a tough test").

Jack's grades through the end of his sophomore year were very good, but he no longer had a perfect GPA. He was more confident and at ease in sessions than he had been at the start of therapy. In some ways he was starting to become more mature and to consider his future, including applying for a program in which he would spend a summer studying in Europe. Jack attended periodic booster sessions during his junior year and consistently appeared more at ease. He continued his stable, medication regimen and no longer discussed a temptation to take additional stimulant pills, even during mid-term and final exams. Just as important, he described an improved balance in his life of schoolwork, friendships, and pursuing a variety of other interests. Jack recognized the change in his attitudes and core beliefs, often shaking his head when he considered how he thought about and handled his life during his freshman year. He represented the embodiment of the phrase *less is more*.

Nonetheless, Jack continued to engage in some risky or impulsive behaviors, such as his marijuana use, but he reported that his use had decreased as his anxiety improved. Booster sessions focused on discussing his marijuana use and ways to further reduce it (though he was ambivalent about giving up social smoking altogether). Jack also considered his future plans, particularly the upcoming challenges of studying abroad. However, Jack now had a framework for understanding and facing problems he would likely encounter in his life in an adaptive and resilient way.

CASE EXAMPLE 3: LAUREN

Lauren is a single 33-year-old woman employed as a public relations consultant in a small business consultation firm. Her job is to work with small- to medium-sized local businesses in order to help them develop strategies for advertising their products and establishing a positive image with the public. As she noted during the phone screening before her initial evaluation, Lauren felt as though much of her life was spent trying to maintain a positive image in order to mask her many struggles that she thought could be related to undiagnosed ADHD.

Lauren sought an evaluation for ADHD after receiving below average feedback on several sections of her most recent work performance evaluation for the third consecutive review cycle, resulting in automatic probation status at work. She always knew she had a very ineffective work style, dating back to high school and college where teachers regularly complained of her lateness with work and general disorganization.

However, she had been able to cover it up and come across as doing passable work, even if it was lower quality than what she had the potential to produce with adequate preparation and effort. The fact that her disorganization and poor time management had been identified as deficiencies at work and now threatened her job understandably scared her and motivated her to seek help.

A psychotherapist she had been seeing for stress management had suggested that Lauren might have ADHD. In subsequent years, Lauren recognized many of her tendencies whenever she read about ADHD in magazines. However, she had not taken steps to seek out an ADHD specialist until now. In addition to her difficulties at work, Lauren sought help because she recognized that her problems were spilling over into her social life, affecting both friendships and romantic relationships. Lauren worried that she was not yet growing out of some of the immature behaviors of her youth.

Assessment

Presenting Problems

Lauren reported that her negative work evaluations were the end result of several incidents in the previous two years in which she missed appointments with clients and was late with reports. She admitted that she always experienced difficulties keeping up at work and that she often waited until the last minute to complete projects. There had previously been more support staff employed by her company to take charge of scheduling, reminding her of appointments, and writing the body of her reports, allowing Lauren to make some minor edits before signing off. The support staff positions had been reduced in an effort to cut costs, and the consultants were now expected to manage their own schedules and reports, which proved to be overwhelming for Lauren.

Lauren said that she had been disorganized at work prior to staff cuts, however. She said she had a reputation as a hard, dedicated worker and she was the last to leave the office but Lauren admitted that the latter habit was because she wasted a lot of time and did not start doing work until the afternoon. Staying late was a desperate attempt to catch up on work that could have been done earlier. Lauren reported having difficulty keeping track of paperwork and managing her time. Because much of her job involved meetings with clients, she often evaded facing her paperwork by scheduling appointments that required her to travel to other sites. Although she performed very well during these meetings, they resulted in increased paperwork above and beyond the work that was already incomplete, putting her farther behind. On the other hand, she viewed herself as good at her job and said that clients viewed her as insightful and helpful, characteristics that were corroborated in her work performance evaluation. In fact, it was because of these strengths that many of her clients overlooked it when she delivered her reports to them many days, sometimes weeks, later than promised.

Lauren said that she has similar difficulties coping with life in her apartment. She lives alone and has difficulty keeping up with household chores and with personal paperwork. She said she regularly pays late fees on credit cards and periodically has had her electricity and cell phone service cut off because she either misplaced or forgot to pay the bills. Lauren said that she has difficulty overcoming her procrastination even when there is a strong incentive, witnessed by the fact she is owed nearly $15,000 in tax refunds over the past several years but still has yet to file these tax returns because she becomes overwhelmed at the thought of tracking down and organizing her records and filing the tax forms (or even to pass them along to an accountant). Her recent substandard work evaluation was the final straw that led to seeking an ADHD evaluation to determine the nature of her difficulties and to develop a course of treatment to help her gain control of her life.

Diagnostic Interview

Lauren reported a history of brief episodes of depressed mood in the past, sometimes with a mixture of mild anxiety. In the 6 months prior to her assessment, she reported growing more depressed, frequently describing bouts of low energy and tearfulness. She denied the presence of suicidal thoughts but had become much more self-critical, particularly about her difficulties at work, and said that she felt more pessimistic about the future. Lauren's score on the Beck Depression Inventory II (BDI-II) fell at the high end of the moderate range for depression. Her current symptoms fulfilled diagnostic criteria for major depression.

Lauren denied that she ever experienced problems related to excessive alcohol or substance use. She said she sometimes had too much to drink or would smoke marijuana with friends but these habits had greatly decreased since college. However, she noted that since feeling more stressed at work, she was more likely to have a glass or two of wine at night by herself to unwind and manage stress. Though not representing alcohol abuse, her recent drinking pattern was viewed by her as a measure of her current distress as she formerly would only drink in social settings.

ADHD Assessment

Lauren completed several self-report symptom measures and recruited her mother and sister to fill out retrospective and current observer reports. There was consistency across time and across reporter that Lauren had problems related to distractibility and inattention since childhood. Lauren's sister added a note that she remembered teachers expressing concern to her mother that Lauren was not fulfilling her potential. In addition to the inattentive symptoms, there were some behaviors related to impulsivity, particularly being talkative, argumentative, and speaking out of turn, that were consistently endorsed.

Responses on objective ratings scales of adult ADHD revealed a similar pattern of difficulties primarily associated with inattention and memory problems. Her CAARS subscale score for Problems with Self-Concept was elevated, suggesting her difficulties were negatively affecting her sense of self. Specific problem areas revealed by the BADDS included Activation and Effort: getting started and sustaining effort on tasks until they are complete. The combination of symptom checklists, objective ADHD questionnaire responses, and interview indicated a diagnosis of ADHD, predominantly inattentive type.

Neuropsychological Screening

Lauren's performance on the intelligence scale subtests each fell in either the superior or very superior range, except for tests measuring cognitive processing speed (that is, Digit Symbol Coding) and auditory working memory for numbers (that is, Digit Span), which fell in the low average range. Likewise, her performance on the SRT, a test of auditory working memory in which she was asked to remember a word list, revealed significant deficits in the encoding and consistent retrieval of aurally presented information. Lauren said that she is aware that she has difficulty remembering information. She tried to write things down but would soon stop because it is inconvenient and she feels embarrassed that others do not seem to need to record things.

Tests of attention and continuous performance indicated that she tends to be able to solve problems well but that it takes her longer than others to do so. Moreover, in addition to a slow reaction time, her reactions tend to become more erratic during longer tasks and she tends to make errors of omission, missing important information and signals. Thus, the testing reinforced what Lauren maintained: "I think I'm smart enough but I have a hard time following through in ways that will prove it to others."

Medical and Psychiatric History

Lauren had two brief counseling experiences in the past for episodes of depression and anxiety that she attributed to stress in college and, later, at work. She said that therapists focused on helping her to recognize her emotions and raise her insight about her unconscious motivations and defenses. Lauren said she learned a lot about herself and felt better for a while but was unable to change her day-to-day bad habits.

Lauren said that no one in her family had ever been officially diagnosed with ADHD, but she said that both parents exhibited many of the same behaviors as she does. Lauren's mother reportedly did not graduate from college because she took too many incompletes during her senior year and was never able to get organized to complete them (or request extensions) before they turned into failing grades. Her mother worked making and selling arts and crafts, sometimes selling her work at local craft fairs or festivals, but was never able to keep a job outside the home. Lauren described her as "an ADD housewife" and noted that her mother appeared to have periods of depressed mood, remembering her as being easily frustrated when Lauren was growing up. Her maternal grandmother was described in similar terms.

Her parents divorced when Lauren was a teenager and she said that her father never seemed to settle down in life. She described him as intelligent, though he did not complete college because he "partied too much." Lauren said that he was arrested for drunk driving while he was dating her mother and entered an AA program to stop drinking. Subsequently, he found a professional niche in a variety of sales positions but Lauren noted that he changed jobs every few years and appeared to be disorganized in his personal life, though she described him as being a loving father. Her personal and family medical histories were otherwise unremarkable.

Developmental History

Lauren reported a long history of problems similar to those that led her to seek help as an adult. She said that she always considered herself intelligent in school but never seemed to earn grades commensurate with her abilities. She said that she frequently lost papers or handed in work that was sloppy when she was younger, resulting in mediocre grades. As she got older, Lauren said she learned that she could earn passing grades with minimal effort. Moreover, when she attempted to put forth her best effort in a class or a project, she found herself easily frustrated due to disorganization and that it seemed to take her longer than her peers to complete the same amount of work. She also was reticent to speak in classes because she often daydreamed and felt lost because she could not follow the topic of conversation.

College was similarly difficult for her and she said she did not have the attentional endurance for college classes. She often fell behind in her work due to procrastination and ended up taking incompletes, which she would finish over breaks. On a few occasions, she forgot to complete the necessary paperwork and her incompletes would have turned into failed grades if not for the good graces of some of her teachers, though she ended up failing a few courses. Lauren did much better in small seminars requiring class participation and when she worked as an intern, though she was not immune to the effects of her disorganization and poor time management in those settings, either. Lauren was very interested in her business courses related to public relations and advertising and she established strong relationships with her mentors. Between her incompletes, failing grades, and change in major, Lauren took 6 years (including some summer sessions) to complete college, though she said she hardly did any reading and did not feel particularly prepared for the work world.

Lauren had difficulty maintaining a steady job after graduation. She worked several different jobs until her late twenties, in part because she could not a find a position in public relations or advertising, which had been her major in college. She took a variety of odd jobs, such as being a waitress or working as an administrative assistant in an office. Lauren said she either grew bored with a job and quit or was fired due to lateness or unreliability resulting from her disorganization. She landed her current position because one of her mentors from college knew the employer and personally recommended Lauren for an entry-level public relations position. Lauren performed well at the outset and was promoted within her first year there. She experienced progressively more difficulties as the newness of the job wore off and she developed a larger list of clients and was expected to assume more professional responsibilities, culminating in the poor performance evaluation that led her to seek help.

Lauren's social and romantic life has been similarly chaotic since college. She experienced difficulties with friends when she was younger because she would show up late for movies or forget engagements and dates altogether. Even when she was with trusted friends and family, she would receive complaints that she did not listen well and did not remember important information. Further, she said that boyfriends often complained that she did not pay attention to them and Lauren admitted that she had been caught cheating on them with other men. More recently, she said that it was difficult to keep up with the minimal demands of friends and boyfriends considering the amount of time and energy she devoted to keeping her job. Lauren said that she did not intentionally try to alienate anyone but felt out of control of her life and increasingly discouraged by its direction.

Assessment Conclusions and Treatment Plan

Based on the assortment of information gathered during the assessment process, we determined that Lauren's symptoms fit the diagnostic profile for ADHD, primarily inattentive type with comorbid major depression. Although not yet reflecting a pattern of abuse, her increased alcohol use was noted as a potential focus for treatment. On a less clinical note, Lauren seemed very scattered and disorganized in her overall approach to life, expending most of her time and energy on "catching up" with tasks or handling an immediate stressor. Her life seemed to be a rudderless boat at the mercy of the tides. Lauren's goals for treatment were to increase her efficiency at work, to reduce procrastination at work and at home, to improve her mood, and challenge her increasing sense of pessimism. It was agreed that she could benefit from a combination of medications and CBT to treat her symptoms, decrease her avoidance, and increase her coping skills.

Course of Treatment

Medication

Lauren was started on a trial of mixed amphetamine salts (MAS) (ADDerall®) 5 mg twice daily increasing incrementally to 10 mg and then to 15 mg twice daily. As reported on her medication log, the optimal dose of MAS was 10 mg twice daily. While she acknowledged that the medication was helping her to concentrate a little better and to get somewhat more accomplished at work, Lauren also reported irregular adherence to the regimen. She would often forget to take the second dose or she would skip the medication entirely because of concerns that she might become dependent on it. She also expressed disappointment that the medication was not as dramatically effective as she had heard from others that it would be. She was switched to 20 mg of extended-release MAS, which she tolerated well and began to use more regularly after discussing her concerns and disappointments about its partial efficacy.

Because Lauren was reporting only modest improvement in her ADHD symptoms, and because she was still depressed much of the time, it was decided to add an antidepressant to her medication regimen. She was started on bupropion extended release 150 mg daily and told to observe for any signs of being overly stimulated or anxious. After 2 weeks of only minimal response, her dose was increased to 300 mg daily. While she initially felt some improvement in her mood with the dose increase, this was not sustained over the ensuing several weeks.

It was decided to switch her antidepressant from bupropion to sertraline, which was accomplished with a cross-titration schedule over a 2-week period. After an additional 2 weeks on 100 mg daily of sertraline along with MAS XR 20 mg, Lauren reported improved mood, reduced anxiety, and an improved ability to concentrate.

CBT

Lauren was somewhat ambivalent at the start of CBT, unsure whether she had either the time or wherewithal to make substantial changes in her life. Furthermore, she had started in pharmacotherapy a week prior to her first CBT session and was frustrated that her first few doses of a stimulant medication had not resulted in the sort of stunning awakening she had read of in some ADHD books, though she acknowledged a subjective sense of being able to focus somewhat better.

She and her therapist spent some time in the first two sessions reviewing her magical expectations for treatment; namely, Lauren's understandable wish that her problems would quickly and easily evaporate after accurate diagnosis and treatment with some "ADHD experts." CBT was reframed as an investment on her part to establish new behaviors and coping strategies for her long-term benefit, using her unrealistic expectations for the speed with which medications and CBT would work as examples of automatic thoughts that could lead to her becoming impatient with treatment. Lauren recognized that her attempts at "quick fixes" in the past had not yielded desired results. However, while Lauren said she felt better at the end of her early sessions, she described difficulties implementing between session homework tasks and seeing progress in her life.

Lauren's first 3 months of CBT could be characterized as erratic, which mirrored experiences in her personal life. She often arrived late for appointments or had to reschedule at the last minute due to conflicts with work or because she had unwittingly scheduled something else. All in all, she probably attended about half of the meetings scheduled during that time. Lauren was appropriately contrite and she verbalized being invested in treatment when she attended sessions but her inconsistent attendance made it difficult to develop a sense of continuity.

Lauren arrived for a CBT session after about 3 months in our program and soon became tearful, saying that it seemed to her that treatment was not helping and she was considering dropping out and "just trying to work harder on (her) own." We focused on her thought that "Treatment is not working for me." The therapist acknowledged that sometimes certain treatments do not work for all individuals but asked Lauren to clarify whether treatment was not working because, despite Lauren and the therapist's best efforts, it had not produced the desired results or because she had not experienced the full effect of what CBT has to offer because of inconsistent attendance and follow-through on homework between sessions. The therapist likened the latter scenario to a piece of exercise equipment gathering dust from lack of use and the owner determining, "This treadmill has not helped me get in shape."

Lauren smiled at this example and said that she understood the point. She also acknowledged that she was having difficulty following through with treatment, including the fact she only sporadically took her prescribed medications. Lauren agreed that it would be useful to discuss at length her possible decision to discontinue treatment in terms of her decision-making process, not the least of which was the possible effect on her job.

First, Lauren said that she did not like the notion of taking medications. It seemed to her as though she was "cheating" and getting an unfair advantage. Specifically, her thought was, "If I do better on medications, it means that it is not really 'me' getting things done." Further exploration of this thought revealed underlying beliefs that helped to shed light on her ambivalence and difficulty committing to treatment.

Therapist (T): Okay. Let's do an exercise. Let us assume for a moment that, first, you would end up doing better on medications than off of them if you took them as prescribed and, second, that this would, in fact, be cheating, artificial improvements that are not the "real you." If that were the case, what would that say about you?

Lauren (L): That I'm not capable of doing things others can do without meds.

T: Suppose that is the case—what would that say about you?

L: That I'm different from everybody else

T: And what would that mean to you?

L: That I'm fundamentally flawed. I'm damaged goods [defectiveness schema].

T: Taking this a step further, if that is the case, what does it mean for you?

L: That I'm a failure [failure schema]. I've achieved nothing in my life. It took me more than five years to finish college and even getting my job was a stroke of luck because my college advisor recommended me. I would never have been able to get it on my own. I'm sure not doing a good job keeping it.

T: So, the prospect of doing better on medications means that it would confirm your sense that you are "fundamentally flawed" and have "failed." Looking at it that way, it makes perfect sense why you have been ambivalent about both medications and CBT.

L: I already know I feel bad about myself. I really doubt that anything can help me change how I do things. I've been trying to do it on my own for so long.

T: What's an example of something you've tried to change?

L: Doing my work earlier in the day rather than wasting time until the afternoon.

T: What did you try to change first?

L: I tried to go to my desk first thing in the morning, just as everyone else does, and to start working on something.

T: How did it work out?

L: It didn't. I'd sit there for a few moments, feel overwhelmed, and would end up checking my e-mail or walking around wasting time.

T: When that plan didn't work, what did you try next?

L: What do you mean? What other way is there? I just couldn't do it. I tried every day for a while but I always ended up not working anyway.

T: Did you ever hear Freud's definition of insanity: doing the same thing over and over but expecting a different outcome? It sounds to me as though you tried approaching your work the same way as your non-ADHD coworkers and found that their way—"just doing it"—did not work for you. Because this result was consistent with your negative beliefs, you may have assumed it was further confirmation of them and felt hopelessness about change. Does that sound accurate to you?

L: Yeah, I hadn't thought of it that way. But I'm still stuck at what I should do about it. I still don't know what I would do different to get started on my work earlier in the day.

T: You're right. It will be important for us to come up with new plans to try. However, let's first spend some time finishing our look at a conceptualization of how your life experiences, particularly living with ADHD, your belief system, reactions and emotions might fit together and contribute to the problems you are facing now, particularly your frustration with treatment. This might give us a blueprint of how to make the changes you want. Would you be willing to spend some time looking at this?

L: Yes.

Lauren and her therapist proceeded to "start small" and to reexamine many other recurring difficulties she encountered in daily life, employing the same "downward arrow" (Burns, 1980) to elicit the thoughts and beliefs associated with her ADHD-related issues. Identifying some candidate schema and core beliefs, more specifically *defectiveness* ("There's something wrong with me. I'm flawed.") and *failure* ("I've not achieved what others have in life."), lent itself to a discussion of various developmental experiences contributing to her chronic sense of frustration. The conceptualization also unwound the tangled knot of Lauren's ADHD symptoms, emotional reactions, negative attributions, and behavior reactions. Embedded in this discussion was also the acknowledgment of Lauren's many strengths and abilities and how these were often undermined by aspects of ADHD and self-defeating behaviors.

Lauren developed some conditional beliefs and rules, based on the schemas identified in the aforementioned review of the underlying beliefs affecting her ambivalence about medications that affected her in daily life. Discussion of her reaction to treatment and other areas of her life revealed a rule that, "If I'm perfect, I'm okay and not defective," but that led to the converse assumption that, "If I'm less than perfect, I'm defective." Thus, she engaged in comparative thinking when assessing her sense of self, resulting in her discounting her achievements of completing college and holding a good job in her chosen profession because she did not achieve them in the right way (for example, graduate college in 4 years and get a job without using her connections).

Lauren's perception that she had not achieved adequate improvement in either CBT or pharmacotherapy was viewed as a personal failure for Lauren inasmuch as it was a failure of the treatments. She described an overgeneralized sense of failure such that when she encountered initial (though normal) difficulties in treatment, she assumed that it was the result of her own defectiveness or inadequacy and that these hitches represented the inevitable start of the downward spiral to failure. She responded to these interpretations by convincing herself that treatment was not working and that she should preemptively drop out of therapy for fear of confirming her sense of inadequacy. Thus, perfectionism served as a compensatory strategy for her because, according to her belief system, only straightforward, trouble-free progress could be free from the specter of failure.

A companion compensatory strategy to emerge from the case conceptualization discussion was Lauren's tendency to be self-critical. The underlying conditional beliefs were, "If I'm hard on myself, I work better and will not fail," and, conversely, "If I allow myself to be satisfied, I'll get lazy and fail." Again, Lauren's inadequacy schema contributed to her core sense that she was flawed and had failed when compared with others. However, she learned that if she could inspire herself through self-criticism to strive for perfection, she could get herself to function adequately. Thus, self-criticism was another compensatory strategy that ultimately seemed to reinforce her sense of inadequacy because it was not a sustainable coping strategy and insidiously left her feeling more inadequate when she could not meet her unrealistic expectations.

Because of these tendencies to be self-critical and perfectionistic, Lauren experienced great difficulties making decisions and addressing problems in her life. She often tried to keep as many options open to her for as long as possible in an effort to avoid making the wrong choice. Thus, similar to her ambivalence about CBT, she had difficulties sustaining friendships and romantic relationships. These problems were compounded by her impulsivity, such that she would engage in all-or-nothing thinking at the first sign a relationship was not perfect. Subsequently she gave into temptations to cheat on boyfriends or abandon promising relationships without cause. To observers, she appeared flighty and insensitive to others' feelings, though she in fact cared deeply but was plagued by self-doubt and self-criticism and had difficulty managing her emotions and sorting through her many reactions.

Lauren's strategies worked adequately enough when she was younger and the demands on her, such as in high school, were manageable and social missteps were considered to be part of growing up. However, the demands of adult life, including work and managing her personal life, were difficult for her, and the negative consequences of poor coping were severe. Whereas she could pull things together in high school or college at the end of an academic term and then start anew with a clean slate, there were no such points in work life that allowed her the time to catch up.

As the demands of her job exceeded her perceived ability to cope with them, she construed increased distractibility, stress, and other uncomfortable sensations in all-or-nothing terms as signals of impending failure. Likewise, the first sign of doubt in a budding friendship or dating relationship was viewed as evidence of trouble. Over time, she developed automatic and visceral negative reactions to tasks that required sustained attention, organization, and effort to complete. In order to avoid facing these distressing sensations and companion thoughts of inadequacy and failure, she would disengage and avoid tasks until the stress of dodging them outweighed the stress required to face them, such as each afternoon at work when she realized she had frittered away the day. In effect, by procrastinating she was attempting to avoid failure and defectiveness, a strategy that provided emotional relief in the immediate moment but that ultimately was self-defeating and unhealthy.

Lauren's eyes lit up and she became increasingly interested as she saw the case conceptualization take shape. She said that she was surprised by how well it encapsulated and made sense of the confusing mix of reactions she had dealt with for a long time. She agreed that, in light of this formulation, her compensatory strategies of avoidance and procrastination, self-criticism, keeping options open and not committing to long-term projects or relationships, and a relentless drive to prove herself to others seemed to add up. In fact, Lauren made the observation that she seemed to attract chaos in her life and perhaps it was because she was able to focus better during a compelling predicament than when managing everyday affairs and hassles. Lauren did not enjoy the consequences of chaos in her life but observed that it provided an external excuse for possible failure instead of her typical internal attribution.

With the backing of this conceptualization, the therapist revisited a recent incomplete homework task in which Lauren said that she needed to complete and mail some forms related to a personal loan consolidation in order to meet a deadline. Lauren, with her therapist's guidance, identified the automatic thoughts associated with the task, her emotional reactions, and her likely behavior response. She also noted how ADHD further contributed to her poor follow-through on completing the forms. In addition to thinking through the benefits of facing the task and focusing on specific strategies for implementation, Lauren identified, using the case conceptualization form, how the task also activated strongly negative visceral feelings related to her core beliefs. The task was subsequently reframed as an opportunity to challenge some of these assumptions and to experiment with facing a challenge. The feelings of emotional discomfort and the procrastination thoughts she would likely encounter were predicted and ways to handle them were developed. Lauren said that she felt up to the challenge and, in fact, proudly reported at the next session that she had successfully completed and mailed the forms, though she admitted that it took her two days to follow through. Lauren and her therapist reviewed her experience of the process, including how she handled the various negative thoughts and reactions she experienced along the way.

The case conceptualization was an important intervention for fostering Lauren's commitment to CBT. It was also an important cognitive intervention because it provided a visual representation of the diverse influences on her and helped to reframe her sense of confusion in concrete behavioral terms. While continuing to come to terms and understand the effects of ADHD on her life, Lauren now had a framework for understanding mistakes instead of automatically attributing them to personal defectiveness. The conceptualization also provided a rationale for the seemingly small steps she was asked to take in therapy and connected them to the larger framework.

By no means did the case conceptualization provide the magical awakening that Lauren still secretly hoped for. CBT focused on helping her to take greater responsibility for her behaviors and to learn to face and tolerate discomfort in order to handle problems head on instead of avoiding them. Lauren was better able to handle difficulties by boiling them down to specific behaviors (for example, "I forgot to write down the appointment in my planner") rather than schema-driven attributions (for example, "I'm unreliable. I'm flawed."). She dealt with her ambivalence about medication treatment for ADHD by considering alternative thoughts about their potential benefit and whether or not it was cheating to use them (for example, "Medications are a tool that might allow me to be less sensitive to distractions. The content and quality of my work are still up to me"). Lauren soon decided to commit to a fair trial of medication use to determine whether or not she viewed it as a useful tool, in her case 3 months of a daily dose. This plan gave her the opportunity to learn that medications, while potentially helpful for reducing the interference of symptoms, are not ultimately the source of one's actions or abilities.

The case conceptualization served as a useful touchstone throughout the difficult process of behavior change. It was difficult for Lauren at the outset because she had become accustomed to taking steps to avoid stressful feelings and uncomfortable emotions. It was scary for her to enact new coping behaviors while on probation at work. However, as she came to realize, her previous methods for handling problems only deferred them. She recognized that her thoughts about various situations represented important choice points. Lauren slowly got better at asking herself "What am I thinking right now? How do I want to handle this situation?" and being able to tolerate emotional discomfort in order to face tasks and problems rather than automatically procrastinating. Further, Lauren became better at giving herself partial credit in situations rather than engaging in all-or-nothing thinking. She applied similar strategies in her personal life in order to prioritize her behaviors and to reserve time for friends and dating partners. Finally, she also used similar evaluations to keep her alcohol use at a reasonable level of social drinking and to avoid drinking to forget her problems.

Lauren had periodic slips and setbacks in the course of CBT, including missing meetings without notice, finding herself in a crisis situation due to procrastination, or questioning her progress in treatment. However, she was much better about giving advance notice to her therapist and working hard not to miss consecutive appointments. Lauren moved to booster sessions after 6 months of therapy, after she was removed from probationary status at work. Although her work evaluation was not stellar and there remained some room for improvement, Lauren received passing ratings.

Lauren subsequently dropped out of CBT altogether after another 6 months of booster sessions or about a year since her initial evaluation. Therapy ended after she missed an appointment and did not respond to several attempts (by phone, e-mail, and postal mail) to reconnect.

Lauren clearly had more work to do in CBT in order to reinforce and stabilize her coping strategies. Despite her drifting out of treatment without an opportunity to appropriately wind up CBT, Lauren made some noticeable progress. Rather than viewing her medications as controlling her actions, she reframed them as a tool for buying time in order to find a solution. CBT also helped Lauren to develop and implement some sustainable organizational habits in her home life and to better manage stress at work. Lauren's therapist may have wished to have had more sessions and it is impossible to know how well treatment gains and the use of coping strategies persist after patients discontinue regular sessions. However, the case conceptualization served as a useful tool with which Lauren could better understand and manage the effects of ADHD on her life, one that hopefully she still finds useful.

CHAPTER 5

Complicating Factors

> Most people don't realize that some people expend tremendous energy merely to be normal. (Albert Camus)

Research and clinical experience suggest that the combination of medications and cognitive behavioral therapy (CBT) should be helpful for most adults seeking treatment for attention-deficit/hyperactivity disorder (ADHD). However, there are many complicating factors that could arise and conspire to hinder treatment. In fact, the same core symptoms and associated problems characteristic of ADHD and for which people seek treatment may also interfere with the effectiveness and delivery of treatment. Finally, ADHD potentially affects functioning in a number of important domains of life, such as school, work, and relationships. Thus, some individuals may seek help to address emergent crises in their lives or struggle with significant difficulties trying to manage daily affairs that most people take for granted.

The CBT case conceptualization provides a useful framework for understanding and addressing the various complications that may arise in treatment. It allows therapists and patients to collaboratively and systematically assess the relevant issues at hand in order to make an informed decision about how to (or, in some cases, whether to) proceed in treatment. Considering the difficult road most adults with ADHD must travel simply to find specialized care and the low frustration tolerance characteristic of ADHD, identifying and resolving complications that arise in treatment is particularly important. If not adequately addressed, many adults with ADHD may drop out of treatment altogether, consequently losing potentially helpful therapeutic support and insidiously reinforcing the sense that "nothing will help me." On the other hand, effectively managing such difficulties in the course of treatment provides opportunities for adults with ADHD to gain confidence in their abilities to handle problems that they used to avoid and thereby to develop a sense of resilience. What follows is a review of some commonly encountered complicating factors that may arise in a course of treatment for adult ADHD.

READINESS FOR CHANGE

We subscribe to the conceptualization of ADHD as a neurobiological syndrome of impaired executive functions that creates significant problems with self-regulation. Said differently, individuals with ADHD have fundamental problems managing the vast array of external and internal information and behavioral choices that inundate people every day. Adults with ADHD have difficulties consistently and effectively processing information and managing behaviors in order to actualize their long-range goals and plans. Many of our patients have voiced frustration about the fact that they have seemingly realistic and achievable personal goals and understand the consequences of their actions but nevertheless have difficulties taking steps to follow through on them despite their genuine best intentions.

Although we do not view ADHD as fundamentally an amotivational syndrome (although executive dysfunction certainly undermines many of the cognitive processes involved in fostering self-directed motivation and intention), we do appreciate the influence of motivational issues at the outset of treatment. It is important to spend time clarifying and elaborating patients' rationales for undertaking and committing to their stated behavioral goals.

Participating in treatment for adult ADHD is not a passive process. It requires a degree of motivation and commitment in order for patients to obtain the best results from what treatment has to offer. Although after receiving a diagnosis of adult ADHD many patients are eager to start treatment, some individuals may be unsure of whether they are ready to make such a commitment. Furthermore, throughout the change process, individuals may face different issues or behaviors about which they are ambivalent, making patients' motivation an important clinical issue to conceptualize and discuss.

We have found Prochaska and colleagues' (Prochaska et al. 1992; Prochaska & Norcross, 2001) *stages of change* model very helpful in conceptualizing and intervening with patients' attitudes toward the diagnosis and treatment of ADHD. This transtheoretical model was developed in research on how people change addictive and health-related behaviors, notoriously difficult behaviors to modify. Considering the chronic and pervasive nature of ADHD, it has proven to be a useful framework for tailoring interventions to the needs of each patient.

In particular, patients who are deemed to be in either the *precontemplation* or *contemplation* stages, characterized by denial of problems or begrudging recognition of some problems paired with ambivalence about making changes, respectively, may not be ready to commit to doing the work required of CBT or pharmacotherapy. For such patients, it is clinically appropriate to spend time exploring their thoughts about their circumstances, what is called *consciousness raising* (Prochaska et al., 1992). Portions of sessions or perhaps several sessions may be spent identifying assumptions individuals hold about ADHD, about treatment, or about their ability to change. Reviewing the relative costs and benefits of changing versus staying the same also can be useful to clarify patients' motivations for treatment. Matching the pace and focus of therapy to individuals' particular stages of change helps decrease the likelihood of patients dropping out of therapy, particularly in the case of ambivalent patients.

We have observed that newly diagnosed college students with ADHD—particularly if they participated in a diagnostic evaluation solely at the urging of family or representatives of their college—struggle with the implications of the diagnosis and the adjustment in coping style it often requires. Motivational interviewing techniques are useful to attempt to find examples in patients' terms of areas of dissatisfaction in their lives which they may be motivated to address (Miller & Rollnick, 1991).

For example, Jen was a college freshman recently diagnosed with ADHD after her parents and her college advisor insisted she get an evaluation. She had nearly been placed on academic probation after her first semester and was forced to drop some courses she had been failing because she had difficulty organizing and keeping up with her work. Jen refused to consider medications as a treatment option and questioned how therapy could help her: "I don't have time for these appointments. I just have to do a better job staying on top of things." Her therapist steered the conversation away from academic matters and inquired about aspects of college that had not been meeting her expectations. Jen admitted that she was having some social problems with other girls in her dorm because her disorganization resulted in her being late for or missing various social events. She agreed that it might be helpful to have a few sessions to address organization and time management to help her improve her social life.

Individuals in the *preparation* stage have started to make some minor behavioral changes but have not yet committed to making wholesale modifications. It can appear that individuals in this stage are attempting to make changes without having it hurt too much. For example, Jen agreed to practice writing down her social arrangements in order to decrease the likelihood of forgetting them. However, she said she did not want to use an organizer because that was too "geeky" and, instead, agreed to use scraps of paper that she kept in her purse. Although reflecting an effort at behavior change on her part, Jen eventually noted that the available-scrap-of-paper system only contributed to her sense of disorganization and she subsequently agreed to reconsider the use of a personal organizer.

Once patients have fundamentally changed their coping patterns in adaptive and sustainable ways, they are considered to be in the *action* stage. The therapeutic focus shifts to reinforcing and maintaining these new coping behaviors and handling inevitable slipups and setbacks that may arise. Finally, the *maintenance* stage refers to the point at which the adaptive coping patterns have become solidified as the new behavioral norm. The main tasks in this stage are relapse prevention and looking to consolidate treatment gains.

Individuals often cycle through these stages several times during the change process and may simultaneously exhibit characteristics of several different stages. The stage model provides a useful clinical heuristic for understanding the experiences of individuals attempting to make changes in their lives in order to more effectively match interventions to a particular stage. Although most motivational issues occur at the outset of treatment, there may be various issues and interventions that arise in the course of treatment that necessitate a reassessment of the readiness for change. In some cases, adults with ADHD may decide that they are not ready to engage in this process. As we have said before, our goal is to help insure that treatment refusal is an informed decision rather than an impulsive one.

COMORBIDITY

Comorbidity, the coexistence of two or more psychiatric or medical disorders, is the rule rather than the exception in the assessment and treatment of adult ADHD. The comorbidity rates in published literature on adult ADHD range upwards of 75% (Angold et al., 1999; Biederman, 2004; Wilens et al., 2002). In many cases, it is the distress associated with these other problems, such as depression, anxiety, or substance abuse, that compels individuals to seek an evaluation or treatment. However, the existence of these added difficulties requiring intervention creates additional layers of diagnostic and clinical complexity that could affect treatment outcome. Below, we discuss some of the challenges of managing comorbid disorders in the treatment of adult ADHD.

Substance Abuse

Untreated ADHD is a risk factor for substance abuse (Wilens, 2004). The popular notion is that individuals use illicit drugs or alcohol in an effort to self-medicate their symptoms and there is some support for this model in research on nicotine use (e.g., Whalen et al., 2003). It may also be the case that poor impulse control puts individuals with ADHD at risk for using substances, or there may be some combination of these factors. Regardless of the source of the problem, ADHD and substance abuse is a problematic combination.

Effective pharmacotherapy has been found to reduce rates of substance abuse, presumably by treating the core symptoms of ADHD, thus helping individuals to decrease impulsivity and to increase their abilities to consider the long-range consequences of their actions (Wilens, 2004). Additional psychosocial treatment focused on ADHD and addiction issues may help to address the various substance-related cues and impulses to use in addition to improving other aspects of overall well-being that may reduce the substance use (Aviram, Rhum, & Levin, 2001). However, substance use has not yet been an outcome variable targeted in the psychosocial treatment outcome literature for adults with ADHD.

As with other aspects of ADHD, it is useful to conceptualize the role of substance abuse in the lives of affected patients (e.g., Beck, Wright, Newman, & Liese, 1993). What are the external and internal triggers that increase the likelihood of using a substance? What are the beliefs about substance use and the specific permission-giving beliefs (that is, rationalizations) that immediately precede its use? Although it sounds counterintuitive for those not familiar with the treatment of substance abuse, it is useful to review with patients both the benefits and drawbacks of their habits. In particular, starting off with a review of the benefits often yields important hints for intervention. For example, an individual who says alcohol use helps him to "quiet [his] mind" and to forget about problems may provide clues that he is experiencing problematic levels of distractibility and stress he feels unable to handle.

For another example, Jerry is a 21-year-old college junior who was diagnosed with ADHD during his first year of college after being placed on academic probation. He became overwhelmed by academic demands and eventually stopped attending classes. After his diagnosis, he was prescribed a medication for ADHD by a psychiatrist and responded well. However, he did not give up his regular use of marijuana. Jerry was open about marijuana use with his psychiatrist and he had not abused his prescribed medications. He was able to keep up with the demands of school, though he admitted that he could be doing better. Thus, his psychiatrist regularly assessed with Jerry the risks of his substance use during their regular appointments until Jerry encountered serious academic problems during his junior year. At his psychiatrist's urging, Jerry agreed to start CBT for ADHD and also said he would be willing to discuss his substance use, though he did not promise he would agree to change his behavior.

In the spirit of "starting small," Jerry's therapist invited him to keep track of times he smoked marijuana when he had planned on doing something else, such as schoolwork. Such instances were considered examples of how his marijuana use might interfere with his goals. In one case, Jerry said that he hoped to read a chapter for a difficult class. He said he had enough time to complete the work and to still go out with friends afterward. However, he noted that he started to feel tense when he thought of opening the textbook. With some exploration, Jerry said his thought was, "I really don't want to read this. It will be boring." He imagined himself struggling to get through the reading an hour later and felt physically uncomfortable at this prospect. Jerry said that his thoughts were related to an overarching belief that "I'm not good at reading," based on the difficulties he had with comprehension prior to his being prescribed ADHD medications. The thought of putting off his reading mixed with the notion of "chilling out with some pot" led him to start smoking some marijuana he had in his room. He also noted that he was aware that when he smokes marijuana, he is no longer able to work productively the rest of the day. Using these insights, Jerry and his therapist conceptualized that his marijuana use, in addition to its chemical effects, served to save him from doing boring work and also reduced his physical feelings of discomfort. He acknowledged that the pattern was ultimately self-defeating. Sessions focused on helping Jerry to challenge his avoidant thoughts with more proactive ones (for example, "I'll read the first ten pages and see if I'm still bored"). He also agreed to experiment with other ways to handle physical discomfort, such as relaxation, and challenging these feelings with brief exposure to the task he wanted to avoid. Jerry did not stop smoking marijuana altogether, but he greatly reduced his use, particularly his use of smoking as a preemptive avoidant strategy.

Depression

Depression is a common psychiatric comorbidity for adults with ADHD, particularly females (Biederman, 2005; Rucklidge & Kaplan, 1997). In fact, a study of a sample of individuals seeking treatment for depression revealed that 16% manifested clinically significant symptoms of ADHD (Alpert et al., 1996). From a CBT standpoint, depression involves thoughts dealing with loss or failure to achieve a desired goal, an emotional state of sadness, and various physical symptoms, such as low energy, anhedonia, and agitation. For adults with ADHD, a common presentation is *learned helplessness*: the belief that nothing will work out as the person desires and, thus, attempts at change are exercises in futility (Seligman,

1991). Consequently, depression compounds the already low frustration tolerance experienced by many adults with ADHD, leading them to avoid handling problems or to give up on their plans at the first sign of adversity.

Non-ADHD adults who are depressed often come to recognize in the course of treatment that their thoughts have become excessively negative and distorted. However, many individuals with ADHD may declare that their negative thoughts are not distorted and may point to a litany of setbacks that seem to confirm their pessimistic mindsets as being accurate. Thus, a depressed college student who had previously always earned passing grades may respond to a low grade on a test with the thought, "I'm going to fail out of school" but is soon able to recognize that there is no evidence of likely failure. A depressed college student with ADHD, on the other hand, may also respond to a low grade on a test with the thought, "I'm going to fail out of school." When asked for evidence supporting this thought, the student with ADHD may respond, "I also failed the previous two tests in this class." This might seem to be hard evidence that confirms the student's deduction that failure in college is a foregone conclusion. However, from a CBT problem management standpoint, the question becomes, "Did you try to make changes in how you prepared for the exam following previous disappointments; or did you use the same study strategies each time, regardless of the outcome?" More often it comes to light that the depressed ADHD individual feels helpless and hopeless about the prospect of different study strategies. Thus, CBT focuses on helping the individual to implement new study strategies and to assess their outcome.

In a similar fashion, treating the combination of ADHD and depression often involves overcoming learned pessimism and developing the ability to maintain a resilient mindset in the face of difficulties. Rather than judging outcomes in all-or-nothing terms (that is, success or failure), problem management becomes a trial-and-error process in which trying new things and revising strategies is the rule.

Anxiety

Whereas depressed individuals struggle with cognitions associated with loss and a sense of having failed, anxious individuals struggle with anticipatory thoughts related to threats and a recurring sense that something bad will happen. These thoughts are often associated with feelings of worry and associated physiological symptoms, such as tension, quickened heart rate, and generally feeling "on edge."

In fact, it may be that small amounts of anxiety can be adaptive and helpful for adults with ADHD. That is, we have heard many patients report that it is usually their sense of worry about the consequences of not completing a task that helps them overcome procrastination. For example, concerns about submitting income taxes after the deadline have helped many a person (with ADHD and without) overcome inertia and to complete the necessary forms. Thus, a little bit of tension can be a good motivator insofar as the individual is able to adequately complete the task at hand.

Many of the patients with ADHD and anxiety we treat report that their worry helped them keep up with work through high school, though they often said that they could have done better had they been able to start working earlier (rather than waiting until the last minute) and more effectively. However, these patients subsequently discovered that this procrastinate-worry-work cycle ultimately proved unsuccessful once they moved on to higher education, the work force, or the daily demands of raising a family and managing a household. The consequences of procrastination and disorganization in adulthood were more severe than they had been in high school and it was harder for them to catch up once they fell behind. Thus, their worry about the consequences of not keeping up with their responsibilities was often overmatched by their sense of inadequacy about their inability to catch up on work. Some individuals found ways to get things done at the last minute, but others faced difficulties, such as academic probation, dropping out of school, poor evaluations at work, or even losing jobs as a consequence. These near misses or negative outcomes further created a heightened sense of anxiety about their ability to handle their responsibilities.

Similar to dealing with depression, CBT for the combination of ADHD and anxiety involves helping individuals to challenge their negative assumptions by attempting new experiences and assessing the results. Anxious individuals often approach new situations with thoughts of how things could go wrong (for example, overappraisal of risk). In the case of ADHD adults, individuals may be able to cite evidence from their past of their fears being realized.

For example, Janet is a 32-year-old single mother with ADHD who had dropped out of college but found a career in sales that was a good fit with her effusive personality. She had numerous experiences in college and at her job in which her disorganization and poor time management left her unprepared for class or for some aspect of her work. In one case, she walked into the office and faced an important presentation for a prospective client for which Janet was totally unprepared (mistakenly thinking she was scheduled for the next week). She felt supremely embarrassed and anxious as she struggled through an off-the-cuff presentation that did not win over the client. Janet described that event as one of many that left her chronically worried about forgetting things and concerned about others' opinions of her. In some ways, she viewed this pressure as helping her to keep up with the mundane paperwork involved in her job and to be able to make a good presentation to others. However, Janet engaged in significant procrastination when it came to making initial contacts with prospective customers or doing follow-ups with difficult clients, and her distractibility was magnified whenever she felt anxious.

Janet's CBT sessions focused on clarifying the connection between her thoughts about contacting customers (for example, "The customer will think I'm unprofessional if I forget something or if I'm late"), her anxiety symptoms (for example, feeling nervous, jittery voice), and her avoidant behaviors (for example, "I'll call first thing tomorrow"; focus on doing paperwork instead of making calls). The suggestion that she do an experiment of calling one of her difficult clients at the same time she used some basic relaxation strategies was met with the thought: "What if he is angry that I called and tells me he no longer wants to do business?" We explored her thoughts of the potential consequences (for example, "Okay. Let's assume for a moment that this worst-case happens? What would that mean for you?"). Janet slowly explored the risks associated with being rejected and determined that they were twofold. First, she was worried about not doing well in her job, getting fired, and not being able to support herself and her son. Second, she was concerned about appearing to be inadequate or as an imposter who was found to have been hired as a mistake. Janet said that her worries reminded her of how she often felt in college, at work, and at other times in her life when her ADHD symptoms created difficulties that left her feeling different and less adequate than others.

Bipolar Disorder

The essential feature of bipolar spectrum disorders is significant affective lability or mood swings that include at least one swing toward depression and one toward hypomania or mania. There are various types of such cyclical mood disorders that involve different constellations and severity of mood and mania symptoms, including cyclothymia, bipolar I disorder, and bipolar II disorder. There are many similarities between bipolar disorder and ADHD that sometimes make it difficult to make a differential diagnosis, such as rapidly changing moods, feeling energized for periods of time, and inconsistent functioning. In general, the mood episodes observed in bipolar disorder are discrete and the diagnostic symptom requirements for hypomania and mania are distinct from the impulsivity observed in ADHD (Biederman, 1998; Ramsay, 2005c). Many individuals with bipolar disorder report a return to a semblance of relative normalcy and stability between mood episodes, whereas adults with ADHD often describe daily struggles with issues related to poor time management and disorganization.

That being said, some individuals present for treatment with both ADHD and bipolar disorder, a combination that creates unique challenges for both medication management and CBT. Individuals with this comorbidity pattern face the challenge of trying to establish and maintain stability in their daily lives and to adjust their coping strategies based on their current mood states. Furthermore, it is important to assess the relative priority in the treatment plan of treating each set of symptoms. Some individuals may struggle with bipolar I disorder but recognize that they also struggle with the effects of secondary symptoms of ADHD. Some individuals, on the other hand, may experience most of their difficulties as a result of ADHD but find that their mood patterns suggest a cyclothymic pattern that may complicate coping efforts. Finally, some individuals may experience a complicated mishmash of both symptoms, requiring a great deal of coping to manage.

Managing the combination of bipolar disorder and ADHD requires that patients become versed in recognizing the various risk factors involved in their distinct mood states and develop commensurate coping strategies (e.g., Newman, Leahy, Beck, Reilly-Harrington, & Gyulani, 2002). For example, an individual with ADHD who is in the midst of a depressive episode may be at risk for skipping work because he thinks he does not have the energy to get dressed. Furthermore, he may experience difficulties prioritizing and organizing a plan for what he hopes to accomplish at work, further contributing to his conclusion he should skip work. CBT would help this individual reconsider the costs and benefits of skipping work by addressing both the mood issue (for example, "I do not have enough energy") and the ADHD issue (for example, "I do not know what I would do first if I got to work").

Episodes of elevated mood combined with ADHD, on the other hand, may require a focus on impulse control. For example, an individual in the throes of hypomania may feel particularly energized and be especially productive in completing some long-avoided tasks. However, during such periods she may also be at risk for taking on new projects, such as agreeing to take on additional assignments at work at the same time that she decides to paint the living room of her apartment. She also finds herself able to get by on fewer hours of sleep each night, so she orders several books from an online bookseller, feeling she will easily be able to read them all. However, in her misguided zeal she may underestimate the time and energy required of her in other areas of her life.

Furthermore, as her mood stabilizes she may start to feel less energized and be left facing a partially painted apartment (and the realization that she chose the wrong color), credit card bills for a pile of unread books, and numerous responsibilities at work that her ADHD-related distractibility and disorganization leave her feeling overwhelmed at the thought of facing. CBT sessions would focus on helping the patient to identify her risk factors in a hypomanic state. Sessions would provide an opportunity to slow down her decision-making process and to consider each choice more deliberately, drawing on past experiences in previous similar mood states to determine the best course of action.

Although by definition impulsivity involves acting without thinking, cognitions arise as individuals face different situations that provoke questionable actions (for example, "This is a great opportunity and I have to take advantage of it") and minimize the potential negative consequences of actions (for example, "It will all work out somehow—I work best under pressure"). Moreover, decisions are often made without thinking through the implications of one's actions. Homework tasks might involve instituting a 24-hour delay when considering a new endeavor and/or eliciting feedback from trusted individuals about her plans (e.g., Newman et al., 2002).

Changes in mood may affect patients' follow-through on treatment, affecting management of both mood and ADHD symptoms. That is, when depressed, individuals may assess treatment more negatively, focusing on apparent evidence that they are not getting better, and be at risk for dropping out. On the other hand, when in a hypomanic or manic state and feeling energized, individuals may assume that because they are *feeling* better that they are also *functioning* better and may be at risk for leaving treatment. Consequently, it is useful to monitor patients' thoughts about treatment and to refer to their stated goals for treatment as a means for assessing treatment progress.

Learning Problems

Considering the negative effects of ADHD on the academic performance and learning experiences of those affected, it could easily be considered to be a learning disability. The executive functions, in fact, play an important role in learning and information processing (Biederman et al., 2004). The existence of comorbid learning and/or language problems may create significant additional functional problems for ADHD adults insofar as they contribute to difficulties with academic achievement and may affect occupational options and earning potential. Furthermore, problems affecting one's ability to read, write, or to perform basic mathematics likely create almost daily frustrations considering the need for these skills to handle the demands of adult life.

Beyond academic skill disorders, many adults with ADHD show signs of nonverbal learning difficulties as manifested by poor visual–spatial perception, left–right directional problems, poor organizational skills, slow writing speed, and extremely poor time management. For these individuals, simply getting from point A to point B to point C during a routine day can prove to be inordinately difficult. What is particularly difficult for them to reconcile is the tremendous gap between their average or above average verbal abilities and their poor performance in these cognitive domains. Another type of nonacademic learning difficulties often seen in patients with ADHD lies in the domain of central auditory processing. These patients have a hard time holding on to verbal information and have trouble discerning linguistic utterances. They lose track of what is being said in lectures or conversations, particularly when speakers are talking quickly or using excessive technical language. They have a terrible time learning foreign languages, and they are frequently overwhelmed in settings where there are different conversations going on at once.

While CBT for adult ADHD is able to conceptualize the effects of a history of learning difficulties on one's belief system and to address some behavioral aspects of learning, such as challenging avoidance and implementing various coping strategies, it does not include specific educational and learning interventions that are the purview of learning specialists. Therefore, when patients present for ADHD assessment and treatment either with a history of learning disorders or evidence emerges that suggests the presence of learning problems, we recommend a separate educational/learning assessment by a learning or educational specialist. For patients involved in academic or occupational settings in which their learning difficulties may interfere with their performance, we recommend additional treatment with professionals who are able to provide more specialized guidance regarding particular learning strategies. However, in many situations, case-specific adjustments of CBT may be sufficient to adapt to individual patients' learning styles, such as writing down the key points of sessions, frequently summarizing the main themes, presenting new information in a variety of ways, et cetera.

Personality Disorders

Personality refers to an integrative bio-psycho-social system of stable psychological structures and processes that are comprised of the biological predisposition and learning history of an individual. It establishes a psychological set point from which an individual makes sense of and adapts to the current environment. Considering its long-standing nature, personality requires a longer time and more concerted effort to change than other aspects of psychological functioning.

Personality disorders, therefore, refer to long-standing, inflexible patterns of perceiving and interacting with one's environment and oneself that make it difficult for individuals to effectively adapt to the demands of the environment, thus creating significant problems functioning. The list of personality disorders set forth in the *DSM-IV-TR* (APA, 2000) is divided into three clusters. Cluster A refers to personality characteristics that appear to be odd or eccentric (for example, schizoid and paranoid personality disorders). Cluster B refers to behaviors that would be considered overly dramatic, emotional, or erratic (for example, antisocial, histrionic, and borderline personality disorders). Finally, chronic tendencies toward appearing anxious, fearful, or passive comprise Cluster C (for example, dependent, avoidant, and obsessive–compulsive personality disorders).

As we mentioned earlier, ADHD has many features of a personality style insofar as it represents an amalgam of genetic and neurobiological predispositions that affect how affected individuals interact with and make sense of themselves and their environments. Consequently, the features of ADHD have a more enduring and pervasive affect on functioning than do relatively transitory mood states. The point we wish to reinforce is that living with ADHD, particularly for adults whose symptoms have gone undiagnosed until adulthood, has significant and pervasive effects on functioning and experience.

Problematic personality characteristics add a layer of complexity to treatment. Such characterological patterns may serve to magnify the effects of ADHD, such as in the case of an individual with obsessive–compulsive personality disorder (OCPD), who counteracts distractibility and disorganization with rigidly high standards for performance and order. Such a combination is a recipe for procrastination and subsequent reliance on brinksmanship for completing tasks (that is, waiting until there is extreme deadline pressure). On the other hand, an individual with antisocial personality disorder and ADHD is at risk for engaging in impulsive behaviors that may have significant legal consequences.

There are diverse psychological theories of personality. The CBT model acknowledges the developmental and bio-psycho-social aspects of personality. From a treatment standpoint, the underlying belief systems (or schema) unique to each personality style provides an orienting framework for intervention (see Beck, Freeman, & Associates, 1990). Thus, again, the case conceptualization becomes a useful integrative heuristic for understanding the various factors affecting a person's reactions to situations. Although personality characteristics are difficult to change, such a conceptualization of the interaction of beliefs, emotions, and behaviors provides a useful framework that empowers individuals to understand and to attempt to modify what seem to be automatic reactions.

Personality characteristics also may become apparent in the course of the therapeutic relationship between therapist and patient. Developmental experiences, particularly attachment and interpersonal experiences, and social learning greatly influence personality development. In some cases, certain characterological features are the direct result of developmental traumas, such as the high incidence of physical and sexual abuse among individuals later diagnosed with borderline personality disorder (Layden et al., 1993).

More specific to the issue of treating ADHD, it is possible that the work in therapy may activate issues related to patients' experiences with family, teachers, peers, previous romantic partners, or other relationships affected by ADHD symptoms that, in turn, affect their reactions toward their therapists. The notion that such previous interpersonal experiences are reenacted with the therapist, whether it is called *transference* or *interpersonal schemas* (Safran & Segal, 1990), is important for therapists to keep in mind in their work with adults with ADHD, particularly those with comorbid personality disorders. In our clinical experience, it is usually patients' emotional reactions (for example, anger) or seemingly extreme behaviors (for example, a patient announcing that he is quitting therapy) that provide a tip-off to the activation of interpersonal issues with the therapist.

For example, Cathy is a 25-year-old woman who has never held a full-time job for longer than 3 months due to problems related to extreme disorganization and impulsivity. She had an angry outburst at the start of a CBT session early in her treatment when her therapist inquired about her experience with the therapeutic homework task from the previous session. Hypothesizing that Cathy's excessive strong response reflected important issues, the therapist gently inquired regarding the various thoughts and feelings she had in response to the homework task. Cathy revealed that she had forgotten what she was supposed to do, had not written it down, and felt too embarrassed to contact the therapist for a reminder. She said it reminded her of similar experiences in school and she would end up being scolded by teachers and parents about her irresponsibility, leaving her feeling hurt and angry. Consequently, as an adult she often used her anger as a preemptive strike when she thought she had failed to do something. Not surprisingly, her argumentativeness in the face of feedback from supervisors was a primary reason she had difficulty keeping a job. After having the opportunity to process her reaction and

having the therapist clarify that therapeutic homework provided opportunities to learn and develop new skills, either by reviewing the outcomes
of what was accomplished or by analyzing the factors that contributed to
not completing tasks, Cathy said that she felt reassured that she would
not be negatively judged in CBT as she had felt elsewhere.

We should note that there are many patient behaviors that are frequently considered to be signs of therapeutic resistance or therapy-interfering behaviors that could be considered as transference reactions,
such as showing up late for or missing an appointment, not completing a homework task, or leaving items behind in the consulting room.
However, in the absence of other clinical data, we have found that such
behaviors are better considered to be manifestations of the common difficulties encountered by adults with ADHD (Ramsay & Rostain, 2005a).

Life Crises and Suicidality

Most individuals who seek assessment and treatment for ADHD want
help managing the recurring difficulties encountered in daily life. Their
symptoms of ADHD create an assortment of functional difficulties with
predictable, though problematic, outcomes, such as running late for
appointments or incurring late fees for bills. For some individuals, however, it is a life crisis that may compel them to finally seek treatment.
Situations such as learning that a spouse plans to file for divorce, getting
fired from a job, or taking a mandated leave of absence from school for
poor academic performance are some of the common crises reported by
our patients. Less frequent though not uncommon crises involve negative
consequences related to substance abuse (for example, arrest for DUI),
extramarital affairs, impulsive and extensive spending, and the physical
and/or legal consequences of poor driving behavior (for example, loss
of license, fatal accident). These sorts of severe and sometimes tragic
events, of course, are not limited to individuals with ADHD, though the
tendency toward impulsive behavior, poor concentration, and deficient
long-range planning put them at higher risk for these experiences (Barkley & Fischer, 2005; James, Lai, & Dahl, 2004).

Not surprisingly, the occurrence of such extreme events is likely at
the forefront of the reason someone seeks an assessment or the therapeutic agenda when they occur in the course of ongoing psychotherapy. It is
appropriate to adjust the treatment plan in order to address these issues
as a new priority. However, patients who are in the midst of a crisis may
desire more relief and resolution to them than can be reasonably provided. Moreover, clinicians as a professional group want to help patients
effectively handle and get through these situations. This scenario can

lead to a desire on the part of a clinician to "fix" the situation immediately, which is likely unrealistic.

As we suggested in our discussion of setting treatment goals, it is wise to start small. In the case of an active emergency arising during treatment, a crisis management approach of ensuring that the actual crisis situation has ended is a useful starting point. If so, it is important to gather detailed information about the situation. Information-gathering helps the clinician to understand what happened and the potential implication of events, and it helps the patient to start to process and face these same events. In some cases, it may emerge that more information is needed, such as a student assuming he will be placed on academic probation based on a conversation with an advisor. In situations in which it is clear that there is a difficult situation to be handled, patient and clinician can engage in problem management regarding next steps needed to address the situation. In many cases, ongoing crisis management may involve a drawn-out process, such as in the case of an adult with ADHD who is arrested for drunk driving. Regardless of the circumstance, even a crisis provides opportunities for learning to manage symptoms of adult ADHD. At the same time, there would likely be many other psychological issues that are triggered that also warrant attention in therapy, such as feelings of remorse and self-criticism.

Finally, although suicidal thoughts are not typically mentioned in the discussion of adult ADHD, as with any other patient group, it is important to assess for and to address the presence of suicidal ideation. Individuals with comorbid depression or bipolar disorder may experience suicidal thoughts. Clinicians should also assess for suicidality among ADHD adults facing significant life crises. Although most individuals with ADHD are able to face supremely stressful circumstances without entertaining the possibility of ending their own lives, a few may regard their problems as confirmatory evidence of their defectiveness and conclude, based on a sequence of distorted and emotionally driven thoughts, that they should no longer live. In particular, adults with ADHD who view themselves as responsible for severe or fatal automobile accidents, or who face severe legal, financial, or relationship ramifications associated with impulsive behaviors, should be explicitly asked if they are experiencing thoughts of hurting themselves or someone else and regularly reassessed if they answer in the affirmative.

MEDICATION-RELATED COMPLICATIONS

While most patients find medications useful in reducing the symptoms of ADHD, there are predictable complications that arise in the course of treatment. These include ambivalence about taking a medication, unrealistic expectations about the effects of medication, distorted beliefs about the meaning of taking a medication, nonadherence and misuse of medications, and side effects of medications. Clinicians should anticipate that any of these issues can become a focus of concern and, when they arise, should be approached in a straightforward and nonjudgmental manner.

Most adult patients express some degree of ambivalence about the necessity of taking a medication for their ADHD symptoms. This can take the form of open acknowledgment ("Gee, I really wish I didn't have to take something to keep me focused on what I am doing...") or of more indirect questioning ("Do you think I will need to take a medication for the rest of my life?"). In whatever way it is expressed, ambivalence is a completely normal reaction to the situation. Few of us ever want to take medications, especially if we are expected to take them on a daily basis for the foreseeable future. Clinicians are on solid ground if they acknowledge the patient's ambivalence as an understandable reaction and if they offer support to an ongoing exploration of the patient's negative reactions to being on medication. If the ambivalence is strong enough to lead the patient to resist taking the medication, it is best to face this option as a positive choice on the patient's part. This can take the form of a reframe as follows: "It looks like you have come to the conclusion that the medication is not worth taking. Perhaps this is a good time to take a break from it. You can always restart it in the future." (Note: Therapists who do not have prescription privileges should encourage patients to discuss medication adjustments with their prescribing physician and also be willing to consult with the physician—with the expressed permission of patients.)

In a fair number of cases, patients are disappointed with the effects of a medication regimen they are following. Their ADHD symptoms may not be remitting enough to make a difference in their lives, or they may be experiencing intolerable side effects. In cases of nonresponse, partial response, or serious adverse effects, it is best to advise the patient to discuss this with the prescribing physician. Modifications might be made to improve outcome or reduce side effects, or the medication regimen might be changed altogether. The important point to remember is that there are "different strokes for different folks," and that it might take several medication trials before an effective and tolerable regimen is devised.

Unrealistic hopes for a magic bullet to cure ADHD and all of its sequelae are not uncommon among our patients. It is understandable that individuals who have spent their lives struggling with a disabling condition that was not diagnosed until adulthood would harbor a strong wish for an instant remedy for all their woes. Most people can see this as an unfulfillable wish and can move beyond the stage of mild disappointment to a more realistic appraisal of what potential benefits might be derived from medication treatment.

Occasionally, however, the disappointment is more profound, and the patient becomes embittered about his situation and the failure of modern medicine to provide any real relief. In these cases, it is most helpful to offer a supportive comment of concern and compassion: "It must be very difficult for you to feel so hopeless about your situation. It would be wonderful if a cure for ADHD were available for you. But at the moment, we have imperfect tools to work with..." Allowing the patient to grieve their loss often leads to a renewed commitment to working in a more realistic framework.

By contrast, it is not unusual for patients to respond to positive medication effects with statements like: "I am not sure that it's really me that's doing better or if it's just the medication." This is often based on uncertainty about the legitimacy of the diagnosis of ADHD and about its treatment with medication. It also reflects a moral sentiment that is rooted in broader cultural notions of fairness—namely, if taking a medication makes it easier to work and get things done, then it must be bad because it is cheating. Much of the controversy surrounding the increased use of stimulants on college campuses, for instance, evokes strong condemnations of stimulants as "cognitive steroids." This direct analogy to the use of performance enhancers in sports leads to excessive guilt on the part of patients who legitimately need and benefit from taking a medication for ADHD. The most effective way to handle this reaction first is to point out that it reflects a common cultural prejudice about ADHD and that the patient will have to figure out a way of coming to terms with the actual reality of the disorder and its treatment. Secondly, it is useful to draw a metaphor between taking medication and wearing glasses. Glasses help to improve eyesight, but they do not eliminate the need for an individual to exert some effort in order to read, write, etc. Similarly, the medication works to sharpen one's focus but it does not do the work for the individual. Eventually, most patients come to see this issue in a more balanced light.

Nonadherence to medication treatment is quite common in clinical practice. Even when patients report clear benefit from their medications, they often skip doses or stop taking the medication for extended periods of time. It is important to review the actual circumstances that are leading to nonadherence in order to address the problem. If the patient is simply forgetting to take the pill, it is helpful to set up a reminder system and see whether it can improve adherence. If the patient is not comfortable with the medication's side effects, it is important to discuss ways to minimize their impact.

At times, patients will skip doses because it allows them to be "more like themselves." This is particularly true of young adult patients who experience some stifling of personality from the medication or who see that the effects of alcohol or other recreational substances are reduced when the patient takes the prescribed medication. In these situations, it is best to suggest that the patient take ownership of this decision and to discuss her pattern of use and nonuse with the prescribing physician.

Misuse of stimulant medications includes taking inappropriate doses and/or at inappropriate times for nonintended purposes such as staying up all night, cramming for examinations, suppressing appetite, et cetera. Abuse of stimulants refers to using them for recreational purposes (to induce euphoria), commonly done via snorting. Both of these sets of behaviors are serious risks to the patient's health and should be handled by direct confrontation.

Finally, the occurrence of side effects from ADHD medications requires careful review of medication usage patterns and of the frequency, severity, and impact of the negative effects that the patient is encountering. Many of the side effects of stimulants are mild and transient in nature and subside after several weeks of usage. However, if potentially serious side effects are being reported (for example, heart arrhythmias, shortness of breath, severe dizziness, fainting, mood swings, involuntary movements), the patient should call the prescribing physician immediately and make her aware of the situation. In the case of stimulants, it is safe to stop them immediately if any serious concerns are being raised. Other medications require a tapering process, although with atomoxetine and bupropion this can be achieved relatively quickly (within a few days). SSRIs and SNRIs require a much longer period of time to discontinue and this should be done with great care to avoid a discontinuation syndrome.

PROFESSIONALS' REACTIONS TO ADHD PATIENTS

As can be seen, the obligations of adult life can prove to be very demanding for many ADHD adults. Treatment obligations may also be demanding for adult ADHD patients, such as balancing daily medication regimens, attending regular CBT sessions, and instituting new coping strategies while keeping up with the ordinary responsibilities of daily life. While attention is rightly focused on patients and helping them to recognize the influence of their cognitive, emotional, and behavioral patterns, it is important for treating clinicians to identify the potential influence of their reactions to their patients insofar as they may negatively affect a course of treatment.

Some clinician reactions may, upon reflection, represent psychological issues specific to the therapist that negatively impinge on treatment. These countertransference issues reflect distorted reactions by the therapist toward the patient, such as feeling irritated with an older male patient because he reminds the therapist of her difficult relationship with her controlling father. The onus is on therapists to recognize these patterns and to adjust their demeanor with patients, often while having supervision consultations with a professional colleague for quality control.

Though not necessarily representing the bubbling up of therapists' deep psychological issues, some therapist reactions may run the risk of replicating embarrassing and invalidating experiences that patients with ADHD have had with other influential people in their lives. Thus, clinicians' thoughts, such as, "This patient just does not want to get better," or "We have been discussing procrastination for the past month and she still does not get it" may reflect frustration on the part of the therapist and losing sight that change is difficult for adults with ADHD. Feelings of frustration or boredom toward ADHD patients also may signal that therapists may have negative thoughts about their patients. It is useful for therapists to conceptualize their own reactions and to develop a reframe and action plan for the next session. Thus, therapists' reactions can be used to inform and to improve treatment.

For example, a therapist recognized that he expected to have a boring session with a young adult with ADHD who was struggling with his job search and, more specifically, committing to a final decision of which job offer to accept. The therapist thought, "We've been over this a hundred times and he should just make a choice." The therapist recognized his exaggeration and his distorted "should" thought. He took some time to reflect on the case conceptualization and to empathize with what the patient might be experiencing while facing the job search. Thus, the therapist started the next session by mentioning to the patient that it seemed they had been spending a lot of time on the job search topic in recent sessions. The therapist wondered aloud whether this continued to be the primary issue or whether there were other topics that might deserve a place on the therapeutic agenda. The patient said that he found it helpful to review his decision-making options but that he also worried how his job choice might affect his relationship with his girlfriend. Thus, a potentially boring session had been revitalized by the introduction of a slightly different issue that had implications for the patient's job search. Such examples provide reminders for clinicians to be aware of their own automatic thoughts and beliefs, and to test them out with their patients in constructive ways in order to ultimately improve the quality of treatment.

SIGNIFICANT IMPAIRMENT

The symptoms of ADHD lie at the extreme end of a continuum of adaptive executive functioning capacities. Similarly, within the group of individuals diagnosed with ADHD there is a continuum of severity of impairment, ranging from individuals who are generally functioning well in life but have mild, circumscribed problems (for example, work performance) to those with severe impairment pervading through most domains of their lives.

Psychotherapists who specialize in treating adults with ADHD recognize that they must adapt their typical therapeutic strategies because ADHD symptoms may interfere with patients getting the most out of therapy (e.g., Ramsay & Rostain, 2005a). However, some individuals present for treatment with symptoms severe enough to significantly interfere with their ability to engage in treatment. For example, individuals may have significant organizational problems or comorbid learning disorders that impede their ability to perform written therapeutic tasks, to complete suggested readings, or even to manage basic organizational tasks in daily life, such as keeping track of important papers or the next appointment. Some individuals with ADHD may have difficulties related to auditory processing that interfere with the ability to listen to, understand, and apply insights gained during therapy sessions. Emotional regulation difficulties may further complicate patients' abilities to attend to information during session, not to mention the fact that many of these difficulties may result in functional difficulties that create crises in patients' lives, so much so that therapy becomes crisis oriented rather than oriented toward better management of the symptoms of ADHD.

Our discussion of severe impairment as a complicating factor is not meant to imply that there are hopeless cases or that clinicians should give up. Rather, we hope to encourage clinicians and patients to collaborate to set realistic expectations for treatment and to adapt interventions to where the patient is at, particularly when facing complex and numerous problems.

In terms of starting treatment, it is important to identify the specific problems faced by patients in the different domains of their lives. Itemizing patients' presenting issues into discrete problems helps to sort out the individual therapeutic issues, which is more manageable and less overwhelming than facing their sum total. That is not meant to say that the problems are not serious, but making problems specific and behavioral often opens up a discussion of specific behavioral steps to be taken to manage them.

Some patients may face many severe and stressful life circumstances, such as the prospect of divorce, unemployment, bankruptcy, or even, in extreme cases, homelessness. In such cases it is important to prioritize issues that can be reasonably addressed in CBT, to determine whether a referral to another professional is indicated (for example, medical consultation, social worker), and to strategically defer focusing on other issues. Our first concerns for high-priority clinical issues are patient safety and meeting basic needs, such as shelter, health issues, and other issues that immediately affect well-being. Thus, suicidal ideation, untreated substance dependence, or pending loss of housing or employment require immediate intervention. Patients should be encouraged to follow through on steps necessary to take care of these important issues. Often this is done in coordination with other helping professionals, such as psychiatrists or social workers.

For individuals with relatively stable living situations who are meeting basic needs, there may still be significant life stressors, such as unemployment, divorce, and poor living environment. In such cases, it is useful to identify with the patient one or two items that are priorities for therapy. We further recommend that longer range goals that are only partially within the control of the individual (for example, "I'd like to be in a romantic relationship") be deferred in order to focus on more immediately achievable and influential tasks (for example, "I'd like to organize my monthly bills so that my power is not turned off again"). It should be noted that such prioritization is not meant to dismiss the importance of the other goals but to focus efforts on immediate problems. The plan is that skills gained while addressing these short-term problems will help individuals in the pursuit of their long-term goals.

Creating a manageable pace and expectations for treatment, including the rationale for interventions and predicting likely complications, reduces the likelihood that patients will misinterpret treatment as failing. Using the stage of change model to monitor motivation issues also helps avoid premature termination at the very time it is most needed. Finally, as was mentioned earlier, it is important for clinicians to monitor their own reactions to their patients struggling with severe impairment to avoid emotionally disengaging from them and giving up on the benefits treatment may provide. Instead, adopting an attitude of unfailing resilience and willingness to seek ways to manage problems increases the likelihood that treatment may contribute to functional improvements.

SOCIAL SKILLS AND RELATIONSHIP PROBLEMS

Increasing attention is being paid to the negative effects of the symptoms of ADHD on social functioning. More research is needed to pinpoint specific social skill deficits, but studies of children with ADHD have suggested that these youngsters are at higher risk for relationship problems, including with peers and siblings, and there are continued relationship problems in adulthood (Charman, Carroll, & Sturge, 2001; Friedman et al., 2003; Greene et al., 2001; Paulson, Buermeyer, & Nelson-Gray, 2005).

Adults with ADHD are known to experience higher rates of divorce and have greater difficulties with peers, coworkers, and employers (Weiss & Hechtman, 1993). A study of married couples in which one spouse had been diagnosed with ADHD and one spouse without ADHD revealed that the symptoms have a negative effect on their marital satisfaction and that there was much agreement regarding the problem areas (Robin & Payson, 2002). Our clinical experience has been that typical ADHD-related impulsivity, distractibility, inattention, and memory problems create difficulties in conversations, such as missing or forgetting important information, speaking out of turn, or making impulsive, inappropriate statements that others may find off-putting. Individuals without ADHD may misinterpret these behaviors as signs that the individual with ADHD is not interested in them.

In addition to the social effects of ADHD symptoms, adults with ADHD may develop compensatory strategies based on their past social frustrations that end up being self-defeating and magnifying their sense of interpersonal rejection. For example, Larry thought that he was a burden to his wife because he often forgot to follow through on promises and appeared distracted while she was talking with him. He worried that she would grow frustrated and seek a divorce because of his many foibles. Thus, whenever she asked a favor of him, he felt pressure to make it up to her and he agreed to do things that were unrealistic for him to accomplish. Not surprisingly, he was unable to keep the majority of his promises, which was interpreted by his wife as Larry's lack of regard for her. Larry viewed his mistakes as evidence that he was, in fact, unreliable and was headed for divorce. Fortunately, Larry was accurately diagnosed with ADHD and entered CBT in addition to being prescribed a medication. Considering the significance of their marital problems, Larry's wife agreed to attend a number of marital sessions to focus on improving their relationship.

Psychoeducation about ADHD helped Larry's wife to recognize that many of Larry's behaviors were not intentional but reflected his problems with information processing. On the other hand, Larry learned that he dealt with his wife as though he had an ever-mounting debt to repay her that was related to his history of unreliable behaviors. He strove to erase his debt by making promises he could not keep, which set him up for failure and greater debt. Having this mutual understanding of their interaction patterns, Larry's wife was able to provide unconditional reassurance to Larry of her love for him, which, of course, Larry was encouraged to reciprocate. For his part, Larry was better able to speak up for himself and to negotiate reasonable expectations, thus demonstrating increased (though not perfect) reliability. He also learned to ask for help from his wife and to spend more time talking with her about how his symptoms affected his daily life, leading them to experience greater intimacy owing to his self-disclosure.

Medications may improve attention and reduce impulsivity, allowing individuals to be better listeners. Additional counseling or coaching regarding appropriate social behaviors may be required for individuals who may not have developed them earlier due to the severity of their symptoms or due to social withdrawal.

SYSTEMIC COMPLICATIONS

Individuals with ADHD do not live in a vacuum. As much as we encourage self-awareness, acceptance, and restructuring environments to make them ADHD-friendly, there are many situations in which ADHD adults must adapt to the constraints of particular environments or systems of society. Dealing with the politics and rules of school or the workplace can be challenging for adults with ADHD and may have considerable effects on their lives insofar as these issues influence employment and quality of life for most individuals. The demands placed on executive functioning by college, graduate, or professional school education may create hardships for individuals with ADHD who are otherwise qualified for admission and capable of completing degree requirements, given some reasonable accommodations. For adults with ADHD in the work force, there are similar sorts of workplace accommodations that help reduce various barriers that might interfere with full expression of their productivity and creativity.

For example, college students with ADHD may be granted reasonable academic accommodations for their particular areas of disability. A student with distractibility and slow cognitive processing speed may have difficulties reading and comprehending questions on an exam that is administered during class time and thus be granted an extra 30 minutes to complete tests.

To our knowledge, there are no data guiding the recommendation of specific academic accommodations for ADHD. In fact, it could be that some accommodations, such as taking an exam alone in a quiet, distraction-free room, may end up making no difference or even being more distracting for some students with ADHD. Furthermore, deadline extensions and taking incompletes for courses that must be completed before final grades can be issued may be a form of avoidance, leaving many students saddled with the prospect of completing work from a previous semester while attempting to keep up with the workload of the current semester. Thus, while we wholeheartedly support the granting of academic accommodations (or housing accommodations; that is, single room without a roommate) for students with ADHD based on logical compensations for specific disabilities, the selection of specific accommodations must be individualized until there is more empirically based guidance.

Workplaces often have greater flexibility for granting accommodations because employers are invested in improving worker productivity and do not have to address concerns related to academic competition. A few of our patients working in professional settings have reported positive experiences associated with disclosing their ADHD diagnoses to their supervisors. These individuals were able to arrange for reasonable workplace modifications that resulted in improved work performance and job satisfaction.

The majority of workers with ADHD, however, may find if difficult to take steps to modify their work environments. One reason for this problem is that many workers with ADHD are unsure whether or not to share their diagnosis for fear that they would be penalized for disclosing or due to understandable concerns about personal privacy. In some cases, informal negotiations with a supervisor may yield a mutually agreeable accommodation without the need to disclose one's diagnosis. For example, a worker with ADHD who has difficulty getting to work by 9 a.m. and whose productivity is at its best in the late morning and in the afternoon may negotiate a later starting time and agree to stay later at the end of day. Such an experiment could be monitored for 3 months to determine whether, in fact, the employee's attendance and work efficiency improve. The situation would be no different than a worker requesting flexible hours in order to accommodate child care arrangements. If such adjustments can be viewed as win–win scenarios for both employer and employee, they are more likely to be instituted.

In rare cases we have been asked and granted expressed permission by patients to communicate with their supervisors regarding the effects of ADHD on the patients' work performance and to share the steps these workers have been taking to modify their behaviors. While we would not recommend this approach in all cases, our limited anecdotal experience has been that, similar to helping clarify ADHD-related behaviors for non-ADHD spouses, our consultations seem to have helped to correct misattributions by supervisors. The supervisors, to their immense credit, were willing to experiment with suggested strategies and accommodations for helping their ADHD workers perform their job duties (for example, provide a follow-up e-mail summarizing the project, provide more frequent check-ins regarding progress).

In many cases, however, adults with ADHD, facing limited employment options due to frequent job changes, lack of training or educational attainment, or other factors, may be in jobs with little flexibility in terms of seeking accommodations, such as working as a server in a restaurant, as a retail sales clerk, or in entry-level positions. In such cases, the burden for adaptation may fall on the shoulders of workers with ADHD. These work-related coping issues can be addressed in CBT or by working with an ADHD coach versed in workplace issues.

There are many other systems and bureaucracies with which adults with ADHD may become involved, such as the Internal Revenue Service (IRS), institutions that administer standardized tests required for admission to various colleges, graduate and professional programs, or, in unfortunate cases, the legal system (Hurley & Eme, 2004). In general, we encourage individuals to understand their particular ADHD symptom profiles in order to better manage and take responsibility for their behavior. However, in many cases, with appropriate clinical assessment evidence and documentation of ADHD, the pursuit of reasonable accommodations is indicated, though the response of the system or agency may be uncertain.

Mental health professionals must determine on a case-by-case basis, in collaboration with their patients, the reckoning of whether or not to disclose the diagnosis when dealing with various organizations, such as the request of a letter as part of an appeal regarding IRS penalties for tardy filing of income taxes as a consequence of poor time management and disorganization. Clinicians must be mindful of issues related to secondary gain and, in rare cases, malingering, particularly when individuals present for assessment of ADHD as a means for securing special assistance without considering comprehensive treatment support.

SUMMARY

There are many issues associated with the core symptoms of adult ADHD that create complications for patients and clinicians. There are additional complexities that may arise in the course of assessment and ongoing treatment that add degrees of difficulty for patients and clinicians alike. We have described some of the complicating factors we have observed in our clinical work in order to help helping professionals identify them and to address them within the case conceptualization for each patient. By doing so, our experience is that these factors can most often be addressed collaboratively and effectively by patients and their clinicians to get the most out of treatment. Hopefully, the focus of CBT switches to the issue of maintaining treatment gains, which is the topic of the next chapter.

CHAPTER 6

Maintenance and Follow-Up

There is no cure for attention-deficit/hyperactivity disorder (ADHD). It is a developmental syndrome requiring ongoing coping and maintenance in order to manage the effects of executive dysfunction, mood dysregulation, and behavioral disinhibition. Consequently, the conceptualization and treatment of ADHD (and other developmental disorders) can be thought of as operating from a habilitation model in which the goal is to adapt to and optimize one's particular style of functioning by making desired coping behaviors automatic and routine (compare Solanto et al., in press). This approach is different from a rehabilitation model in which the goal is to restore a previous level of emotional functioning, which is used with most psychiatric disorders, such as depression or anxiety.

For example, treatment for depression ends when there is remission of depressed mood. Due to the pervasive and chronic nature of developmental disorders, however, it is difficult to draw the line defining when treatment is finished. Even when patients reach a point at which their ADHD symptoms are considered to be effectively managed, ongoing maintenance of gains is an active process. As Shakespeare wrote, "What wound did ever heal but by degrees?" (*Othello*, Act II, Scene iii).

Both cognitive behavioral therapy (CBT) and pharmacotherapy progress through different phases as patients make therapeutic progress and learn to independently manage their symptoms and take control of their lives.

CBT for adult ADHD is designed to start with regular and relatively frequent meetings in order to identify and address specific functional problems and to understand the interplay of ADHD and comorbid symptoms. As patients grow more confident with the use of new coping strategies and their improved functioning, later sessions are scheduled at longer intervals, such as every second or third week. The ultimate objective is to switch to periodic booster sessions and, eventually, move toward termination of meetings. As was stated earlier, the goal of CBT is for the individual to be her or his own therapist.

The early phase of pharmacotherapy for adult ADHD involves developing a medication regimen that targets problematic symptoms related to executive dysfunction and comorbid conditions. Depending upon patients' individual responses to medications, subsequent follow-up appointments focus on monitoring the response to medications. Initial follow-up pharmacotherapy appointments help establish the correct therapeutic dose or, in some cases, the need to change medications if the initial agents do not provide adequate symptom improvement or produce intolerable side effects. When a stable and effective dose of medication(s) has been achieved, meetings with the prescribing physician are scheduled at longer intervals, allowing for sufficient follow-up monitoring of treatment response. In optimal circumstances, follow-up consultations involve brief assessments to confirm ongoing effectiveness of the medications and the absence of side effects and to renew a prescription. In some cases, the use of particular medications or the medical history of certain patients warrants additional medical examinations or lab tests to monitor the effects of medications on cardiac health, liver functioning, or other specific aspects of general health.

Treatment does not always unfold and end so smoothly, however. Individuals with ADHD may return to CBT in order to address new problems in their lives that they feel unable to handle. Similarly, some adults with ADHD may eventually stop taking their medications and cease meeting with their psychiatrists, only to later find themselves struggling with recurrent symptoms. The purpose of this chapter is to discuss how to decide when to stop treatment for adult ADHD and how to prepare to maintain treatment gains after the discontinuation of regular clinical appointments. More specifically, we will discuss how these issues are addressed differently in CBT and pharmacotherapy, as the decision to stop each treatment is a distinct one that must be made on its own merits.

MAINTENANCE AND FOLLOW-UP: CBT

One of the benefits of CBT that consistently emerges in research on its use in the treatment of various psychiatric disorders is the maintenance of treatment gains after the completion of treatment. CBT usually fares well when compared with medications for depression, with some studies finding slight benefits for CBT and other studies showing medications with a slight advantage, leading to the suggestion that a combination of CBT and medications is often most effective (DeRubeis et al., 2005; Gloaguen et al., 1998).

An important feature of these studies, however, is that individuals who had been taking medications often report a recurrence of symptoms once they stop active treatment. That is, once the pharmacologic agent, such as an antidepressant medication, is no longer in their system, individuals risk a relapse of symptoms. Individuals completing a course of CBT, on the other hand, are less likely to experience such backslides, presumably because CBT involves increasing an awareness of individuals' cognitive, behavioral, and emotional patterns and developing specific strategies for handling them (Fava et al., 2004; Gloaguen et al., 1998; Hollon et al., 2005; Ludgate, 1995). This makes intuitive sense because the active ingredient in medication management is the pharmacologic agent; the active ingredient in CBT is the ability to recognize and modify automatic cognitive and behavioral patterns (Ramsay, in press).

Research of treatments for depression indicates that CBT and pharmacotherapy each make a significant and distinct contribution to recovery (Goldapple et al., 2004). Similarly, both CBT and pharmacotherapy are important treatment options to consider in the management of adult ADHD. It is also important to consider the role of each of these treatments in the ongoing, long-range coping plan for each individual.

As was mentioned above, there is no definitive time frame for when CBT for adult ADHD should end apart from a consensus arrived at by therapist and patient that treatment objectives have been reasonably achieved. Studies of psychosocial treatments for adult ADHD thus far have varied in the duration of treatments employed. The length of therapy considered to represent an adequate dose ranges from 4 sessions (Wiggins et al., 1999) to 16 sessions over about 6 months (Rostain & Ramsay, 2006c). Additionally, a retrospective chart review study of CBT and medications revealed a wider range of number of sessions attended (10 to 103 sessions, with an average length of therapy of 36 sessions) and great variability in length of calendar time spent in therapy (3 to 30 months, with an average length of treatment of 12 months) (Wilens et al., 1999).

In general clinical practice of CBT for adult ADHD, treatment progress is assessed through the collaborative observations of the patient and therapist regarding specific targeted behaviors and outcome measures. Measures of mood, anxiety, and ADHD symptoms are also used to provide additional objective clinical data about treatment response. The implementation of new coping skills, such as the use of an organizational aid or DTR to monitor thoughts, or desired behavior changes, such as decreasing frequency and duration of procrastination or increasing time spent planning and prioritizing activities, are concrete examples of change. In cognitive terms, increased recognition of the activation of automatic thoughts and belief systems and considering alternative interpretations also represent positive therapeutic changes. Similar examples of changes related to comorbid problems, such as improved mood or decreased subjective feelings of anxiety, are also markers of progress. These cognitive and behavioral changes can be further documented with follow-up objective measures of ADHD symptoms or measures of mood and anxiety. As with the initial evaluation, it can be invaluable to gather corroborative observations of a patient's functioning, such as inviting a spouse to attend a session. In some cases, we have found that ADHD adults underestimate the improvements they have made in their lives.

Therapists must be mindful of flights into health or patients professing to be doing well in the face of strong evidence to contrary, such as in the case of ongoing problematic substance abuse. In such cases, there may be ambivalence about treatment or secondary gains that need to be addressed. However, in most cases, progress in the form of specific cognitive and behavioral changes are apparent to both therapist and patient. After a reasonable period of sustained improved functioning, and in the absence of new treatment issues to be addressed, attention turns to preparing to end CBT.

Ending CBT

Just as there is little research on psychosocial treatments for adult ADHD, there is even less evidence on the maintenance of clinical improvements after the end of active psychosocial treatment. Researchers who have performed follow-up assessments of participants who had completed psychosocial treatments for adult ADHD have found mixed results, with some improvements gained during treatment being maintained (for example, organization, ADHD symptoms) and others not maintained (for example, anger, self-esteem; Stevenson et al., 2002, 2003).

In terms of striving to maintain treatment gains, a stated objective of CBT is to help individuals to become their own therapists. That is, with heightened insight, self-awareness, and use of coping strategies, individuals are able to recognize and assess their problematic tendencies in order to figure out ways to handle them. Even should change prove difficult, as it often does, such a framework provides a means for making sense of and managing situations rather than reflexively feeling powerless to cope.

In the course of CBT, individuals are encouraged to progressively assume more control of therapy sessions and to set the lead in the problem-management process. The therapist remains as an active collaborator but patients draw on their past experiences and their ability to conceptualization situations to determine a course of action. An important step in this process, particularly for adults with ADHD, is to normalize the occurrence of problems and mistakes.

The relapse rate for ADHD is 100%, meaning that it is certain that ADHD adults, even with a textbook combination of appropriate medications and CBT, will encounter problems resulting from inefficient memory, distraction, impulsivity, disorganization, procrastination, or forgetting to use effective coping skills. Rather than viewing such unavoidable slipups in all-or-nothing terms (for example, "I guess I'm still at square one"), CBT encourages the use of a problem-management approach (for example, "What factors contributed to this situation? What can I do to handle it and to minimize its occurrence?"). Such an approach is appealing because it defines problems in behavioral terms rather than characterological terms, as it is easier to change behaviors than character traits.

Although many extratherapeutic factors may contribute to an abrupt end to CBT, such as a change in insurance coverage, a change in a shift at work that interferes with an appointment time, or simply drifting out of therapy, ideally there is an opportunity to wind down sessions and to complete therapy with the final few meetings devoted to termination and ongoing problem management.

During these sessions, the major take-home points from the course of treatment are reviewed. That is, the relevant schema and core beliefs that are highest risk for being activated are identified. The revised belief system and the experiences on which it is based that have been fostered throughout CBT are also reviewed and reinforced as a counterpoint to the old beliefs. Specific coping strategies that have proven to be useful and effective are highlighted. Examples of problematic situations that arose during treatment and how patients handled them provide a useful blueprint for anticipating future difficulties and potentially useful coping strategies to keep in mind. An important message for ADHD adults to take away from CBT is their documented ability to face problems head-on and to handle them effectively rather than avoiding them—a hallmark of the resilience it is hoped patients will develop with the help of CBT.

Despite these preparations, there are some specific strategies to increase the likelihood of maintaining treatment gains after formal CBT ends.

Problem Management and Decision-Making

CBT not only offers help with handling the problems that brought someone into therapy but also provides a framework that patients can use in order to understand and handle the recurrence of problems or new challenges that may happen after treatment ends. In terms of ADHD, many of the difficulties encountered by patients after completing CBT represent a lineup of the usual suspects: disorganization, procrastination, impulsivity, and so forth. Managing the core symptoms and problems associated with ADHD requires ongoing identification of their effects and use of effective coping strategies.

Of course, adult life is complex, and there are many domains of life that can become complicated. Decisions about getting married, changing a job or career, or having children may involve significant stress and concern about one's ability to cope. ADHD adults also may be sensitive to other changes (even positive ones) in their lives that create a sense of instability, such as getting a promotion, changing work locations, or changes in household routines. Such life events require the faithful use of problem management, decision-making skills, and the ability to adapt to changing circumstances. Such adjustments can be difficult for adults with ADHD, who often must work hard to establish a sense of regularity, predictability, and structure in their lives.

As in similar exercises conducted during CBT sessions, the problem management process involves identifying the problem or decision at hand, gathering information about possible options (including communicating with others involved in the decision), considering the benefits and costs of different options, making and executing a decision, and assessing the outcome. We remind individuals that not all problems necessarily have easy solutions, but there are probably ways to at least contend with issues directly to adequately resolve them.

An important aspect of problem management for adults with ADHD is the ability to normalize problems and setbacks as an unavoidable fact of adult life. Such a cognitive reframe helps to challenge all-or-nothing thinking by reminding individuals that experiencing problems does not mean that they have failed but that such situations inevitably arise in life—ADHD or no ADHD—and that they present learning opportunities. Thus, we try to avoid using the term *relapse prevention* because such difficulties are neither evidence of relapse nor can they be prevented. Managing some complex problems, however, may require adults with ADHD to make some sort of change in their environment, which we discuss below.

Environmental Engineering

Making adjustments to one's environment to make it more ADHD-friendly or using an organizational aid are effective ways to continue to manage symptoms of ADHD. The ability to identify and remove distractions from the environment and to otherwise set up one's surroundings to support the maintenance of effective coping strategies reflects a desirable degree of self-awareness and problem management.

The fact that individuals with ADHD are sensitive to such environmental factors makes it important for patients to develop a sense of what works in terms of their particular styles and sensitivities. Adults with ADHD often report a long history of trying to do things the same way as others do, only to end up feeling frustrated when they are not effective. It is easy to slip back into such patterns after CBT ends and to experience a resurgence of negative automatic thoughts of unfairness (for example, "It's not fair that my roommate can do work while watching television and I can only do work in silence"). The use of cognitive modification strategies, such as recognizing distorted thoughts, helps to reverse-engineer problematic situations such that ADHD adults can hopefully recognize and modify the contribution of environmental distractions.

Self-Advocacy and Asking for Help

The aforementioned suggestions require ADHD adults to identify and develop ways to manage difficult situations that will likely arise after completion of CBT. It could be inferred that the bulk of the responsibility for handling such situations falls on the shoulders of the individuals themselves. In fact, though we fully acknowledge the significant and often negative effects that ADHD can have on many areas of patients' lives, we encourage individuals to assume responsibility for and to take charge of their lives and managing their behaviors. However, this approach includes developing the ability to identify and to pursue necessary services, supportive technology, and assistance from others. We view the ability to ask for help as an aspect of personal responsibility and effective problem management.

Self-advocacy is particularly relevant for individuals in academic or work settings. Being a student with ADHD may require seeking additional support from a professor or academic counselor or going through official channels to apply for reasonable academic accommodations. Students may be reticent to do so because their previous educational experiences have not prepared them for pursuing such interactions or because of thoughts along the lines of "I should be able to do this myself if I just work a little harder." However, when the source of one's difficulties is ADHD rather than lack of effort, such self-advocacy becomes very important.

ADHD adults in the workplace may face a more difficult situation. These individuals may be understandably reticent to share personal information with an employer when they are unsure of how it could be used. What is more, employers vary in their flexibility and willingness to be accommodating to different working styles. Although we hope that ongoing education about adult ADHD will increase employers' awareness of its negative impact on work productivity in traditional work settings and hopefully lead to greater flexibility in allowing workers to use their strengths, we appreciate that discussing a diagnosis of ADHD may not be an option for some workers. Even so, seeking assistance from an ADHD coach or engaging in problem-solving with a supervisor about a specific workplace situation may be alternative ways to handle commonly encountered problems.

Booster Sessions

If the aforementioned self-help strategies do not prove effective in resolving individuals' problems, seeking additional CBT sessions—*booster sessions*—to address a recurrence of difficulties or to figure out how to handle new situations is a feasible option. A single booster session may be sufficient for a patient to get a handle on a situation, such as getting a refresher on counteracting automatic thoughts and avoidant behaviors that might be fueling procrastination on a project at work. Sometimes several sessions may be required to address issues related to a recurrence of mood or anxiety symptoms or to discuss an important decision, such as whether or not to change jobs. Finally, some problems may warrant a resumption of regular sessions, such as handling marital problems, adjusting to a new job, or addressing worsening mood or anxiety symptoms.

As in previous sections, it should be pointed out that many of these issues are not ADHD issues per se. That is, most individuals face relationship or work problems and may resume counseling for them. However, considering the pervasive effects of ADHD on experience, we assume that chronic symptoms, even if well treated, may play a role in these difficulties. Thus, we consider them a continuation of ADHD treatment.

The important take-home point for ADHD adults is to anticipate and to normalize the occurrence of difficulties in life and to remember to utilize their coping repertoire to manage them. Ongoing problem management may involve rededication to the use of previously effective coping strategies or correcting the drift away from healthy habits and environmental modification. An important maintenance issue for many adults with ADHD is ongoing medication management, which we discuss in a separate section below.

MAINTENANCE AND FOLLOW-UP: PHARMACOTHERAPY

Just as individuals have beliefs about medications that affect their willingness to start a course of pharmacotherapy, it is important to assess beliefs about ongoing medication management, particularly after an extended period of stable, improved functioning. At the start of patients' pharmacotherapy, we frequently encounter the question, "How long will I need to take these medications?" When considering ongoing medication management the question becomes, "How much longer will I need to take these medications?"

The answer to this question is variable, and it depends on the goals and beliefs that patients have about medication treatment. If patients are unrealistically hoping for a medication to repair their faulty neurobiology, it is important to reinforce the notion that ADHD is hard-wired and that medications only meliorate the neural mechanisms that underlie the disorder. While CBT, environmental reengineering, new strategies for problem-management, and improved social support can all contribute to an improved quality of life for patients, the ADHD brain remains disordered to greater or lesser degrees. While this is very difficult for patients to accept on an emotional level, it is a basic truth about all neurodevelopmental disorders, and it needs to be acknowledged by patients in order for them to make appropriate decisions about taking medications on a long-term basis. Like other chronic disorders, this decision needs to be made on the basis of cost–benefit analysis. That is, what are the risks, hazards, and costs (financial, medical, and psychological) as well as the benefits of continuing versus discontinuing medication treatment? This is the basic set of questions that patients and clinicians must face over the long term.

To help patients answer this, we find it is useful to draw an analogy between ADHD and a medical disorder like hypertension. Even after following a healthy diet, losing weight, exercising regularly, and maintaining a positive mental attitude, many patients are still plagued by high blood pressure as a result of abnormal cardiovascular physiology. What are the hazards, risks, and costs versus the benefits of taking blood pressure medication versus not taking medication? This decision faces millions of Americans on a daily basis. It is well established that lowering blood pressure reduces the incidence of stroke, heart attacks, and premature deaths from the complications of hypertension, but it is also well recognized that most patients do not comply with their prescribed medical treatments. While it is clear that hypertension is different from ADHD, we find the analogy compelling because it emphasizes to patients that there are no clear-cut right or wrong answers.

Many individuals adopt an "If it's not broke, don't fix it" attitude and are satisfied with maintaining a stabilized and effective medication regimen. In other cases, we hear individuals who say "I'm ready to try things on my own" as they plan to discontinue their medications. While it is usually preferable for patients to continue pharmacotherapy, there is nothing wrong with deciding to discontinue medications periodically to observe what happens. This approach serves to reinforce for the patient that he or she is the ultimate decision-maker. It also enables the patient to conduct an empirical trial to determine if indeed the medication is contributing to his or her daily functioning. Whenever the decision is made to discontinue pharmacotherapy, it is best if the patient does so in a careful and well-thought-out way and in collaboration with the clinician. The medication(s) should be tapered or discontinued in a manner that minimizes potential side effects from discontinuation. The patient should observe his concentration, mood, and behavior prior to and immediately after stopping the medication, preferably by utilizing the medication log or some other standardized record of target symptoms. Finally, it is best to schedule a follow-up appointment in approximately one month to reassess how the patient is doing and how the cessation of medication has impacted on ADHD and comorbid symptoms.

College students in particular seem to struggle with issues related to ongoing use of prescribed medications, even when they acknowledge their benefits. In our experience, it is best to adopt a flexible clinical stance with respect to the ambivalence expressed by patients at this developmental stage. Young adults are particularly worried about how they can combine medications with alcohol, marijuana, and other recreational drug use. We point out that it is up to them to learn how to regulate the medication regimen to best suit their treatment goals, and we emphasize the value of moderation in all aspects of daily living. At times, there are concerns about long-term dependence on medication. The best response to these issues is to reinforce the notion that this is up to the patients to decide, and that the choices will become clearer as they enter the next phase of their lives after college.

SUMMARY

Managing the effects of ADHD is an ongoing proposition. It is a chronic neurodevelopmental syndrome that affects everyday functioning and, therefore, requires coping everyday. We frequently refer to the need for resilience throughout our combined treatment approach. That is, it is normal for individuals to experience difficulties and setbacks, both during treatment and after it ends. Effective coping for adult ADHD is not defined by the absence of problems but by having ways to understand them and to manage them. Our notion of an attitude of resilience that we wish for all our patients is captured by a quote attributed to an anonymous college student–athlete who reportedly said, "I'm going to graduate on time, no matter how long it takes me."

Informational Resources about Adult ADHD

Online Resources and Organizations Regarding Adult ADHD

- Attention Deficit Disorder Association (ADDA): www.add.org (Largest organization solely dedicated to ADHD issues faced by adults)
- Children and Adults with Attention Deficit Disorder (CHADD): www.chadd.org
- National Resource Center for ADHD: www.help4add.org (CHADD-sponsored Web site providing information about ADHD across the life span)
- ADDISS: www.addiss.co.uk (British organization providing information about ADHD across the life span)
- University of Pennsylvania's Adult ADHD Treatment and Research Program: www.med.upenn.edu/add/ (Drs. Ramsay and Rostain's Adult ADHD Clinic)

RECOMMENDED READINGS ABOUT ADULT ADHD: FOR CONSUMERS

Adler, L. A., & Florence, M. (2006). *Scattered minds: Hope and help for adults with attention deficit hyperactivity disorder.* New York: Putnam.

Hallowell, E. M., & Ratey, J. J. (1994). *Driven to distraction.* New York: Touchstone.

Kelly, K. M., & Ramundo, P. (1993). *You mean I'm not lazy, stupid, or crazy?* Cincinnati, OH: Tyrell and Jerem Press.

Murphy, K. R., & LeVert, S. (1995). *Out of the fog: Treatment options and coping strategies for adult attention deficit disorder.* New York: Hyperion.

Novotni, M., & Whiteman, T. A. (2003). *Adult AD/HD: A reader-friendly guide to identifying, understanding, and treating adult attention deficit/hyperactivity disorder* (Rev. ed.). New York: Pinion.

Ratey, J. J. (2001). *A user's guided to the brain: Perception, attention, and the four theaters of the brain.* New York: Vintage.

Safren, S. A., Sprich, S., Perlman, C. A., & Otto, M. W. (2005). *Mastering your adult ADHD—Client workbook.* Oxford: Oxford University Press.

RECOMMENDED READINGS ABOUT ADULT ADHD: FOR CLINICIANS

Barkley, R. A. (1997). *ADHD and the nature of self-control.* New York: Guilford.

Barkley, R. A. (Ed.). (2006). *Attention-deficit hyperactivity disorder: A handbook for diagnosis and treatment* (3rd ed.). New York: Guilford.

Brown, T. E. (Ed.). (2000). *Attention deficit disorders and comorbidities in children, adolescents, and adults.* Washington, DC: American Psychiatric Press.

Brown, T. E. (2005). *Attention deficit disorder: The unfocused mind in children and adults.* New Haven, CT: Yale University Press.

Goldstein, S., & Ellison, A. T. (Eds.). (2002). *Clinician's guide to adult ADHD: Assessment and intervention.* San Diego: Academic Press.

Nadeau, K. G. (Ed.). (1995). *A comprehensive guide to attention deficit disorder in adults: Research, diagnosis, and treatment.* New York: Brunner/Mazel.

Nigg, J. T. (2006). *What causes ADHD?: Understanding what goes wrong and why.* New York: Guilford.

Pliszka, S. (2003). *Neuroscience for the mental health clinician.* New York: Guilford.

Resnick, R. J. (2000). *ADHD: The hidden disorder.* Washington, D.C.: American Psychological Association.

Safren, S. A., Perlman, C. A., Sprich, S., & Otto, M. W. (2005). *Mastering your adult ADHD—Therapist manual.* Oxford: Oxford University Press.

Solanto, M. V., Arnsten, A. F. T., & Castellanos, F. X. (Eds.) (2001). *Stimulant drugs and ADHD: Basic and clinical neuroscience.* New York: Oxford University Press.

Weiss, G., & Hechtman, L. T. (1993). *Hyperactive children grown up* (2nd ed.). New York: Guilford.

Weiss, M., Hechtman, L. T., & Weiss, G. (1999). *ADHD in adulthood: A guide to current theory, diagnosis, and treatment.* Baltimore: Johns Hopkins University Press.

Wender, P. H. (1995). *Attention-deficit hyperactivity disorder in adults.* New York: Oxford University Press.

Wender, P. H. (2000). *ADHD: Attention-deficit hyperactivity disorder in children, adolescents, and adults.* New York: Oxford University Press.

Outline of a Typical CBT Session for Adult ADHD

- Check-in: Symptom check (e.g., ADHD, mood, medication issues)

- Agenda setting: Includes review of therapeutic homework and other session issues

- Review homework task: Address any difficulties

- Agenda items: Specific issues to be addressed in session

- Summary and homework task: Wrap-up and develop personal experiment

Outline of a 20-Session Course of CBT for Adult ADHD

SESSION 1: GETTING STARTED

- Develop and define treatment objectives (start small).
- Elicit highly specific examples of problem areas (e.g., thoughts, feelings, behaviors).
- Address readiness for change and motivational issues.
- Develop initial homework task (anticipate potential problems).

SESSION 2: GETTING STARTED (CONTINUED)

- Review initial homework task and assess outcome, handle initial difficulties.
- Prioritize other agenda items and treatment goals (including motivational issues).
- Summary and homework.

SESSIONS 3 THROUGH 6: EARLY PHASE

- Develop initial case conceptualization from review of homework and agenda items.
- Focus on relevant skill-based interventions for ADHD-related difficulties.
- Address relevant interaction of comorbid problems and ADHD.

SESSIONS 7 THROUGH 15: MIDDLE PHASE

- Ongoing focus on coping skills and handling initial setbacks.
- Address comorbidities.
- Use case conceptualization to target relevant beliefs and compensatory strategies.
- Start to increase interval between sessions.

SESSIONS 16 THROUGH 20: FINAL PHASE

- Support trust in patient's new abilities.
- Normalize setbacks and adopt problem-solving attitude (e.g., relapse prevention).
- Generalize treatment gains.
- Review revised beliefs.
- Assess overall functioning.
- Develop long-term coping plan.
- Booster sessions (as needed).
- Address coping skill drift.
- Understand new life issues in terms of impact of ADHD (e.g., new job, parenting, etc.).
- Focus on lingering compensatory strategies.
- Revise schema.
- Continue focus on doing what works.

Typical Medications Prescribed to Treat Adult ADHD

TABLE D.1   Stimulants Used in the Treatment of Adult ADHD

Generic class (brand name)	Daily dosage schedule	Typical dosing schedule
Methylphenidate		
Short-acting (Ritalin, Metadate, Ritadex)	Two to four times	10–40 mg bid to qid
Intermediate-acting (Ritalin SR, Metadate SR)	Once or twice	20–60 mg qid to bid
Extended release (Concerta, Ritalin LA, Metadate CD)	Once or twice	18–108 mg qid (Concerta) 20–40 mg bid (Ritalin LA, Metadate CD)
Transdermal patch (Daytrana)	Apply patch for 9 hr	10–40 mg
Dextromethylpheniate		
Short-acting (Focalin)	Two to four times	5–20 mg bid to qid
Long-acting (Focalin XR)	Once or twice	10–20 mg qid or bid
Dextroamphetamine		
Short-acting (Dexedrine)	Twice or three times	10–30 mg bid or tid
Intermediate-acting (Dexedrine spansules)	Once or twice	10–30 mg bid
Mixed salts of amphetamine		
Intermediate-acting (Adderall)	Once or twice	10–30 mg bid or tid
Extended-release (ADDerall XR)	Once or twice	10–40 mg qid or bid

TABLE D.2   Nonstimulants Used in the Treatment of Adult ADHD

Generic name/class (brand name)	Daily dosage schedule	Typical dosing schedule
Atomoxetine (Strattera)	Once or twice daily	60–100 mg daily
Bupropion (Wellbutrin regular, SR, XL)	Once or twice daily for regular; twice daily for SR; once daily for XL	100–450 mg daily
Tricyclic antidepressants		
Desipramine (Norpramin)	Once at bedtime	100–200 mg daily
Nortriptyline (Pamelor)	Once at bedtime	50–150 mg daily
Alpha-2 adrenergic agonists		
Clonidine (Catapres)	Two or three times daily	0.1 mg bid or tid
Guanfacine (Tenex)	Once or twice daily	1 mg qid or bid
Modafanil (Provigil)	Once or twice daily	100–400 mg qid or bid

References

Acosta, M. T., Arcos-Burgos, M., & Muenke, M. (2004). Attention deficit/hyperactivity disorder (ADHD): Complex phenotype, simple genotype? *Genetics in Medicine, 6,* 1–15.

Adler, L. A., & Chua, H. C. (2002). Management of ADHD in adults. *Journal of Clinical Psychiatry, 63*(Suppl. 12), 29–35.

Adler, L. A., Reingold, L. S., Morrill, M.S., & Wilens, T. E. (2006). Combination pharmacotherapy for adult ADHD. *Current Psychiatry Reports, 8,* 409–415.

Allsopp, D. H., Minskoff, E. H., & Bolt, L. (2005). Individualized course-specific strategy instruction for college students with learning disabilities and ADHD: Lessons learned from a model demonstration program. *Learning Disabilities Research & Practice, 20,* 103–118.

Alpert, J. E., Maddocks, A., Nierenberg, A. A., O'Sullivan, R., Pava, J. A., Worthington III, J. J., et al. (1996). Attention deficit hyperactivity disorder in childhood among adults with major depression. *Psychiatry Research, 62,* 213–219.

American Academy of Child and Adolescent Psychiatry. (1997). Practice parameters for the assessment and treatment of children, adolescents, and adults with attention-deficit/hyperactivity disorder. *Journal of the American Academy of Child and Adolescent Psychiatry, 36*(Suppl. 10), 85S–121S.

American Academy of Child and Adolescent Psychiatry. (2002). Practice parameters for the use of stimulant medications in the treatment of children, adolescents, and adults. *Journal of the American Academy of Child and Adolescent Psychiatry, 41*(Suppl. 2), 26S–49S.

American Psychiatric Association. (1980). *Diagnostic and statistical manual of mental disorders* (3rd ed.). Washington, DC: Author.

American Psychiatric Association. (1987). *Diagnostic and statistical manual of mental disorders* (3rd ed., rev.). Washington, DC: Author.

American Psychiatric Association. (1994). *Diagnostic and statistical manual of mental disorders* (4th ed.). Washington, DC: Author.

American Psychiatric Association. (2000). *Diagnostic and statistical manual of mental disorders* (4th ed., text rev.). Washington, DC: Author.

Angold, A., Costello, E. J., & Erkanli, A. (1999). Comorbidity. *Journal of Child and Adolescent Psychiatry, 40,* 57–87.

Arnsten, A. F. T., & Li, B. M. (2005). Neurobiology of executive functions: Catecholamine influences on prefrontal cortical functions. *Biological Psychiatry, 57,* 1377–1384.

Attention Deficit Disorder Association. (2006). *Guiding principles for the diagnosis and treatment of attention deficit/hyperactivity disorder.* Pottstown, PA: Author.

Aviram, R. B., Rhum, M., & Levin, F. R. (2001). Psychotherapy of adults with comorbid attention-deficit/hyperactivity disorder and psychoactive substance use disorder. *Journal of Psychotherapy Practice and Research, 10,* 179–186.

Barkley, R. A. (1997a). *ADHD and the nature of self-control.* New York: Guilford.

Barkley, R. A. (1997b). Behavioral inhibition, sustained attention, and executive functions: Constructing a unifying theory of ADHD. *Psychological Bulletin, 121,* 65–94.

Barkley, R. A. (2001). The executive functions and self-regulation: An evolutionary neuropsychological perspective. *Neuropsychology Review, 11,* 1–29.

Barkley, R. A. (2002). Major life activity and health outcomes associated with attention-deficit/hyperactivity disorder. *Journal of Clinical Psychiatry, 63*(Suppl. 12), 10–15.

Barkley, R. A. (Ed.). (2006a). *Attention-deficit hyperactivity disorder: A handbook for diagnosis and treatment* (3rd ed.). New York: Guilford.

Barkley, R. A. (2006b). Driving risks in adults with ADHD: Yet more evidence and a personal story. *The ADHD Report, 14*(5), 1–9.

Barkley, R. A., & Fischer, M. (2005). Suicidality in children with ADHD, grown up. *The ADHD Report, 13*(6), 1–6.

Barkley, R. A., Fischer, M., Smallish, L., & Fletcher, K. (2002). The persistence of attention-deficit/hyperactivity disorder into young adulthood as a function of reporting source and definition of disorder. *Journal of Abnormal Psychology, 111,* 279–289.

Barkley, R. A., Fischer, M., Smallish, L, & Fletcher, K. (2006). Young adult outcome of hyperactive children: Adaptive functioning in major life areas. *Journal of the American Academy of Child and Adolescent Psychiatry, 45,* 192–202.

Barkley, R. A., & Murphy, K. R. (2006a). *Attention-deficit hyperactivity disorder: A clinical workbook* (3rd ed.). New York: Guilford.

Barkley, R. A., & Murphy, K. R. (2006b). Identifying new symptoms for diagnosing ADHD in adulthood. *The ADHD Report, 14*(4), 7–11.

Barkley, R. A., Murphy, K. R., & Bush, T. (2001). Time perception and reproduction in young adults with attention deficit hyperactivity disorder. *Neuropsychology, 15,* 351–360.

Barkley, R. A., Murphy, K. R., Du Paul, G. J., & Bush, T. (2002). Driving in young adults with attention deficit hyperactivity disorder; Knowledge, performance, adverse outcomes, and the role of executive functioning. *Journal of the International Neuropsychological Society, 8,* 655–672.

Barkley, R. A., Murphy, K. R., & Kwasnik, D. (1996a). Motor vehicle driving competencies and risks in teens and young adults with attention deficit hyperactivity disorder. *Pediatrics, 98,* 1089–1095.

Barkley, R. A., Murphy, K. R., & Kwasnik, D. (1996b). Psychological adjustment and adaptive impairments in young adults with ADHD. *Journal of Attention Disorders, 1,* 41–54.

Beck, A. T. (1967). *Depression: Causes and treatments.* Philadelphia: University of Pennsylvania Press.

Beck, A. T. (1976). *Cognitive therapy and the emotional disorders.* New York: Meridian.

Beck, A. T. (2005). The current state of cognitive therapy: A 40-year retrospective. *Archives of General Psychiatry, 62,* 953–959.

Beck, A. T., Freeman, A., & Associates. (1990). *Cognitive therapy of personality disorders.* New York: Guilford.

Beck, A. T., Rush, A. J., Shaw, B. F., & Emery, G. (1979). *Cognitive therapy of depression.* New York: Guilford.

Beck, A. T., & Steer, R. A. (1987). *Manual for the revised Beck Depression Inventory.* San Antonio, TX: The Psychological Corporation.

Beck, A. T., & Steer, R. A. (1989). *Manual for the Beck Hopelessness scale.* San Antonio, TX: The Psychological Corporation.

Beck, A. T., & Steer, R. A. (1990). *Beck Anxiety Inventory manual.* San Antonio, TX: The Psychological Corporation.

Beck, A. T., Steer, R. A., & Brown, G. K. (1996). *Beck Depression Inventory—Second edition manual.* San Antonio, TX: The Psychological Corporation.

Beck, A. T., Wright, F. D., Newman, C. F., & Liese, B. S. (1993). *Cognitive therapy of substance abuse.* New York: Guilford.

Beck, J. S. (1995). *Cognitive therapy: Basics and beyond.* New York: Guilford.

Bemporad, J., & Zambenedetti, M. (1996). Psychotherapy of adults with attention-deficit disorder. *Journal of Psychotherapy Practice and Research, 5,* 228–237.

Bemporad, J. R. (2001). Aspects of psychotherapy with adults with attention deficit disorder. *Annals of the New York Academy of Sciences, 931,* 302–309.

Biederman, J. (1998). A 55-year-old man with attention-deficit/hyperactivity disorder. *Journal of the American Medical Association, 280,* 1086–1092.

Biederman, J. (2004). Impact of comorbidity in adults with attention-deficit/hyperactivity disorder. *Journal of Clinical Psychiatry, 65*(Suppl. 3), 3–7.

Biederman, J. (2005). Attention-deficit/hyperactivity disorder: A selective overview. *Biological Psychiatry, 57,* 1215–1220.

Biederman, J., & Faraone, S. V. (2004). Attention deficit hyperactivity disorder: A worldwide concern. *The Journal of Nervous and Mental Disease, 192,* 453–454.

Biederman, J., & Faraone, S. V. (2005, October). *Economic impact of adult ADHD.* Poster session presented at the 17th CHADD Annual International Conference, Dallas, TX.

Biederman, J., Faraone, S. V., Mick, E., Williamson, S., Wilens, T. E., Spencer, T. J., et al. (1999). Clinical correlates of ADHD in females: Findings from a large group of girls ascertained from pediatric and psychiatric referral sources. *Journal of the American Academy of Child and Adolescent Psychiatry, 38,* 966–975.

Biederman, J., Faraone, S. V., Spencer, T. J., Mick, E., Monuteaux, M. C., & Aleardi, M. (2006). Functional impairments in adults with self-reports of diagnosed ADHD: A controlled study of 1001 adults in the community. *Journal of Clinical Psychiatry, 67,* 524–540.

Biederman, J., Faraone, S. V., Spencer, T., Wilens, T., Norman, D., Lapey, K. A., et al. (1993). Patterns of comorbidity, cognitions, and psychosocial functioning in adults with attention deficit hyperactivity disorder. *American Journal of Psychiatry, 150,* 1792–1798.

Biederman, J., Kwon, A., Aleardi, M., Chouinard, V. A., Marino, T., Cole, H., et al. (2005). Absence of gender effects on attention deficit hyperactivity disorder: Findings in nonreferred subjects. *American Journal of Psychiatry, 162,* 1083–1089.

Biederman, J., Mick, E., & Faraone, S. V. (2000). Age-dependent decline of symptoms of attention deficit hyperactivity disorder: Impact of remission definition and symptom type. *American Journal of Psychiatry, 157,* 816–818.

Biederman, J., Mick, E., Faraone, S. V., Braaten, E., Doyle, A., Spencer, T., et al. (2002). Influence of gender on attention deficit hyperactivity disorder in children referred to a psychiatric clinic. *American Journal of Psychiatry, 159,* 36–42.

Biederman, J., Monteaux, M. C., Doyle, A. E., Seidman, L. J., Wilens, T. E., Ferrero, F., et al. (2004). Impact of executive function deficits and attention-deficit/hyperactivity disorder (ADHD) on academic outcomes in children. *Journal of Consulting and Clinical Psychology, 72,* 757–766.

Biederman, J., Wilens, T., Mick, E., Faraone, S. V., & Spencer, T. (1998). Does attention-deficit hyperactivity disorder impact the developmental course of drug and alcohol dependence? *Biological Psychiatry, 44,* 269–273.

Biederman, J., Wilens, T., Mick, E., Spencer, T., & Faraone, S. V. (1999). Pharmacotherapy of attention-deficit hyperactivity disorder reduces risk for substance abuse disorder. *Pediatrics, 104,* e20–e25.

Brown, T. E. (1996). *Brown Attention Deficit Disorder scales.* San Antonio, TX: The Psychological Corporation.

Brown, T. E. (2005). *Attention deficit disorder: The unfocused mind in children and adults.* New Haven, CT: Yale University Press.

Brown, T. E. (2006). Executive functions and attention deficit hyperactivity disorder: Implications of two conflicting views. *International Journal of Disability, Development and Education, 53,* 35–46.

Brown, T. E., Patterson, C., & Quinlan, D. M. (2003, October). *Cognitive strengths and impairments in 126 high-IQ patients with ADHD.* Poster session presented at the 15th CHADD Annual International Conference, Denver, CO.

Burns, D. D. (1980). *Feeling good.* New York: Signet.

Buschke, H. (1973). Selective reminding for analysis of memory and learning. *Journal of Verbal Learning and Verbal Behavior, 12,* 543–550.

Bush, G., Frazier, J. A., Rauch, S. L., Seidman, L. J., Whalen, P. J., Jenike, M. A., et al. (1999). Anterior cingulate cortex dysfunction in attention-deficit/hyperactivity disorder revealed by fMRI and the Counting Stroop. *Biological Psychiatry, 45,* 1542–1552.

Bush, G., Valera, E. M., & Seidman, L. J. (2005). Functional neuroimaging of attention-deficit/hyperactivity disorder: A review and suggested future directions. *Biological Psychiatry, 57,* 1273–1284.

Carlson, C. L., & Mann, M. (2002). Sluggish cognitive tempo predicts a different pattern of impairment in the attention deficit hyperactivity disorder, predominantly inattentive type. *Journal of Clinical Child and Adolescent Psychology, 31,* 123–129.

Castellanos, F. X., Giedd, J. N., Berquin, P. C., Walter, J. M., Sharp, W., Tran, T., et al. (2001). Quantitative brain magnetic resonance imaging in girls with attention-deficit/hyperactivity disorder. *Archives of General Psychiatry, 58,* 289–295.

Castellanos, F. X., Giedd, J. N., Eckburg, P., Marsh, W. L., Vaituzis, C., Kaysen, D., et al. (1994). Quantitative morphology of the caudate nucleus in attention deficit hyperactivity disorder. *American Journal of Psychiatry, 151,* 1791–1796.

Castellanos, F. X., Giedd, J. N., Marsh, W. L., Hamburger, S. D., Vaituzis, D. P., Dickstein, S. E., et al. (1996). Quantitative brain magnetic resonance imaging in attention-deficit hyperactivity disorder. *Archives of General Psychiatry, 53*, 607–616.

Cephalon, Inc. (2006). *Cephalon reports no benefit from Provigil in a study of adults with ADHD.* Retrieved November 30, 2006, from http://phx.corporate-ir.net/phoenix.zhtml?c=81709&p=irol-newsArticle&ID=18727&highlight=adhd.

Charman, T., Carroll, F., & Sturge, C. (2001). Theory of mind, executive function and social competence in boys with ADHD. *Emotional and Behavioural Difficulties, 6*, 31–49.

Cohen, J. (1992). A power primer. *Psychological Bulletin, 112*, 155–159.

Conners, C. K. (2004). *The Conners' Continuous Performance Test-II.* North Tonawanda, NY: Multi-Health Systems.

Conners, C. K., Erhardt, D., & Sparrow, E. (1999). *Conners' adult ADHD rating scales.* North Tonawanda, NY: Multi-Health Systems.

Conners, C. K., March, J. S., Frances, A., Wells, K. C., & Ross, R. (2001). Treatment of attention-deficit/hyperactivity disorder: Expert consensus guidelines. *Journal of Attention Disorders, 4*(Suppl. 1), S7–S128.

Coolidge, F. L., Thede, L. L., & Young, S. E. (2000). Heritability and the comorbidity of attention deficit hyperactivity disorder with behavioral disorders and executive function deficits: A preliminary investigation. *Developmental Neuropsychology, 17*, 273–287.

Denckla, M. B. (1991). Foreword. In B. F. Pennington (Ed.), *Diagnosing learning disorder: A neuropsychological framework* (pp. vii–x). New York: Guilford.

DeRubeis, R. J., Hollon, S. D., Amsterdam, J. D., Shelton, R. C., Young, P. R., Salomon, R. M., et al. (2005). Cognitive therapy vs medications in the treatment of moderate to severe depression. *Archives of General Psychiatry, 62*, 409–416.

Dodson, W. W. (2005). Pharmacotherapy of adult ADHD. *Journal of Clinical Psychology, 61*, 589–606.

DuPaul, G. J., Schaughency, E. A., Weyandt, L. L., Tripp, G., Kiesner, J., Ota, K., et al. (2001). Self-report of ADHD symptoms in university students: Cross-gender and cross-national prevalence. *Journal of Learning Disabilities, 34*, 370–379.

Faraone, S. V. (2005). The scientific foundation for understanding attention-deficit/hyperactivity disorder as a valid psychiatric disorder. *European Child and Adolescent Psychiatry, 14*, 1–10.

Faraone, S. V. (2006, May). ADHD "Not otherwise specified:" Conceptual issues. In T. Wilens (Chair), *Understanding and managing the transition of ADHD from adolescence to young adulthood: The maturation of the disorder.* Industry-supported symposium, 159th Annual Meeting of the American Psychiatric Association, Toronto, Canada.

Faraone, S. V., & Biederman, J. (2005, October). *Adolescent predictors of functional outcome in adult ADHD: A population survey.* Poster session presented at the 17th CHADD Annual International Conference, Dallas, TX.

Faraone, S. V., Biederman, J., Spencer, T., Wilens, T., Seidman, L. J., Mick, E., et al. (2000). Attention-deficit/hyperactivity disorder in adults: An overview. *Biological Psychiatry, 48,* 9–20.

Faraone, S. V., & Khan, S. A. (2006). Candidate gene studies of attention-deficit/hyperactivity disorder. *Journal of Clinical Psychiatry,* 67(Suppl. 8), 13–20.

Faraone, S. V., Perlis, R. H., Doyle, A. E., Smoller, J. E., Goralnick, J. J., Holmgren, M. A., et al. (2005). Molecular genetics of attention deficit hyperactivity disorder. *Biological Psychiatry, 57,* 1313–1323.

Faraone, S. V., Sergeant, J., Gillberg, C., & Biederman, J. (2003). The worldwide prevalence of ADHD: Is it an American condition? *World Psychiatry, 2,* 104–113.

Faraone, S. V., Tsuang, M. T., & Tsuang, D. W. (1999). *Genetics of mental disorders: A guide for students, clinicians, and researchers.* New York: Guilford.

Fava, G. A., Ruini, C., Rafanelli, C., Finos, L., Conti, S., & Grandi, S. (2004). Six-year outcome of cognitive behavior therapy for prevention of recurrent depression. *American Journal of Psychiatry, 161,* 1872–1876.

Ferrari, J. R., Johnson, J. L., & McCown, W. G. (Eds.). (1995). *Procrastination and task avoidance: Theory, research, and treatment.* New York: Plenum.

Filipek, P. A., Semrud-Clikeman, M., Steingard, R. J., Renshaw, P. F., Kennedy, D. N., & Biederman, J. (1997). Volumetric MRI analysis comparing subjects having attention-deficit hyperactivity disorder with normal controls. *Neurology, 48,* 589–601.

First, M. B., Spitzer, R. L., Gibbon, M., & Williams, J. B. W. (1997). *User's guide for the structured clinical interview for DSM-IV Axis I disorders.* Washington, DC: American Psychiatric Press.

Fischer, M., Barkley, R. A., Smallish, L., & Fletcher, K. (2002). Young adult follow-up of hyperactive children: Self-reported psychiatric disorders, comorbidity, and the role of childhood conduct problems and teen CD. *Journal of Abnormal Child Psychology, 30,* 463–475.

Freeman, A. (1993). A psychosocial approach for conceptualizing sche-matic development for cognitive therapy. In K. T. Kuehlwein & H. Rosen (Eds.), *Cognitive therapies in action: Evolving innovative practice* (pp. 54–87). San Francisco: Jossey-Bass.

Friedman, S. R., Rapport, L. J., Lumley, M., Tzelepis, A., VanVoorhis, A., Stettner, L., et al. (2003). Aspects of social and emotional com-petence in adult attention-deficit/hyperactivity disorder. *Neuropsy-chology, 17,* 50–58.

Gallagher, R., & Blader, J. (2001). The diagnosis and neuropsycho-logical assessment of adult attention deficit/hyperactivity disorder: Scientific study and practical guidelines. *Annals of the New York Academy of Sciences, 931,* 148–171.

Gaub, M., & Carlson, C. L. (1997). Gender differences in ADHD: A meta-analysis and critical review. *Journal of the American Acad-emy of Child & Adolescent Psychiatry, 36,* 1036–1045.

Gilger, J. W., Pennington, B. F., & DeFries, J. C. (1992). A twin study of the etiology of comorbidity: Attention-deficit hyperactivity disor-der and dyslexia. *Journal of the American Academy of Child and Adolescent Psychiatry, 31,* 343–348.

Gingerich, K. J., Turnock, P., Litfin, J. K., & Rosén, L. A. (1998). Diver-sity and attention deficit hyperactivity disorder. *Journal of Clinical Psychology, 54,* 415–426.

Glahn, D. C., Cannon, T. D., Gur, R. E., Ragland, J. D., & Gur, R. C. (2000). Working memory constrains abstraction in schizophrenia. *Biological Psychiatry, 47,* 34–42.

Gloaguen, V., Cottraux, J., Cucherat, M., & Blackburn, I. -M. (1998). A meta-analysis of the effects of cognitive therapy in depressed patients. *Journal of Affective Disorders, 49,* 59–72.

Goldapple, K., Segal, Z., Garson, C., Lau, M., Bieling, P., Kennedy, S., et al. (2004). Modulation of cortical-limbic pathways in major depression: Treatment-specific effects of cognitive behavior ther-apy. *Archives of General Psychiatry, 61,* 34–41.

Goldstein, S. (2005). Coaching as a treatment for ADHD. *Journal of Attention Disorders, 9,* 379–381.

Gollwitzer, P. M. (1999). Implementation intentions: Strong effects of simple plans. *American Psychologist, 54,* 493–503.

Gollwitzer, P. M., & Schaal, B. (1998). Metacognition in action: The importance of implementation intentions. *Personality and Social Psychology Review, 2,* 124–136.

Greene, R. W., Biederman, J., Faraone, S. V., Monuteaux, M. C., Mick, E., DuPre, E., et al. (2001). Social impairment in girls with ADHD: Patterns, gender comparisons, and correlates. *Journal of the Amer-ican Academy of Child and Adolescent Psychiatry, 40,* 704–710.

Greenhill, L. L., Abikoff, H. B., Arnold, L. E., & Cantwell, D. P. (1996). Medication treatment strategies in the MTA study: Relevance to clinicians and researchers. *Journal of the American Academy of Child & Adolescent Psychiatry, 35*, 1304–1313.

Gur, R. C., Ragland, J. D., Moberg, P. J., Bilker, W. B., Kohler, C., Siegel, S. J., et al. (2001). Computerized neurocognitive scanning: II. The profile of schizophrenia. *Neuropsychopharmacology, 25*, 777–788.

Hallowell, E. M. (1995). Psychotherapy of adult attention deficit disorder. In K. G. Nadeau (Ed.), *A comprehensive guide to attention deficit disorder in adults: Research, diagnosis, and treatment* (pp. 146–167). New York: Brunner/Mazel.

Hallowell, E. M., & Ratey, J. J. (1994). *Driven to distraction*. New York: Touchstone.

Hammen, C., & Zupan, B. A. (1984). Self-schemas, depression, and the processing of personal information in children. *Journal of Experimental Child Psychology, 37*, 598–608.

Hart, E. L., Lahey, B. B., Loeber, R., Applegate, B., & Frick, P. J. (1995). Developmental change in attention-deficit hyperactivity disorder in boys: A four-year longitudinal study. *Journal of Abnormal Child Psychology, 23*, 729–749.

Hartman, C. A., Willcutt, E. G., Rhee, S. H., & Pennington, B. F. (2004). The relation between sluggish cognitive tempo and DSM-IV ADHD. *Journal of Abnormal Child Psychology, 32*, 491–503.

Heiligenstein, E., Conyers, L. M., Berns, A. R., & Smith, M. A. (1998). Preliminary normative data on *DSM-IV* attention deficit hyperactivity disorder in college students. *Journal of American College Health, 46*, 185–188.

Hervey, A. S., Epstein, J. N., & Curry, J. F. (2004). Neuropsychology of adults with attention-deficit/hyperactivity disorder: A meta-analytic review. *Neuropsychology, 18*, 485–503.

Hesslinger, B., van Elst, L. T., Nyberg, E., Dykierek, P., Richter, H., Berner, M., et al. (2002). Psychotherapy of attention deficit hyperactivity disorder in adults: A pilot study using a structured skills training program. *European Archives of Psychiatry and Clinical Neuroscience, 252*, 177–184.

Hill, J. C., & Schoener, E. P. (1996). Age-dependent decline of attention deficit hyperactivity disorder. *American Journal of Psychiatry, 153*, 1143–1146.

Hinshaw, S. P. (2001). Is the inattentive type of ADHD a separate disorder? *Clinical Psychology: Science and Practice, 8*, 498–501.

Hollon, S. D., DeRubeis, R. J., Shelton, R. C., Amsterdam, J. D., Salomon, R. M., O'Reardon, J. P., et al. (2005). Prevention of relapse following cognitive therapy vs medications in moderate to severe depression. *Archives of General Psychiatry, 62,* 417–422.

Hornig-Rohan, M., & Amsterdam, J. D. (2002). Venlafaxine versus stimulant therapy in patients with dual diagnosis ADD and depression. *Progress in Neuro-psychopharmacology & Biological Psychiatry, 53,* 112–120.

Horvath, A. O. (2001). The alliance. *Psychotherapy: Theory, Research, Practice, Training, 38,* 365–372.

Hurley, P. J., & Eme, R. (2004). *ADHD and the criminal justice system: Spinning out of control.* Charleston, SC: Book Surge.

Hynd, G. W., Semrud-Clikeman, M., Lorys, A. R., Novey, E. S., & Eliopulos, D. (1990). Brain morphology in developmental dyslexia and attention deficit disorder/hyperactivity. *Archives of Neurology, 47,* 919–926.

James, A., Lai, F. H., & Dahl, C. (2004). Attention deficit hyperactivity disorder and suicide: A review of possible associations. *Acta Psychiatrica Scandinavica, 110,* 408–415.

Kessler, R. C., Adler, L. A., Ames, M., Barkley, R. A., Birnbaum, H., Greenberg, P., et al. (2005). The prevalence and effects of adult attention deficit/hyperactivity disorder on work performance in a nationally representative sample of workers. *Journal of Occupational and Environmental Medicine, 47,* 565–572.

Kessler, R. C., Adler, L. A., Barkley, R. A., Biederman, J., Conners, C. K., Demler, O., et al. (2006). The prevalence and correlates of adult ADHD in the United States: Results from the national comorbidity survey replication. *American Journal of Psychiatry, 163,* 716–723.

Kessler, R. C., Adler, L. A., Barkley, R. A., Biederman, J., Conners, C. K., Faraone, S. V., et al. (2005). Patterns and predictors of attention-deficit/hyperactivity disorder persistence into adulthood: Results from the national comorbidity survey replication. *Biological Psychiatry, 57,* 1442–1451.

Khantzian, E. J. (1985). The self-medication hypothesis of addictive disorders: Focus on heroin and cocaine dependence. *American Journal of Psychiatry, 142,* 1259–1264.

Klein, R., & Mannuzza, S. (1991). Long-term outcome of hyperactive children: A review. *Journal of the American Academy of Child and Adolescent Psychiatry, 30,* 383–387.

Kolberg, J., & Nadeau, K. (2002). *ADD-friendly ways to organize your life.* New York: Brunner-Routledge.

Krause, K. H., Dresel, S. H., Krause, J., la Fougere, C., & Ackenheil, M. (2003). The dopamine transporter and neuroimaging in attention deficit hyperactivity disorder. *Neuroscience and Behavioral Reviews, 27,* 605–613.

Krause, J., Krause, K. H., Dresel, S. H., la Fougere, C., & Ackenheil, M. (2006). ADHD in adolescence and adulthood, with a special focus on the dopamine transporter and nicotine. *Dialogues in Clinical Neuroscience, 8,* 29–36.

Lahey, B. B. (2001). Should the combined and predominantly inattentive subtypes of ADHD be considered distinct and unrelated disorders? Not now, at least. *Clinical Psychology: Science and Practice, 8,* 494–497.

Lambert, M. J., & Barley, D. E. (2001). Research summary on the therapeutic relationship and psychotherapy outcome. *Psychotherapy: Theory, Research, Practice, Training, 38,* 357–361.

Layden, M. A., Newman, C. F., Freeman, A., & Morse, S. B. (1993). *Cognitive therapy of borderline personality disorder.* Boston: Allyn & Bacon.

Levy, F., Hay, D. A., McStephen, M., Wood, C., & Waldman, I. (1997). Attention-deficit hyperactivity disorder: A category or a continuum? Genetic analysis of a large-scale twin study. *Journal of the American Academy of Child and Adolescent Psychiatry, 36,* 737–744.

Linehan, M. M. (1993). *Cognitive-behavioral treatment of borderline personality disorder.* New York: Guilford.

Ludgate, J. W. (1995). *Maximizing psychotherapeutic gains and preventing relapse in emotionally distressed clients.* Sarasota, FL: Professional Resource Press.

Mannuzza, S., & Klein, R. G. (1999). Adolescent and adult outcome in attention-deficit hyperactivity disorder. In H. C. Quay & A. E. Hogan (Eds.), *Handbook of disruptive behavior disorders* (pp. 279–294). New York: Kluwer.

Mannuzza, S., Klein, R. G., Bessler, A., Malloy, P., & LaPadula, M. (1993). Adult outcome of hyperactive boys: Educational achievement, occupational rank, and psychiatric status. *Archives of General Psychiatry, 50,* 565–576.

Mannuzza, S., Klein, R. G., Bessler, A., Malloy, P., & LaPadula, M. (1998). Adult psychiatric status of hyperactive boys grown up. *American Journal of Psychiatry, 155,* 493–498.

McDermott, S. P. (2000) Cognitive therapy for adults with attention-deficit/hyperactivity disorder. In T. E. Brown (Ed.), *Attention deficit disorders and comorbidities in children, adolescents, and adults* (pp. 569–606). Washington, DC: American Psychiatric Press.

McGough, J. J., & Barkley, R. A. (2004). Diagnostic controversies in adult attention deficit hyperactivity disorder. *American Journal of Psychiatry, 161,* 1948–1956.

McGough, J. J., Smalley, S. L., McCracken, J. T., Yang, M., Del'Homme, M., Lynn, D. E., et al. (2005). Psychiatric comorbidity in adult attention deficit hyperactivity disorder: Findings from multiplex families. *American Journal of Psychiatry, 162,* 1621–1627.

McGuffin, P., Riley, B., & Plomin, R. (2001, February 16). Toward behavioral genomics. *Science, 291,* 1232–1233.

Michelson, D., Adler, L., & Spencer, T. (2003). Atomoxetine in adults: Two randomized, placebo-controlled studies. *Biological Psychiatry, 58,* 125–131.

Mick, E., Faraone, S. V., & Biederman, J. (2004). Age-dependent expression of attention-deficit/hyperactivity disorder symptoms. *Psychiatric Clinics of North America, 27,* 215–224.

Milich, R., Balentine, A., & Lynam, D. (2001). ADHD combined type and ADHD predominantly inattentive type are distinct and unrelated disorders. *Clinical Psychology: Science and Practice, 8,* 463–488.

Miller, W. R., & Rollnick, S. (1991). *Motivational interviewing: Preparing people to change addictive behavior.* New York: Guilford.

Millstein, R. B., Wilens, T. E., Biederman, J., & Spencer, T. J. (1997). Presenting ADHD symptoms and subtypes in clinically referred adults with ADHD. *Journal of Attention Disorders, 2,* 159–166.

Mostofsky, S. H., Reiss, A. L., Lockhart, P., & Denckla, M. B. (1998). Evaluation of cerebellar size in attention-deficit hyperactivity disorder. *Journal of Child Neurology, 13,* 434–439.

Murphy, K. R. (2005). Psychosocial treatments for ADHD in teens and adults: A practice-friendly review. *Journal of Clinical Psychology: In Session, 61,* 607–619.

Murphy, K. R., & Barkley, R. A. (1996a). Attention deficit hyperactivity disorder adults: Comorbidities and adaptive impairments. *Comprehensive Psychiatry, 37,* 393–401.

Murphy, K. R., & Barkley, R. A. (1996b). Prevalence of DSM-IV symptoms of ADHD in adult licensed drivers: Implications for clinical diagnosis. *Journal of Attention Disorders, 1,* 147–161.

Murphy, K. R., & Gordon, M. (2006). Assessment of adults with ADHD. In R. A. Barkley (Ed.), *Attention-deficit hyperactivity disorder: A handbook for diagnosis and treatment* (3rd ed., pp. 425–450). New York: Guilford.

Murphy, K. R., & LeVert, S. (1995). *Out of the fog: Treatment options and coping strategies for adult attention deficit disorder.* New York: Hyperion.

Newman, C. F., Leahy, R. L., Beck, A. T., Reilly-Harrington, N. A., & Gyulai, L. (2002). *Bipolar disorder: A cognitive therapy approach.* Washington, DC: American Psychological Association.

Nierenberg, A. A., Miyahara, S., Spencer, T., Wisniewski, S. R., Otto, M. W., Simon, N., et al. (2005). Clinical and diagnostic implications of lifetime attention-deficit/hyperactivity disorder comorbidity in adults with bipolar disorder: Data from the first 1000 STEP-BD participants. *Biological Psychiatry, 57,* 1467–1473.

Nigg, J. T. (2006). *What causes ADHD?: Understanding what goes wrong and why.* New York: Guilford.

Paulson, J. R., Buermeyer, C., & Nelson-Gray, R. O. (2005). Social rejection and ADHD in young adults: An analogue experiment. *Journal of Attention Disorders, 8,* 127–135.

Persons, J. B. (1989). *Cognitive therapy in practice: A case formulation approach.* New York: Norton.

Persons, J. B. (2006). Case formulation-driven psychotherapy. *Clinical Psychology: Science and Practice, 13,* 167–170.

Pinker, S. (1997). *How the mind works.* New York: Norton.

Pliszka, S. R. (2002). Neuroimaging and ADHD: Recent progress. *The ADHD Report, 10*(3), 1–6.

Pliszka, S. R. (2003). *Neuroscience for the mental health clinician.* New York: Guilford.

Pliszka, S. R. (2005). Recent developments in the neuroimaging of ADHD. *The ADHD Report, 13*(2), 1–5.

Pomerleau, O. F., Downey, K. K., Stelson, F. W., & Pomerleau, C. S. (1995). Cigarette smoking in adult patients diagnosed with attention deficit hyperactivity disorder. *Journal of Substance Abuse, 7,* 373–378.

Prochaska, J. O., DiClemente, C. C., & Norcross, J. C. (1992). In search of how people change: Applications to addictive behaviors. *American Psychologist, 47,* 1102–1114.

Prochaska, J. O., & Norcross, J. C. (2001). Stages of change. *Psychotherapy, 38,* 443–448.

Ramsay, J. R. (2002). A cognitive therapy approach for treating chronic procrastination and avoidance: Behavioral activation interventions. *Journal of Group Psychotherapy, Psychodrama, & Sociometry, 55,* 79–92.

Ramsay, J. R. (2005a). Cognitive behavioral therapy: The invisible ropes of adult ADHD. *Focus Magazine,* Spring 12.

Ramsay, J. R. (2005b). Managing time and getting organized—Again! *Focus Magazine,* Winter, 4–5.

Ramsay, J. R. (2005c). Masks of adult ADHD. *Focus Magazine,* Summer, 10–11.

Ramsay, J. R. (in press). Current status of cognitive behavioral therapy as a psychosocial treatment for adult attention-deficit/hyperactivity disorder. *Current Psychiatry Reports.*

Ramsay, J. R., & Rostain, A. L. (2003). A cognitive therapy approach for adult attention-deficit/hyperactivity disorder. *Journal of Cognitive Psychotherapy: An International Quarterly, 17,* 319–334.

Ramsay, J. R., & Rostain, A. L. (2004). Cognitive therapy: A psychosocial treatment for ADHD in adults. *The ADHD Report, 12*(1), 1–5.

Ramsay, J. R., & Rostain, A. L. (2005a). Adapting psychotherapy to meet the needs of adults with attention-deficit/hyperactivity disorder. *Psychotherapy: Theory, Research, Practice, Training, 42,* 72–84.

Ramsay, J. R., & Rostain, A. L. (2005b). CBT for adult ADHD. In A. Freeman (Ed.), *Encyclopedia of cognitive behavior therapy* (pp. 52–54). New York: Springer.

Ramsay, J. R., & Rostain, A. L. (2005c). Cognitive therapy for adult ADHD. In L. Vandecreek (Ed.), *Innovations in clinical practice* (pp. 53–63). Sarasota, FL: Professional Resource Press.

Ramsay, J. R., & Rostain, A. L. (2005d). Girl, repeatedly interrupted: The case of a young adult woman with ADHD. *Clinical Case Studies, 4,* 329–346.

Ramsay, J. R., & Rostain, A. L. (2006a). Issues in ADHD in adults. *The ADHD Report, 14*(6), 5–8.

Ramsay, J. R., & Rostain, A. L. (2006b). Cognitive behavior therapy for college students with attention-deficit/hyperactivity disorder. *Journal of College Student Psychotherapy, 21*(1), 3–20.

Ramsay, J. R., & Rostain, A. L. (in press). Psychosocial treatments for attention-deficit/hyperactivity disorder in adults: Current evidence and future directions. *Professional Psychology: Research and Practice.*

Rasmussen, P., & Gillberg, C. (2000). Natural outcome of ADHD with developmental coordination disorder at age 22 years: A controlled, longitudinal, community-based sample. *Journal of the American Academy of Child and Adolescent Psychiatry, 39,* 1424–1431.

Ratey, J. J., Greenberg, M. S., Bemporad, J. R., & Lindem, K. J. (1992). Unrecognized attention-deficit hyperactivity disorder in adults presenting for outpatient psychotherapy. *Journal of Child and Adolescent Psychopharmacology, 2,* 267–275.

Ratey, J. J., & Johnson, C. (1997). *Shadow syndromes.* New York: Pantheon.

Ratey, N. A. (2002). Life coaching for adult ADHD. In S. Goldstein & A. T. Ellison (Eds.), *Clinician's guide to adult ADHD: Assessment and intervention* (pp. 261–277). San Diego: Academic Press.

Reimherr, F. W., Marchant, B. K., Strong, R. E., Hedges, D. W., Adler, L., Spencer, T. J., et al. (2005). Emotional dysregulation in adult ADHD and response to atomoxetine. *Biological Psychiatry, 58,* 125–131.

Rhee, S. H., Waldman, I. D., Hay, D. A., & Levy, F. (1999). Sex differences in genetic and environmental influences on DSM-III-R attention-deficit hyperactivity disorder. *Journal of Abnormal Psychology, 108,* 24–41.

Riccio, C. A., Wolfe, M., Davis, B., Romine, C., George, C., & Lee, D. (2005). Attention deficit hyperactivity disorder: manifestation in adulthood. *Archives of Clinical Neuropsychology, 20,* 249–269.

Robin, A. L. (1998). *ADHD in adolescents.* New York: Guilford.

Robin, A. L., & Payson, E. (2002). The impact of ADHD on marriage. *The ADHD Report, 10*(3), 9–11, 14.

Rostain, A. L., & Ramsay, J. R. (2006a). Adult with ADHD? Try medication + psychotherapy. *Current Psychiatry, 5*(2), 13–16, 21–24, 27.

Rostain, A. L., & Ramsay, J. R. (2006b). College and high school students with attention-deficit/hyperactivity disorder: New directions in assessment and treatment. In American College Health Association (Ed.), *Use and misuse of stimulants: A guide for school health professionals.* Englishtown, NJ: Princeton Media Associates.

Rostain, A. L., & Ramsay, J. R. (2006c). A combined treatment approach for adults with attention-deficit/hyperactivity disorder: Results of an open study of 43 patients. *Journal of Attention Disorders, 10,* 150–159.

Rucklidge, J. J., & Kaplan, B. J. (1997). Psychological functioning of women identified in adulthood with attention-deficit/hyperactivity disorder. *Journal of Attention Disorders, 2,* 167–176.

Safran, J. D., & Segal, Z. V. (1990). *Interpersonal process in cognitive therapy.* New York: Guilford.

Safren, S. A. (2006). Cognitive-behavioral approaches to ADHD treatment in adulthood. *Journal of Clinical Psychiatry, 67*(Suppl. 8), 46–50.

Safren, S. A., Lanka, G. D., Otto, M. W., & Pollack, M. H. (2001). Prevalence of childhood ADHD among patients with generalized anxiety disorder and a comparison condition, social phobia. *Depression and Anxiety, 13,* 190–191.

Safren, S. A., Otto, M. W., Sprich, S., Winett, C. L., Wilens, T. E., & Biederman, J. (2005). Cognitive-behavior therapy for ADHD in medication-treated adults with continued symptoms. *Behaviour Research and Therapy, 43,* 831–842.

Safren, S. A., Perlman, C. A., Sprich, S., & Otto, M. W. (2005). *Mastering your adult ADHD: A cognitive-behavioral treatment program—Therapist guide*. Oxford: Oxford University Press.

Safren, S. A., Sprich, S., Perlman, C. A., & Otto, M. W. (2005). *Mastering your adult ADHD: A cognitive-behavioral treatment program—Client workbook*. Oxford: Oxford University Press.

Satterfield, J. H., & Schell, A. (1997). A prospective study of hyperactive boys with conduct problems and normal boys: Adolescent and adult criminality. *Journal of the American Academy of Child & Adolescent Psychiatry, 36*, 1726–1735.

Scahill, L., Chappell, P. B., Kim, Y. S., Schultz, R. T., Katsovich, L., Shepherd, E., et al. (2001). A placebo-controlled study of guanfacine in the treatment of children with tic disorders and attention deficit hyperactivity disorder. *American Journal of Psychiatry, 158*, 1067–1074.

Schatz, D. B., & Rostain, A. L. (2006). ADHD with comorbid anxiety: A review of the current literature. *Journal of Attention Disorders, 10*, 141–149.

Schulz, K. P., Fan, J., Tang, C. Y., Newcorn, J. H., Buchsbaum, M. S., Cheung, A. M., et al. (2004). Response inhibition in adolescents diagnosed with attention deficit hyperactivity disorder during childhood: An event-related fMRI study. *American Journal of Psychiatry, 161*, 1650–1657.

Seligman, M. E. P. (1991). *Learned optimism*. New York: Knopf.

Semrud-Clikeman, M., Steingard, R., Filipek, P. A., Biederman, J., Bekken, K., & Renshaw, P. F. (2000). Using MRI to examine brain-behavior relationships in males with attention deficit disorder with hyperactivity. *Journal of the American Academy of Child and Adolescent Psychiatry, 39*, 477–484.

Shekim, W., Asarnow, R. F., Hess, E., Zaucha, K., & Wheeler, N. (1990). An evaluation of attention deficit disorder-residual type. *Comprehensive Psychiatry, 31*(5), 416–425.

Shire Pharmaceutical. (2006). *Shire announces study results with once-daily guanfacine extended release (GXR) in ADHD patients aged 6–17*. Retrieved December 1, 2006, from http://www.investorrelations.co.uk/shire/uploads/press/shire/1SPD503_2006_USPMHC_Releaseuti_161106.pdf.

Simpson, D., & Plosker, G. L. (2004). Atomoxetine: A review of its use in adults with attention deficit hyperactivity disorder. *Drugs, 64*, 205–222.

Singer, H., Brown, J., Quaskey, S., Rosenberg, L., Mellits, E., & Denckla, M. (1995). The treatment of attention-deficit hyperactivity disorder in Tourette's syndrome: A double-blind placebo controlled study with clonidine and desipramine. *Pediatrics, 95*, 74–81.

Solanto, M. V., Etefia, K., & Marks, D. J. (2004). The utility of self-report measures and the continuous performance test in the diagnosis of ADHD in adults. *CNS Spectrums, 9*, 649–659.

Solanto, M. V., Marks, D. J., Mitchell, K. J., Wasserstein, J., & Kofman, M. D. (in press). Development of a new psychosocial treatment for adults with AD/HD. *Journal of Attention Disorders.*

Solden, S. (1995). *Women with attention deficit disorder.* Grass Valley, CA: Underwood Books.

Spencer, T., Biederman, J., & Wilens, T. (2004a). Nonstimulant treatment of adult attention-deficit/hyperactivity disorder. *Psychiatric Clinics of North America, 27*, 373–384.

Spencer, T., Biederman, J., & Wilens, T. (2004b). Stimulant treatment of adult attention-deficit/hyperactivity disorder. *Psychiatric Clinics of North America, 27*, 361–372.

Spencer, T., Biederman, J., Wilens, T., & Faraone, S. V. (2002). Overview and neurobiology of attention-deficit/hyperactivity disorder. *Journal of Clinical Psychiatry, 63*(Suppl. 12), 3–9.

Spencer, T. J., Biederman, J., Wilens, T., Harding, M., O'Donnell, D., & Griffin, S. (1996). Pharmacotherapy of attention deficit hyperactivity disorder across the lifecycle: A literature review. *Journal of the American Academy of Child and Adolescent Psychiatry, 35*, 409–432.

Spreen, O., & Strauss, E. (1991). *A compendium of neuropsychological tests: Administration, norms, and commentary.* New York: Oxford University Press.

Sprich, S., Biederman, J., Crawford, M. H., Mundy, E., & Faraone, S. V. (2000). Adoptive and biological families of children and adolescents with ADHD. *Journal of the American Academy of Child and Adolescent Psychiatry, 39*, 1432–1437.

Stevenson, C. S., Stevenson, R. J., & Whitmont, S. (2003). A self-directed psychosocial intervention with minimal therapist contact for adults with attention deficit hyperactivity disorder. *Clinical Psychology and Psychotherapy, 10*, 93–101.

Stevenson, C. S., Whitmont, S., Bornholt, L., Livesey, D., & Stevenson, R. J. (2002). A cognitive remediation programme for adults with attention deficit hyperactivity disorder. *Australian and New Zealand Journal of Psychiatry, 36*, 610–616.

Still, G. F. (1902/2006). Some abnormal psychical conditions in children: Excerpts from three lectures. *Journal of Attention Disorders,* *10,* 126–136.

Swanson, J. M., Oosterlaan, J., Murias, M., Schuck, S., Flodman, P., Spence, M. A., et al. (2000). Attention deficit/hyperactivity disorder children with a 7-repeat allele of the dopamine receptor D4 gene have extreme behavior but normal performance on critical neuropsychological tests of attention. *Proceedings of the National Academy of Science, 97,* 4754–4759.

Swartz, S. L., Prevatt, F., & Proctor, B. E. (2005). A coaching intervention for college students with attention deficit/hyperactivity disorder. *Psychology in the Schools, 46,* 647–656.

Tannock, R. (2000). Attention-deficit/hyperactivity disorder with anxiety disorders. In T. E. Brown (Ed.), *Attention-deficit disorders and comorbidities in children, adolescents, and adults* (pp. 125–170). Washington, DC: American Psychiatric Press.

Taylor, F. R., & Russo, J. (2000). Efficacy of modafinil compared to dextroamphetamine for the treatment of attention deficit hyperactivity disorder in adults. *Journal of Child and Adolescent Psychopharmacology, 10,* 311–320.

Taylor F. B., & Russo, J. (2001). Comparing guanfacine and dextroamphetamine for the treatment of adult attention-deficit hyperactivity disorder. *Journal Clinical Psychopharmacology, 21,* 223–228.

Taylor, L. A., & Ingram, R. E. (1999). Cognitive reactivity and depressotypic information processing in children of depressed mothers. *Journal of Abnormal Psychology, 108,* 202–210.

Thapar, A., Hervas, A., & McGuffin, P. (1995). Childhood hyperactivity scores are highly heritable and show sibling competition effects: Twin study evidence. *Behavior Genetics, 25,* 537–544.

Thapar, A., Holmes, J., Poulton, K., & Harrington, R. (1999). Genetic basis of attention deficit and hyperactivity. *British Journal of Psychiatry, 174,* 105–111.

The MTA Cooperative Group. (1999). A 14-month randomized clinical trial of treatment strategies for attention-deficit/hyperactivity disorder. Multimodal treatment study of children with ADHD. *Archives of General Psychiatry, 56,* 1073–1086.

The Tourette's Syndrome Study Group. (2002). Treatment of ADHD in children with tics: A randomized controlled trial. *Neurology, 58,* 527–536.

Turner, D. C., Clark, L., Dowson, J., Robbins, T. W., & Sahakian, B. J. (2004). Modafinil improves cognition and response inhibition in adult attention-deficit/hyperactivity disorder. *Biological Psychiatry, 55,* 1031–1040.

Tzelepis, A., Schubiner, H., & Warbasse III, L. H. (1995). Differential diagnosis and psychiatric comorbidity patterns in adult attention deficit disorder. In K. G. Nadeau (Ed.), *A comprehensive guide to attention deficit disorders in adults: Research, diagnosis, and treatment* (pp. 35–57). New York: Brunner/Mazel.

Ward, M. F., Wender, P. H., & Reimherr, F. W. (1993). The Wender Utah rating scale: An aid in the retrospective diagnosis of childhood attention deficit hyperactivity disorder. *American Journal of Psychiatry, 150,* 885–890.

Wechsler, D. (1997). *Wechsler Adult Intelligence Scale (3rd ed.): Administration and scoring manual.* San Antonio, TX: The Psychological Corporation.

Weinstein, C. E., Palmer, D. R., & Schulte, A. C. (2002). *The learning and study strategies inventory.* Clearwater, FL: H&H Publishing Co.

Weiss, G., & Hechtman, L. T. (1993). *Hyperactive children grown up* (2nd ed.). New York: Guilford.

Weiss, M., Hechtman, L. T., & the Adult ADHD Research Group. (2006). A randomized double-blind trial of paroxetine and/or dextroamphetamine and problem-focused therapy for attention-deficit/hyperactivity disorder in adults. *Journal of Clinical Psychiatry, 67,* 611–619.

Weiss, M., Hechtman, L. T., & Weiss, G. (1999). *ADHD in adulthood: A guide to current theory, diagnosis, and treatment.* Baltimore, MD: Johns Hopkins University Press.

Weiss, M., & Murray, C. (2003). Assessment and management of attention-deficit hyperactivity disorder in adults. *Canadian Medical Association Journal, 168,* 715–722.

Weiss, M., Murray, C., & Weiss, G. (2002). Adults with attention-deficit/hyperactivity disorder: Current concepts. *Journal of Psychiatric Practice, 8,* 99–111.

Wender, P. H. (1995). *Attention-deficit hyperactivity disorder in adults.* New York: Oxford University Press.

Wender, P. H. (2000). *Attention-deficit hyperactivity disorder in children, adolescents, and adults.* New York: Oxford University Press.

Whalen, C. K., Jamner, L. D., Henker, B., Gehricke, J. G., & King, P. S. (2003). Is there a link between adolescent cigarette smoking and pharmacotherapy for ADHD? *Psychology of Addictive Behaviors, 17,* 332–335.

Wiggins, D., Singh, K., Getz, H. G., & Hutchins, D. E. (1999). Effects of brief group intervention for adults with attention deficit/hyperactivity disorder. *Journal of Mental Health Counseling, 21,* 82–92.

Wilens, T. E. (2003). Drug therapy for adults with attention-deficit/hyperactivity disorder. *Drugs, 63,* 2395–2411.

Wilens, T. E. (2004). Attention-deficit/hyperactivity disorder and the substance use disorders: The nature of the relationship, who is at risk, and treatment issues. *Primary Psychiatry, 11*(7), 63–70.

Wilens, T. E., Biederman, J., Mick, E., Faraone, S. V., & Spencer, T. (1997). Attention deficit hyperactivity disorder (ADHD) is associated with early onset substance use disorders. *The Journal of Nervous and Mental Disease, 185*(8), 475–482.

Wilens, T. E., Biederman, J., Mick, E., & Spencer, T. J. (1995). A systematic assessment of tricyclic antidepressants in the treatment of adult attention deficit/hyperactivity disorder. *Journal of Nervous and Mental Disorders, 183*, 48–50.

Wilens, T. E., Biederman, J., Prince, J., Spencer, T. J., Faraone, S. V., Warburton, R., et al. (1996). Six-week, double-blind, placebo-controlled study of desipramine for adult attention deficit hyperactivity disorder. *American Journal of Psychiatry, 159*, 1147–1153.

Wilens, T. E., Biederman, J., & Spencer, T. J. (2002). Attention deficit/hyperactivity disorder across the lifespan. *Annual Review of Medicine, 53*, 113–131.

Wilens, T. E., Haight, B. R., Horrigan, J. P., Hudziak, J. J., Rosenthal, N. E., Connor, D. F., et al. (2005). Buproprion XL in adults with attention-deficit/hyperactivity disorder: A randomized, placebo-controlled study. *Biological Psychiatry, 57*, 793–801.

Wilens, T. E., McDermott, S. P., Biederman, J., Abrantes, A., Hahesy, A., & Spencer, T. (1999). Cognitive therapy in the treatment of adults with ADHD: A systematic chart review of 26 cases. *Journal of Cognitive Psychotherapy: An International Quarterly, 13*, 215–226.

Wilens, T. E., Spencer, T. J., & Biederman, J. (2000). Pharmacotherapy of attention-deficit/hyperactivity disorder. In T. E. Brown (Ed.), *Attention deficit disorders and comorbidities in children, adolescents, and adults* (pp. 509–535). Washington, DC: American Psychiatric Press.

Wilens, T. E., Spencer, T. J., & Biederman, J. (2001). A controlled clinical trial of bupropion for attention-deficit/hyperactivity disorder in adults. *American Journal of Psychiatry, 158*, 282–288.

Willcutt, E. G., Doyle, A. E., Nigg, J. T., Faraone, S. V., & Pennington, B. F. (2005). Validity of the executive function theory of attention-deficit/hyperactivity disorder: A meta-analytic review. *Biological Psychiatry, 57*, 1336–1346.

World Health Organization. (1993). The ICD-ID classification of mental and behavioral disorders: Diagnostic criteria for research. Geneva, Switzerland: Author.

Young, J. E. (1999). *Cognitive therapy for personality disorders: A schema-focused approach* (3rd ed.). Sarasota, FL: Professional Resource Press.

Young, J. E., Klosko, J. S., & Weishaar, M. E. (2003). *Schema therapy: A practitioner's guide.* New York: Guilford.

Zametkin, A. J., Nordahl, T. E., Gross, M., King, A C., Semple, W. E., Rumsey, J., et al. (1990). Cerebral glucose metabolism in adults with hyperactivity of childhood onset. *New England Journal of Medicine, 323,* 1361–1366.

Index

A

Abstraction, Inhibition, and Working Memory Test (AIM) (Penn, The), 31
Academic accommodations, 168–169
Academic achievement
  difficulties in, 12–13, 155
  inattentive type effect on, 7
Academic history, 24
ADDerall, 100, 194
ADHD Checklist (ADHD-CL), 93
Adolescents, 14
Agitation, 35
Alcohol abuse, 36–37
All-or-nothing thinking, 47, 75
Alpha-2 adrenergic antagonists, 81–82, 102
Amphetamine (AMP)
  mechanism of action, 100
  mixed salts of, 194
  research evidence regarding, 100–101
  selective serotonin reuptake inhibitors with, 80–81
Anger, 35
Anterior cingulate gyrus, 18
Anticipatory avoidance, 49
Anxiety
  adaptive benefits of, 152
  case study of, 152–153
  Clinical Global Impression of Severity, 94
  cognitive-behavioral therapy for, 152
  description of, 34
  prevalence of, 12
  symptoms of, 151
  treatment of, 81–82

Assertiveness, 77
Assessments
  academic history, 24
  developmental history, 23
  diagnostic interview, 25–26
  family history, 23–24
  medical history, 25
  psychiatric history, 25
  review and history of presenting problems, 22–23
  self-awareness gained through, 54
  summary of, 38
  vocational history, 24–25
Atomoxetine, 82–83
Atomoxetine hydrochloride
  description of, 86
  dosing of, 80
  research evidence regarding, 101–102
  side effects of, 80, 101
Attention, 44
Attention deficit, 2–3, 6
Attention-deficit/hyperactivity disorder (ADHD)
  cultural prejudice against, 162
  discovery of, xiii
  misconceptions about, xi–xii, 3
  relapse rate for, 177
Automatic thoughts
  changing of, 62
  description of, 50–51
  focus of, 62–63

B

Basal ganglia, 17
Beck Depression Inventory (BDI), 93–94

D

E

F